D1570732

PLACE IN RETURN BOX to remove this checkout from your record.
TO AVOID FINES ret ··
MAY BE RECALLED ·· ·

DATE DUE

154

THOMISTIC PSYCHOLOGY

THE MACMILLAN COMPANY
NEW YORK · BOSTON · CHICAGO · DALLAS
ATLANTA · SAN FRANCISCO

MACMILLAN AND CO., Limited
LONDON · BOMBAY · CALCUTTA · MADRAS
MELBOURNE

THE MACMILLAN COMPANY
OF CANADA, Limited
TORONTO

THOMISTIC PSYCHOLOGY

A Philosophic Analysis of the Nature of Man

BY

ROBERT EDWARD BRENNAN, O.P., Ph.D.

PROFESSOR OF PSYCHOLOGY AND DIRECTOR OF THE THOMISTIC INSTITUTE
OF PROVIDENCE COLLEGE

NEW YORK

THE MACMILLAN COMPANY

Nihil Obstat

    CHARLES J. CALLAN, O.P., S.T.M.
    JOHN A. McHUGH, O.P., S.T.M.

Imprimi Potest

    TERENCE S. McDERMOTT, O.P., S.T.Lr.
             Provincial

Nihil Obstat

    ARTHUR J. SCANLAN, S.T.D.
           Censor librorum

Imprimatur

    ✠ FRANCIS JOSEPH SPELLMAN, D.D.
           Archbishop of New York

COPYRIGHT, 1941,

BY THE MACMILLAN COMPANY

ALL RIGHTS RESERVED—NO PART OF THIS BOOK MAY BE
REPRODUCED IN ANY FORM WITHOUT PERMISSION IN WRITING
FROM THE PUBLISHER, EXCEPT BY A REVIEWER WHO WISHES
TO QUOTE BRIEF PASSAGES IN CONNECTION WITH A REVIEW
WRITTEN FOR INCLUSION IN MAGAZINE OR NEWSPAPER

Published August, 1941. Reprinted
March, 1942; June, 1942 ; November,
1944; August, 1945; August, 1946;
October, 1946; January, April,
November, 1948.

PRINTED IN THE UNITED STATES OF AMERICA

3-29-49
31920
Psychol.

5923-419

"There is nothing that We have longer wished for and desired than that you should give largely and abundantly to youths engaged in study the pure streams of wisdom which flow from the Angelic Doctor as from a perennial and copious spring."

LEO XIII: *Aeterni Patris*

TO THE YOUTH OF AMERICA

209933

INTRODUCTION

It may have been a coincidence, but it is not without profound historical meaning, that Cardinal Mercier, who was so closely associated with Pope Leo XIII in the revival of Thomism, should also have made his own special contribution in the field of psychology. What has come to be called the "science of psychology," developed by methods of laboratory and clinical research, was just beginning at the time that Cardinal Mercier, and his colleagues at Louvain, undertook to rethink traditional principles in terms of contemporary problems. He was himself skilled in the experimental techniques of the new science, but unlike most experimentalists and investigators—in his own day and, since his day, up to the present time—he knew that the methods of science were inadequate by themselves for the study of man, and that they could be rightly oriented, and their findings truly interpreted, only if scientific psychology were properly completed by, and ordered to, the philosopher's analysis of human nature. But if the philosophical account were itself distorted and untrue, more harm than good would be done by trying to maintain the unity of psychology as a field in which scientific findings and philosophical principles collaborate. Cardinal Mercier clearly saw the disastrous influence which modern philosophical doctrines had exerted over the minds of his contemporaries, and especially positivism—the living paradox of philosophy denying itself. He saw the need for saving good scientific work from the crippling incubus of a bad philosophical inheritance, and he knew that only wisdom about man, which Aristotle and St. Thomas might teach even us moderns, could meet this need. All this is set forth in his great work, *The Origins of Contemporary Psychology*, but what he therein projected many years ago has only at last come to fruition in this book by Father Brennan. Here in this book at last is the unity of psychology achieved—a body of knowledge, well-defined in subject matter, and unified by a right ordering of philosophy and science.

In writing the Introduction to Father Brennan's book, I cannot help recalling my own career as a student of psychology. The textbooks through which I made my first acquaintance with this subject confessed, in their opening chapters, that psychologists had not been able to reach genuine agreement about the subject matter of their science. They quite belligerently proclaimed the complete independence from philosophy of psychology as a science; and at the same time they summarized the diverse "schools of thought"—each differing from the others, not because of contrary discoveries, but because of the "point of view" which motivated its method of research and determined the restricted field of phenomena it was willing to explore. Even to a sophomore, it was apparent that the psychologists had shut the front door on philosophy only to indulge in some surreptitious "philosophizing" on their own. But, as an undergraduate, I could not discern the causes of the confusions and disorders which increased my bewilderment the more I studied psychology. I patiently performed all the prescribed experiments; I read widely, if not deeply, in all the departments of the experimental literature; I could recite the dogmas of the various schools and was able to tell the difference between a behaviorist, a structuralist, and a functionalist, a Freudian and a Jungian, a *Gestalter* and a mental tester; I studied physiology, endocrinology, and neuroanatomy, and, at times, thought I had found the key which would open the door to all the secrets of man and his behavior in the conditioned reflex or the ductless glands, in *Gestalten* or in complexes; I was indoctrinated with such beliefs as that the founding of the first psychological laboratory marked the opening of real inquiry into human nature, or that Herbart had dealt a death-blow to the "faculty psychology" (which was nothing but a superstitious myth that had dominated the pre-scientific era); I taught experimental psychology for six years and tried my hand at various types of research in pursuance of a doctoral degree; but in all those years of teaching, throughout all my experimental efforts, and at the moment I received the degree—supposedly a competent worker in the field—I could not tell my students, my colleagues, or myself, what psychology was about, what its fundamental principles were, or what was the theoretical significance of all the data and findings that thousands of young men like myself had been collecting and assorting ever since the Ph.D. industry and the research foundations had encouraged such labors. This was the situation between 1920 and 1930; it had been the situation from the beginning of scientific psychology; and it is still the situation among the leading representatives of psychological science, as anyone can tell by reading the books and articles they write or by attending the annual meetings of the American Psychological Association.

The story of my gradual enlightenment can be briefly told. I began to understand the tradition of European thought as I read, and reread, the great books which constitute our intellectual heritage. Reading those books, both philosophical and scientific, I came to see the decisive rôle which Aristotle and St. Thomas Aquinas had played in the formation of fundamental doctrines; for, whether their insights were accepted or rejected by later thinkers, they were always determinative of the basic issues. I found in the *De Anima* of Aristotle and in the Treatise on Man in the *Summa Theologica*, a thoroughly intelligible account of human nature and of the principles and causes of human behavior—not only intelligible in itself, but thoroughly conversant with all the obvious facts of experience, quite compatible with all the physiology and neurology I had learned, and above all, a theory which was neither ashamed nor unable to make its metaphysical foundations both explicit and acceptable to reason. In the light of this theory, I could see at last the crucial errors of modern philosophy—the disastrous Cartesian mistake of regarding body and mind as separate substances, from which all the nonsense of the "mind-body problem" flows; the shallow materialism of Hobbes; the Platonic fallacies of Locke, Berkeley, and Hume; the misunderstanding of faculties as if they were agents rather than principles of operation, with the consequent restriction of psychological subject matter to "states of consciousness" or the "association of ideas." At last I understood why the recently born science of psychology had revolted against philosophy. The only philosophy the embryo scientists knew was this bad modern philosophy and they were quite right in wishing to be rid of it. But unfortunately they had been tainted by it; for, in the very act of revolt, they retained one or another of its dogmas, and this caused the various "schools of thought" which divided scientific psychologists, deprived them of a common subject matter, and inspired the "theorizing" which frustrated their best intentions.

In my first enthusiasm for the knowledge and wisdom about man which Aristotle and St. Thomas had taught me, I went to the opposite extreme—which is the common, and perhaps pardonable, mistake of the neophyte. I rejected all the modern developments, scientific as well as philosophical, the good along with the bad. Though contrary in direction, this was the same mistake my contemporaries had made in rejecting all of ancient and mediaeval psychology, because it contained errors along with its truths. I supposed that the study of human nature had been completed by St. Thomas. Only through coming to understand the distinction between philosophical and scientific knowledge, and the way in which these two methods of knowing supplement one another in the study of nature, did I finally comprehend in my own thinking what Cardinal Mercier had realized, namely, that psychology is pre-eminently a field in which the work of science and philosophy are of mutual assistance. Aristotle and St. Thomas could learn much from modern research, and the novel facts would stimulate and require them to extend and modify their theories in detail, even though fundamental principles remained unaltered. And, on the other hand, research could be more intelligently done if guided by true principles, and its findings would become intelligible if interpreted by an adequate theory. All of these benefits can accrue only if one condition be satisfied: that the subject matter of psychology be properly conceived as man—his nature, and its powers, habits, and acts. When the province of psychology is thus conceived, the philosopher makes his contribution by defining the essence of man, setting forth the essential distinction of his powers, analyzing the nature underlying his habits and acts; the scientist makes his contribution by investigating the phenomenal correlations among human operations, and discovering thereby the material and accidental determinants of his habits and powers. I envisaged such a unified psychology, both traditional in principle and progressive in detail, when, in writing *What Man Has Made of Man*, I tried to indicate the significance of the researches done by the psychoanalyst and the psychometrist, and at the same time tried to suggest certain extensions and revisions in Thomistic principles which modern findings prompted. I envisaged an orderly exposition of all the truths we now know about human nature, both philosophical and scientific. The dream I had has come to life in this book; and though Father Brennan would be the first to insist that his work is only a first approximation to the ideal of which we both have been dreaming, he cannot deny that he has completed the pioneer's work. He has not merely seen the promised land: he has surveyed it, marked its boundaries, laid out its thoroughfares, developed its building sites. However much improvement will come with the future—and there is every reason to expect that it will be profound as well as extensive—the edifice of psychology will not be moved from these foundations.

I have indulged in these reminiscences in order to tell the student, into whose hands this book falls, how fortunate he is that, at the beginning of his career, his interest in human nature is not frustrated by an unintelligible jumble of factual data, further confounded by specious interpretations, which is the picture of psychology as presented in the ordinary textbook. I hope that what I have said will make him appreciate under what happy auspices he is being introduced to a subject matter of momentous significance to anyone who is trying to regain the perennial wisdom of European culture without discarding the inventions and discoveries of modern research. If he is guided by these insights to learn well what this book has to teach, he will ultimately free himself from the privations and negations of modern thought—for a defective and erroneous psychology is at the root of the most crucial errors in modern philosophy, and these errors are, in turn, the cause of many confusions and disorders in contemporary psychology. While it is false to say, without qualification, that the proper study of mankind is man, it is unquestionably true that a right understanding of man is pre-requisite to wisdom in most other fields, both theoretic and practical. Because man is on the boundary line between the corporeal and spiritual worlds, man's understanding of himself both illumines all inferior natures, and throws an analogical light on all that is above. Not only is psychological truth indispensable, in the theory of knowledge, for avoiding the positivism characteristic of modern thought (which rejects theology and philosophy and regards science alone as knowledge); but, in the practical order, all of moral philosophy is corrupted by false notions concerning man's nature, which end in denials of his rationality, his freedom, his destiny. Not only because of the nature of things, but for historical reasons as well, the study of psychology is today probably the best introduction to the whole of philosophy, as well as the best remedy for the failings typical of our culture. In writing this book, Father Brennan has, I think, kept that larger view of its usefulness in mind.

It would be enough to say in praise of Father Brennan's achievement that in the writing of this book, he has never lost sight of his fundamental aim to unify psychology by properly conceiving its subject matter and rightly ordering its philosophical and scientific parts; to say that he has everywhere done justice to the most recent findings of research, at the same time being sufficiently flexible in his reformulation of traditional principles so that they are not antiques just masquerading in modern dress, but living models of a perennially sound analysis. I have, however, one word of higher praise to add. This is not a textbook, but a book of texts with commentaries thereon. Modern scholastic philosophy, as, in fact, all the rest of modern education, has been almost ruined by bad textbooks, which have come between the student and the primary sources of his instruction—the great books. The great books, the great original sources, are the major teachers of every generation. All the rest of us are, at best, minor teachers, and our task must be to mediate between our students and the great minds who are our teachers as well as theirs. We can perform that task well only if we work as media, not as opaque barriers. Father Brennan has understood this obligation and discharged it well by incorporating throughout this book, the most important passages from the writings of Aristotle and St. Thomas, and by helping the student learn how to understand these capital texts by the manner of his commentary. By so doing, he has also avoided the horrible Wolffian errors which have corrupted scholastic textbooks, in psychology as in all other fields. In the sense in which Christian von Wolff was a writer of text-books and clearly not a Thomist, this book is clearly not a textbook and truly a Thomistic work. These traits distinguish it from most of the other secondary books now being offered to students in our educational institutions.

Father Brennan's title, and his quotation from the Encyclical *Aeterni Patris* on the dedicatory page, bespeak the spirit in which he dedicated himself to the writing of this book. But more than zeal is required to accomplish what he had in mind. An intelligent employment of means, a careful avoidance of pitfalls, is indispensable. Pope Leo knew what the difficulties and dangers were, when he wrote:

"We earnestly exhort you . . . to restore the golden wisdom of St. Thomas and propagate it far and wide to the best of your power. 'The wisdom of St. Thomas,' we say; for if there be in the scholastic doctors any excessive subtlety of inquiry, any inconsiderate teaching, anything less consistent with the ascertained conclusions of a later generation, anything in any way improbable, we have no mind to hold that up for imitation. . . . But to the end that supposititious doctrine be not imbibed instead of the true, or the adulterate instead of the genuine, take care that the wisdom of Thomas be drunk from his own fountains."

So well has Father Brennan heeded this advice, and followed these injunctions, that he can rest assured the readers of his book will become, through his aid, better students of Aristotle and St. Thomas.

MORTIMER J. ADLER

UNIVERSITY OF CHICAGO, May, 1941

ACKNOWLEDGMENTS

For reading the entire manuscript and helping with its final revision I wish to thank Professors Mortimer J. Adler, of the University of Chicago; Anton C. Pegis, of Fordham University; Noël Mailloux, O. P., of the University of Montreal; Charles J. Callan, O. P. and John A. McHugh, O. P., editors of *The Homiletic and Pastoral Review;* and Daniel J. O'Neill, of Providence College. To James H. Haberlin, M.D., formerly Professor of the Rhode Island School of Pharmacy, I am indebted for the construction of the index. Finally, to my students who assisted me so generously in the reading of the proofs, I wish to express my sincere thanks and gratitude.

THE AUTHOR

TABLE OF CONTENTS

BOOK ONE: ARISTOTLE

BOOK THREE: THE MODERNS

DIAGRAMS

BOOK ONE

ARISTOTLE

THE PSYCHOLOGY OF ARISTOTLE

i

Introduction

It has often been said that the psychology of Aquinas is rooted in the teaching of Aristotle. What I wish to show, in the opening pages of our work, is the fundamental truth of this statement. Several sections of the Stagirite's writings have been examined; but the basic texts are the *Treatise on the Soul*, the *Treatise on Sense and the Object of Sense*, and the *Treatise on Memory and Recollection*. The first text is, of course, the main source of our information. It is the most synoptic treatment that we possess of the Aristotelian psychology. The second and third texts give us detailed analyses of what are called today the presentative and re-presentative powers of the soul. To complete our survey of the general body of Aristotle's psychology, we must add the *Nichomachean Ethics* which, though professedly moral in tone, is nevertheless full of insights on the rational nature of man, on the relation of his higher and lower appetites, and on the habits formed by these appetites.

There are certain observations that I should like to make about the exposition which follows. In the first place, a systematic order has been given to the Aristotelian doctrines, forecasting the order in which I have developed the psychology of Aquinas in the remainder of the book. Moreover, the perspective exercised on the texts of the Stagirite is derived, in the main, *from the perspective which Aquinas himself reveals in his commentaries on these texts.* Perhaps from this habit of reading Aristotle through the eyes of Aquinas—a habit which the Thomist finds exceedingly difficult to circumvent or eradicate—I have made the distinctions of the Stagirite sharper and his basic propositions clearer than he himself made them. My only defense is that the psychology of both thinkers is woven of one cloth. It is perennial because of the truth which it represents. The genius of Aristotle discovered it. The genius of Aquinas integrated and developed it. Its enduring character is ample testimony to the correctness of its philosophic insights. I should like to stress this point about philosophic insights, because the same thing cannot be said of the nonphilosophic parts of the Aristotelian and Thomistic texts. In matters of empirical observation, both Aristotle and Aquinas were men of their age, which was definitely a prescientific age. This means that extreme caution must be used to dissociate the permanent philosophic analyses from the useless and outmoded scientific formulas with which these analyses are often overlaid. The record of Aristotle's and Aquinas's theories in the field of science is, for the most part, without value, except as a moment in the history of their mental development.

A further word should be added here about the Greek references which are cited in the bibliography. The language of Aristotle, Plato, and the other great Hellenic philosophers is the source of many terms in our modern psychological dictionaries, as every ambitious student will ascertain for himself. Again, not a few of the classic phrases in the texts of Aquinas are simply transliterations of the language of Aristotle. Thus we are able to trace many common psychological dicta directly to their source. Further, in fairness to all the critical labors that have been performed on the Stagirite's writings, it is no more than right that we should make some modest attempt to address ourselves immediately to the symbols in which the Aristotelian thought was first clothed. We need hardly add that a great diversity of opinion is to be found among the commentators and exegetes. Perhaps the meaning which Aquinas attaches to the Greek text—a meaning, let me repeat, that I have employed consistently in my own exposition of Aristotle's psychology—is not always the import that Aristotle himself had in mind. This really is beside the point since, in the building of our psychological edifice, the criterion, always and everywhere, as the Angelic Doctor would insist, is not the authority of the Stagirite, but the truth of the matter. It remains for the competent critic to pass judgment on the rightness or wrongness of Aquinas's interpretation. In any case, what is of capital importance to the Thomist is not so much what Aristotle says as the special use which Aquinas makes of the Aristotelian analysis. To repeat what was said a moment ago: the psychology of the Stagirite is perennial precisely for the reason that it is true; and the psychology of Aquinas is likewise enduring because, having fixed upon the truth of Aristotle's insights into human nature, it has preserved and ordered and systematically expanded upon these insights.

We begin our study, then, in the field of what the ancients called physics. This is the domain of natural philosophy, as distinguished from natural science.[a] [1] We end our inquiry in the province of metaphysics. To explain: man, as a corporeal substance, operative within the dimensions of space and time, equipped with powers and habits that manifest his corporeal essence in acts of different sorts, is a proper subject for physical analysis. The soul of man, as an entity that is intrinsically free of the cosmic movements of matter, is a proper subject

---

[1] The letters a, b, c, etc. refer to certain textual clarifications developed at the end of each chapter.

for metaphysical analysis. Our point of departure, then, in
the study of man, lies within the boundaries of mobile being.
But the end of our speculative journey brings us face to face
with the limitless vision of transcendent and immobile realities.[b]

ii

The Aristotelian Meaning of Soul

A. DEFINITION OF SOUL

Psychology, for Aristotle, is the study of the soul. A knowledge of the soul contributes greatly to the advance of truth
in general, but, above all, to an understanding of the philosophy of nature, since the soul is the principle of natural life.
The philosophy of nature considers being, not in itself, but
in so far as it participates in movement. Its proper province
is sensible or corporeal reality, in which form is conjoined to
matter. The student of nature, therefore, must have some
notion of matter; but, more importantly, he must know the
meaning of form, since form determines matter and specifies
the nature of corporeal being. The psychologist, as a natural
philosopher, is concerned with the living form. His business
is to acquaint himself with the essential definition of soul.
To accomplish this, he must study the acts and powers of the
soul, since by these the ultimate nature of the soul is recognized.

Some of the powers of living entities are uniquely psychic.
They are properties of the soul alone. Others are both psychic
and somatic. They are properties of the *synolon*, that is, of
the soul and body in combination. Is the soul something substantial or is it merely an accident? Is it an actuality or a
potentiality? Is it form or matter? At bottom, the reply is
the same on all three scores: the soul is a substantial entity,

the carrier of several accidents; an actuality that exhibits different kinds of powers or properties; a form which has a basic unitive relation to matter. The soul is the substantial form of a natural body. Substantial form is not any actuality, but always and of necessity first actuality. It is the first actuality of a natural body. Further, the soul is the first actuality, not of any natural body, but of an organized natural body, that is, of a body which has, within the depths of its material bosom, the potentiality to live. It is, in short, *the first actuality of a natural body which is potentially alive.*

The analogy of knowledge is helpful. Thus, one must possess information before he can use it. So, too, the natural body, disposed to live, must actually possess a soul before it can live and exercise the functions of life. Considered apart from the soul, it is only potentially alive. The analogy suggests a further important distinction between the soul as an entitative principle, constituting, with the potentially alive body, a living being or an organism; and the soul as an operational principle or fountainhead and reservoir of all the vital acts of the organism. Moreover, if the soul is the first actuality of the body, it is wholly meaningless to ask if soul and body form a unit substance. One might just as well ask if the wax and the shape given to it by the stamp are really one. The notion of oneness is manifold; but nothing is more properly one than the union of a first actuality with that of which it is the actuality.

Matter and form, in conjunction, yield a fundamental unity or a single substance; wherefore, body and soul, in conjunction, are said to produce a single organism. The ratio of body to soul is like the ratio of the organ of sight to the power of sight. As the material organ plus the visual power constitutes the eye, so the body plus the soul constitutes the organism. The body corresponds to what exists in potentiality. The soul corresponds to what exists in actuality. If the soul is the first actuality of the potentially alive body, the potentially alive body is the first material substrate of the soul. First potentiality, then, and first actuality, or first matter and first form, are the essential constitutive elements of the organism.

B. KINDS OF SOUL

Among the creatures of the cosmic universe, we discern three kinds of besouled organisms: plants, animals, and men. Accordingly, there are three kinds of souls immersed in matter: the threptic or vegetative soul; the aesthetic or sensitive soul; and the dianoetic or rational soul. Each soul is distinct by virtue of the special powers or properties which it manifests in its operations. Plant life reveals itself in acts of nutrition, growth, and reproduction. Animal life is exhibited in acts of sensitive cognition, sensitive appetition, and local movement. Human life, the crowning perfection of physical nature, is manifested in acts of rational cognition and rational appetition. Just as the act of thinking is different from the act of sensing, so the power of thinking is different from the power of sensing. And it is the same with all the other powers of the soul. Because of their distinguishable character, we may refer to the powers as parts of the soul. Such parts, however, are merely virtual. There are no quantitative divisions of the soul, which always and everywhere is a unit substance. It is absurd to speak of the soul as desiring with one part, thinking with another, and so forth, except part be understood here to connote power.

Further, the powers of a lower species of soul are included, virtually and eminently, in the higher species. This means that a man is virtually an animal, and an animal is virtually a plant. To illustrate: there is no mathematical figure apart from the triangle, the quadrangle, the pentagon, and so on. Similarly, there is no soul apart from the three species we have mentioned, unless it belong to another order of being superior to man and endowed, like him, with the power to think. The comparison of figures and souls reveals an exact parallel, since both constitute a series in which each successive term virtually contains its predecessor. Thus, the pentagon virtually contains a quadrangle, and the quadrangle virtually contains a triangle. So, too, the human soul virtually contains an animal soul, and the animal soul virtually contains a plant soul. The soul is not only the substantial form of the organism, but also the efficient and final cause of life.

C. RECAPITULATION

To sum up, with special reference to human psychology: man is a besouled organism. He is a complex creature, made up of matter and form. Matter, here, means first matter, the ultimate material substrate of form. Form, here, means first form or first actuality, the ultimate determining principle of matter. Because man is a besouled organism, his body cannot be the actuality of his soul. On the contrary, his soul must be the actuality of his body. While the soul cannot be a body, it cannot be without a body, so long as man is man. This indicates a definite substantial relationship between man's soul and his body.

Earlier philosophers were unsuccessful in their efforts to fit the soul into a body without adding some specification as to the kind of body which the soul informs. For, an actuality can be realized only in what is potentially able and ready to receive it, that is, in a matter that is appropriate to it. Accordingly, we must define man's soul, entitatively, as the first actuality of a potentially alive body. With this idea of its entitative nature clearly in mind, we can then further specify the human soul, in its operational nature, as *that whereby we primarily live and sense and reason*. This means that the soul is the ultimate source of all our vital actions. Yet it is better to avoid saying that the soul lives, senses, and reasons. Rather, we should say that it is *man* who functions thus, using the powers of his soul.

iii

Plant Life: Vegetation

The adequate object of psychology is every species of soul. Its proper object is the human soul. The vegetative soul is the most primitive and widely distributed kind of vital principle. The acts by which it manifests itself are chiefly two: first, the use of food; second, reproduction. Nothing grows or decays naturally except what feeds itself; and nothing feeds itself except what has a soul in it. Moreover, any besouled organism that has reached its normal state of maturity and is unmutilated naturally generates another organism like itself: an animal producing an animal, a plant producing a plant, in order that, so far as in it lies, it may participate in what is eternal and divine. It is not the individual, however, which survives, but the race represented by the individual.

The nutritional process involves three separate factors: first, that which is fed, and this is the body; second, that whereby the body is fed, and this is food; third, that whereby the food is transformed into the body, and this is the soul. It is obvious that food is essentially related to what has a soul in it. The power of assimilating food, however, is different from the power of increasing the bulk of what is nourished by it. Inasmuch as the organism is a quantum, food may increase its magnitude. But it is only because the organism is a particular something, that is, a substance, that food acts as food. As a nutritive agent, it preserves the life of what is fed. Food, moreover, is an instrument of generation, because it supplies the material by which another individual, like the reproducing agent, is brought into existence.

From the foregoing analysis, we see that the vegetative soul has three fundamental properties: the power of nutrition; the power of growth; and the power of reproduction. Further, because things are rightfully named after the ends they realize, and because the final purpose of the vegetative soul is to perpetuate the race, this most elemental species of vital principle could just as well be called a reproductive soul as a nutritive soul. Since man is virtually a plant, he exhibits all the basic properties of the vegetative organism. He is able to nourish himself, grow, and reproduce after his kind.

iv

Animal Life: Sensation

The continuity of nature manifests a gradual transition from plants to animals. This is so true that it is difficult to discern the exact nature of certain borderline organisms. One thing is certain, that plants are restricted, in their vital processes, to the phenomena of nutrition, growth, and reproduction. Animals, on the other hand, always enjoy at least a rudimentary kind of consciousness. They have sensations. In their more perfect species, they show traces of the intellectual and moral characteristics which distinguish the rational nature of man. The word *aisthesis* means either the act of sensation or the power of sensation. As the act of sensation, it designates a qualitative change wrought in a sense organ by the impinging of an external stimulus. As the power of sensation, it signifies a capacity for receiving sensible forms without their matter. A sense organ is that in which such a power resides.

When we say that sense assimilates form without matter, we mean that it receives an impression of its proper object without changing or destroying the nature of this object. The process here involved is comparable to the process whereby wax receives the impression of a signet ring without absorbing or mutilating the gold or bronze of the ring. It makes no difference to the wax what sort of metal the signet is made of; and, similarly, it makes no difference to the sense what kind of corporeal substance is acting on it. The important thing, in the latter instance, is the quality of the object which, at the moment, is affecting the sense organ, since only qualities can impress themselves on a sense receptor. The power of sensation may be likened to a combustible object which never ignites itself but must be set on fire by an extrinsic agent. Thus, we distinguish between the sense in potency and the sense in act. Further, in its relation to the power of sensation, the object of sense may be similarly differentiated as the sensible in potency and the sensible in act. Here we observe that, in the actual process of sensation, whereby the sensible object is brought to bear on the organ of sense, *the sensible in act is identical with the sense in act*. This means that object and subject become one in the act of knowledge.

Between the sense and the sensible object there must be a certain proportion. Excessive stimulation destroys this balance, just as the harmony of a musical instrument is destroyed by the violent plucking of its strings. Plants have no capacity for taking in forms without matter. Rather, their powers are the other way about, since they assimilate matter and leave aside form in the nutritional procedure. To each external sense is assigned the task of apprehending some material quality of corporeal substance, such as its color, sound, and so forth. The particular quality, in each case, is known as a proper sensible. The animal possesses at least five modalities of sense or five ways of apprehending the sensible qualities of matter.

v

The Outer Senses

Of all our external powers, *tactual sense* is the most fundamental. Without it, the animal cannot exist. Its function is to apprehend body qualities. Its proper object is the tangible. Tangibility implies contact of one body with another and therefore the influx of qualities that may be either beneficial or harmful. Nature, accordingly, has arranged, first, that all animals should have a sense of touch; second, that it should be distributed throughout the whole body. The objects of the other external senses may be reduced to single categories. Not so in the case of touch. All we can say is that tactual distinctions are such as characterize bodies as bodies. Actually, there may be several senses of touch. In matters of tactual sensibility, man is superior to all the other animals. Further, among men themselves, those most highly endowed with a delicate sense of touch usually have the best intelligences.

Gustatory sense is really a special form of touch, since food is something tangible. From this point of view, taste is as necessary as touch, because an animal must eat in order to live. Indeed, the ultimate point of reference for all the senses of the brute is food. Flavor is the proper object of taste. The excellence of man's tactual powers, as compared with those of the animal, also extends to the field of taste, since gustatory sensibility is simply an aspect of tactual sensibility.

Olfactory sense is very poorly developed in man. Here he falls far below the animal's level. The proper object of smell is the odor of bodies. Though relatively obtuse in his olfactory reactions, man is the only creature who has made an art out of the pleasures of smell.

Of all our external powers, *auditory sense* contributes the most, in an indirect way, to the growth of intelligence. Its proper object is the audible. Rational discourse is a medium of instruction because the spoken word, which is a symbol of thought, is an audible sound. Accordingly, of persons unable to see or hear from birth, those who lack auditory sense are at a greater disadvantage, intellectually, than those who lack the power of vision. Voice is common to man and many animals. It is sound with imagination and meaning, and not merely the expulsion of breath.

Visual sense supplies the primary wants of life. In its direct effects, it is the most refined and cultural of all our outer senses. Its proper object is the visible. Because all bodies refract light and are colored, the visual field may be regarded as the most fertile source of information about our cosmic environment.

vi

Common Sense

While sensation is the proper act of an external sense, perception belongs to *common sense.*[c] In vision, only colors are sensed; in hearing, only sounds; in smell, only odors; in taste, only flavors; in touch, only body qualities. Common sense enables us to bring several or all of these proper sensibles together, and, by a single perceptual act, to recognize their simultaneous existence in one and the same object. The perception of a rose, for example, shows us the inherence of color, odor, and tactual qualities in a unit object. This means that the external senses mediate their sensations to a central sensorium, furnishing the proper stimuli for the operation of common sense. Each outer sense has its roots, so to speak, in this central sensorium; so that it is quite correct to say that common sense is the foundation and meeting ground of all the external senses. The eye may be said to perceive colors, and the ear to perceive sounds, inasmuch as the external senses are grounded in common sense and mediate their proper sensibles to common sense.

Moreover, by means of common sense we can identify particular sensations as belonging to ourselves, as subjects. We not only see, hear, smell, taste, and touch objects, but we are aware of the fact of our so doing. In the very act of perceiving an objective world, we also perceive a subjective world. By common sense, therefore, we become object-conscious and subject-conscious, being made aware, in the perceptual process, of both the outer stimulus and the operation of the sense as it responds to the stimulus. Further, the external senses supply us with information about the qualities of corporeal substance; but it is not their office to discriminate between these qualities. Visual experience, for instance, reveals something white; and gustatory experience reveals something sweet. But the eye knows nothing about the sweetness of an object; and the tongue knows nothing about the whiteness of an object. To make such distinctions is the task of common sense. Thus, by holding up before the mirror of animal consciousness all the various sorts of informations that arise from peripheral stimulation, common sense enables us to perceive the differences between the reports of the several senses at the same time that we fuse such discrete informations into a psychological whole. To sum up, then: common sense is the principle of sensitive consciousness and of the analysis and synthesis that we make of our sensations within the field of animal consciousness.

Finally, common sense perceives not only the proper sensibles of the special senses, but also certain other common sensibles which, because they are not peculiar to any one sense, are therefore said to be common to all. These common sensible qualities in an object derive from the fact that every corporeal substance exists within certain spatial and temporal dimensions. We have already listed the proper sensibles as color, sound, odor, flavor, and body qualities. We may enumerate the common sensibles as shape, magnitude, number, motion, and rest. Besides these two classes of objects that affect the senses directly, we may distinguish a further group which falls under the heading of indirect objects. These latter sensibles are really matters for intellection, not sensation or perception, inasmuch as the senses apprehend them only in a roundabout way or by accident. For example, a certain patch of color, which is discerned by the eye as a white object, happens to be the son of Diares; wherefore, Diares's offspring is said to be incidentally an object of sense perception.

vii

Imagination

The primary and basic power of forming images is *imagination.*[d] It is found in all animals. Its operation supposes the persistence of sense impressions after the stimulus which produced these impressions is removed. The proper object of imaginal power, therefore, is something absent. Its product is a phantasm, which is the sensible re-presentation of an original experience. The special function of imagination, accordingly, is to bring back to consciousness the images of objects that have ceased to be present to the external senses. I no longer hear the song, for instance, because the sound waves that carried it have stopped impinging on my ears; yet it continues to exist in my consciousness in a series of auditory images. All perceptual experience can be thus reinstated by imaginal power. Imagination, then, is able to hold the impressions of sense in the form of images, and to revive these impressions after the perceptual object is gone. The ability to perform operations of this sort is vital and essential to both memory and intellect, for, without such a re-presentative power, our consciousness would be an ever-shifting scene of kaleidoscopic sense impressions which, once gone, could never be lived again.

The word "phantasm" contains, etymologically, an implied distinction between the appearance and the reality of things. Thus, while the phantasm is not the real thing but merely the sensible image of the real thing, it may be, nevertheless, a true re-presentation of the real, and, as such, as true as the presentative or perceptual experience from which it is derived. Imagination is the light of the inner world of sensitive consciousness, just as the sun is the light of the cosmic world. The postsensationary process involved in the actual operation of imaginal power is derived from the movement set up in the sense organ by the application of a stimulus. This movement is, fundamentally, of a physiological nature, and it persists after the original stimulus has disappeared. It is like throwing a stone into water and creating a circular movement. The first circle causes a second by its energy; the second circle, in turn, communicates its movement to a third, and so on, the original movement growing fainter and fainter. Just so, the physical stimulus starts a movement in the sense organ which eventually reaches imagination and is the cause of the forming of a phantasm. Because it is removed out of the sphere of perceptual experience, the phantasm is less distinct than the original experience. Accordingly, it is sometimes described as a sort of washed-out sensation. For man, the most significant task of imagination is to supply the schematic forms or phantasms from which intellect abstracts its ideas. Its most vehement exercise occurs during slumber, when the activities of the external senses are largely suppressed. In our dreams, pictures flit across the imagination like clouds across the sky, taking all kinds of shapes and forms in rapid succession.

Two types of imaginal operation are found in man: the first a function of purely sensitive imagination, wherein original experiences are reproduced just as they occurred; the second a function of logistic or dianoetic imagination, sometimes referred to as deliberative imagination, wherein insight and control are exercised to produce images of things that never really occurred, or never happened in the manner that they are pictured. This second kind of imaginal activity is exemplified in the creations of the literary and plastic arts. Thus, it is the distinctive function of logistic or deliberative imagination to clothe the artist's idea in a phantasm, and so to provide a medium between his concept and the actual embodiment of this concept in the matter with which he works. It is not necessary to suppose, however, that sensitive and dianoetic imagination are two separate powers. Rather, they are names for one and the same power which, because of its association with intellect and will, is able to create as well as to simply reproduce.

viii

Memory

Memory, like imagination, is an image-forming power. Its proper object is something past. Its functioning, therefore, is conditioned by the lapse of time; and only those animals that are aware of time can remember. The act of memorial recall may refer to a previous intellectual experience, as when one remembers that the sum of the angles of a triangle is equal to two right angles; or to former perceptual data, as when one remembers something that he saw, or heard, and so on. Yet, because its proper object is always something past, memory belongs to intellect only incidentally, while directly and immediately it falls within the category of the re-presentative senses. The original experience stamps into memory an impression of itself, much as the signet makes its imprint on wax. If the wax is either too soft or too hard, it does not take a perfect impression. Similarly, mnemonic traces are not easily left on the nerve substance of the very young or the very old, or on those who are strongly moved by their passions.

Just as man's imagination is both reproductive and creative, so his memory is both reproductive and recollective. Simple reproductive memory is a purely sensitive type of memory. Recollective memory is guided by intellect and will. If creative imagination is logistic, recollective memory is syllogistic, that is to say, it proceeds in its movements by a sort of syllogism or rational inference. Empirical analysis shows us that the accomplishments of recollective memory are guided by natural rules. These rules are the laws of association. For instance: we may start with a present situation and work our way back, in a temporal series, until we reach the image after which we are searching. The empirical grounds of recollection are threefold: the similarities, contrasts, and propinquities of our experiences. Animals, of course, do not recollect; and so they do not employ such inferential methods in searching for images of the past. Yet the recollective power is composite by nature, like all the other senses of man, since it belongs to body and soul together.

The images of memory also bear the name of phantasms. They, too, like the products of imagination, are sensible representations of material objects. In importance, therefore, they rank equally with the phantasms of imagination since they furnish intellect with schematic forms from which it can abstract its ideas. Thus, imagination and memory both mediate the concrete data of sense to reason, whose task is to interpret such data and structuralize it into various kinds of knowledge, such as science, philosophy, history, art, and morality. As with imagination, so with memory, the distinction between sensitive and dianoetic forms of recall does not signify the possession of two separate powers, but simply that one and the same power can act in two different ways.

ix

Animal Prudence

To explain the actual motion of pursuit and avoidance in animals, two factors must be brought into account: first, the cognitive determination which arises from imaginal power; second, the impulsive determination which springs from appetite. Behind pursuit, there are movements of pleasure. Behind avoidance, there are movements of pain. It is a question here, not only of what is directly and immediately beneficial or harmful, but also of what is only remotely so. Animal life shows a definite planning for the attainment of goods and the eschewing of evils that are only distantly related to its actual perceptual experience. Now, creative imagination, which is proper to man, helps to explain such remote planning; but simple reproductive imagination, which is proper to the animal, cannot satisfactorily account for such a phenomenon. It appears necessary, therefore, to introduce another power into the animal's equipment which would act upon reproductive imagination in the same manner that reason, in man, acts upon creative imagination. It is suggested, accordingly, that the brute possesses a *faculty of sensitive prudence*, comparable to the practical intellect of man.

This power of forming certain insensate images of an object, that is, images not originally given in the content of perceptual or imaginal or memorial experience, is a special ability of nature, conferred on the animal in order to preserve its individual and specific integrity. By it, and without previous knowledge, the brute knows what is friendly and beneficial to its life and welfare, what is inimical and obnoxious, and so on. Because of its critical offices in the estimation of remote goods and evils, such an endowment may be referred to as a kind of power of forethought. The sheep sees an enemy in the wolf; but a thing to be loved in its own offspring. The swallow constructs its nest and the spider spins its web neither by the rules of art, nor after rational inquiry, nor by deliberation, nor by intelligence, but by nature or natural instinct. All such acts are exhibitions of an ability to recognize biological values; and since knowledge of this sort cannot be explained by the operation of the other senses, it must derive from some special faculty in the animal's make-up, which enables it to discern the usefulness or harmfulness of objects that fall under its experience.[e]

x
Passion and Action

A. THE SENSITIVE APPETITES

Whatever has sensitive life also has appetitive life. Just as *aisthesis* means either sense or sensation, so *orexis* signifies either appetite or appetition. The notion of appetite is generic. It is divided, broadly, into sensitive appetite, which is proper to the animal, and dianoetic appetite, which is proper to man. The species of sensitive appetite are reduced to two: *concupiscible appetite*, which generates the passions of desire; and *irascible appetite*, from which the passions of victory and defeat are born. The difference between sensitive and dianoetic appetite is an essential one, being a difference between two levels of powers. The difference between concupiscible appetite and irascible appetite, on the other hand, is a nonessential one, being a difference within the same level. Because of this hierarchical separation, it is possible for man to experience a conflict between the movements of his sensitive and rational appetites. Thus, reason inclines him in one direction, very often, and passion propels him in another. Sensitive appetite seeks the pleasure of the moment; reason looks to the future and total good of man.

All animals, even those that have no knowledge except the scant information supplied by tactual experience, exhibit motions of a concupiscent nature, since they desire things, derive enjoyment from things, suffer pain at things, and so on. Feelings of pleasure give rise to movements of pursuit; feelings of pain originate movements of avoidance. The presence of such pleasurable and painful feelings seems to be ubiquitous in all our vital reactions. Three factors are involved in orectic movements: first, that which moves and is moved, and this is appetite; second, that which moves but is itself not moved, and this is the end or realizable good; third, that which is in motion, and this is the animal.

B. THE POWER OF LOCOMOTION

From the above analysis, we see how appetition is naturally complemented by the *ability to move about from one point in space to another*. Properly speaking, this power belongs to the whole animal, not to any part of it; nevertheless, locomotion involves the several parts of the animal body. If the office of appetite is to issue commands and thereby act as the efficient cause of movement, the office of locomotive power is to carry out such commands. But appetite never functions apart from knowledge of some sort, since nothing is desired unless it is previously known. This means that both cognition and appetition are sources of local movement—but from different points of view. We might sum up the whole matter by saying that the cognitive power directs; the appetitive power issues orders; and the locomotive power executes. Cognitive power here means either sensitive power or rational power, since, in man's case at any rate, direction of movement may come from intellect as well as from sense. Similarly, appetitive power here means either sensitive appetite or rational appetite, since man is moved by volition as well as by passion.

In the cognitive process, there is calculation of means to end; in the locomotive process, there is actual attainment of the end. That, precisely, which is desired by the appetitive power constitutes a principle or starting point for the operation of the cognitive power; for the thing which is desired is always a good, and the function of the cognitive power is to display this good to the appetite. That, on the other hand, which is the term or resting point in the process of cognition constitutes the starting point of action; for the end result of knowledge is to supply the appetite with a motive for setting the executive powers into movement. While it is proper to say, therefore, that cognition and appetition are sources of local movement, it is even more proper to say that it is the end, or thing desired, which moves the animal. By way of comparison, the value of cognition is absolute; the value of appetition is relative. Why? Because desire is always in terms of something else, whereas knowledge is always in terms of itself. To restate briefly: in local movement, as in orectic behavior, three factors are at work: first, that which commands the movement, and this is appetitive power; second, that which induces appetite to issue its orders, and this is the apprehended good; third, that which is moved, and this is the animal. The final purpose of locomotive power, therefore, is to enable the animal to execute the designs of its knowledge and the impulsions of its appetites; and the instruments by which it accomplishes this purpose are the various motile organs of the body.[f]

xi

Human Life: Intellection

A. THE POWERS OF INTELLIGENCE

There are two powers of intelligence in man: one creative or poietic in function; the other receptive or dynamic. *Poietic intellect*, which is essentially an active or energetic faculty, may be defined as the power of making all things understandable. *Dynamic intellect*, which by its very nature is passive, may be defined as the power of becoming or being made all things understandable. The task of making all things understandable is accomplished by the abstraction of intelligible forms from sensible forms. These latter forms are administered to poietic intellect as phantasms, that is, as products of the image-making powers. The soul never exercises its intellectual functions without converting to phantasms. The first stage of ideogenesis, therefore, is reserved to poietic intellect and may be depicted as a process wherein the sensible object is transformed into an intelligible object. As the sun communicates to material entities the light without which their colors would be invisible, so poietic intellect bestows upon the universe of knowable entities an intelligibility without which their natures or essences could not be apprehended. The function of poietic mind, then, is to illuminate the phantasm which conceals beneath the folds of its outer garments a potentially understandable object. In this act of illumination, a marvellous change is wrought in the re-presentation of phantasmal consciousness. For, now, what was only potentially intelligible becomes actually intelligible. A proper stimulus for dynamic or receptive intellect is thus brought into being. Truly, the work of poietic intellect is in the nature of a creation when it is able to disperse the shadows that envelop the data of sense, and, in the very dispersal, to lay bare the intelligible form which the phantasm hides in its bosom. It remains for dynamic intellect to receive this intelligible form, to be determined and specified by it, to respond to such stimulation by generating an idea through whose medium we are able to understand. If poietic or active intellect, therefore, is the instrument of illumination and abstraction, dynamic or receptive intellect is the instrument of conception, judgment, and reasoning.[g]

Intellect is related to the intelligible in the same way that sense is related to the sensible. Now, the sensible in act is identical with the sense in act, as we have already said. So, too, *the intelligible in act is identical with the intellect in act.* Moreover, if sense is the form of sensible forms, intellect is the form of intelligible forms. Because of its intellectual nature, the soul of man is said to be *pos panta*—everything, as it were. Thus, it can become everything that it is able to understand; and the limits of what it actually is are the limits of what it actually knows. Because intellect requires phantasms in the process of thinking, it is never actively aware of anything in the absence of sense. All man's knowledge is derived, basically, from experience or the exercise of his senses. At the beginning, his mind is like a tablet on which nothing is written. He has no innate ideas.

The proper object of sense is concrete corporeal substance, or, better, the concrete determinate qualities of corporeal substance. The proper object of intellect, on the other hand, is the nature or essence of corporeal substance. We are speaking here, of course, of man's intellect. The adequate object of intellect, or the object of understanding *qua* understanding, is any kind of nature or essence. Just as there is no error in external sense which simply apprehends its proper object as it is brought to bear on the sense organ, so there is no error in intellect in its simple apprehension of the essences of things.

Where illusion occurs in the realm of sensitive cognition, it will always be found to exist fundamentally in common sense, whose office is to synthesize and differentiate the products of the external senses. In the same manner, where error occurs in the field of intellectual cognition, it will always be discovered in judicial acts, when intellect composes or divides its ideas.

From what we have just said, it is clear that the difference between sense and intellect is resolvable into a difference of objects. Thus, sense is concerned with singular and concrete entities which, by their very nature, are measured in terms of space and time. Intellect, on the contrary, deals with universal and abstract entities which supersede all spatial and temporal dimensions. Sensitive knowledge, moreover, is intrinsically dependent upon material organs. Intellectual knowledge, by contrast, is intrinsically free of matter or material organs. This being the case, the sensible forms of corporeal substances are received by sense without matter, but not without the conditions of matter, since such forms determine and specify a material power. The intelligible forms of corporeal substances, contrariwise, are received by intellect not only without matter but also without the appendages of matter, since such forms determine and specify a power that is intrinsically independent of matter. Indeed, if intellect is potentially susceptible of all the forms of corporeal substances—being everything, as it were—it must be free of all admixture with a body organ. It cannot, then, be subjectively dependent upon matter. It is a power of the soul alone, and not a composite ability, as are the vegetative and sensitive powers.

To recapitulate, intellect is opposed to sense in several ways: first, because the products of intellect are strictly universal and free, whereas those of sense are particular and restricted; second, because intellect deals with the abstract and ideal aspects of things, whereas sense deals with their concrete and material characteristics; third, because intellect is properly exercised upon substances or essences, whereas sense is properly concerned with accidents or operations; fourth, because intellect is able to reflect on its acts, whereas sense can perform no such function. The two genders of powers are comparable in the same manner that a straight line is related to itself when bent. Thus, sense in action is like the straight line, because it moves directly to its object and reposes there; while intellect in action is like the same line when bent, because it not only reaches its object but also returns upon itself.

In respect to the goals of knowledge and the way in which its information is employed, man's understanding is both theoretic and practical. The task of theoretic intellect is to discriminate between the true and the false. The task of practical intellect is to distinguish between the good and the bad. The former is engaged with knowledge for its own sake. The latter is occupied with knowledge that can be incorporated into practice: either the doing of something or the making of something. Theoretic intellect gives no commands. Practical intellect operates in the form of an epitactic or imperative syllogism. The major premise is a general principle in the practical order. The minor premise is a particular instance. The conclusion is an action, represented, in the concrete, by subsuming the particular instance under the general principle. The ultimate goal of theoretic intellect is demonstrable truth. The ultimate goal of practical intellect is appetible good. Such a good may fall within the field of either art or morals. Knowledge, as knowledge, moves theoretic intellect. Knowledge, as motive, moves practical intellect. The first principles of demonstration bear the same relation to theoretic intellect that the ultimate ends of action bear to practical intellect. This means that the final end is the initial cause of all our practical resolutions. Moreover, although the goal is the first thing that is intended, it is always the last thing that is reached.[h]

B. THE POWER OF VOLITION

The imperative quality of a judgment of practical intellect is meaningless, of course, apart from *will*. Reason can legislate; but only through will can its legislation be translated into action. The task of practical intellect is to guide will by enlightening it. Will, in fact, is to be understood wholly in terms of intellect. If there were no intellect, there would be no will. This is obvious from the way in which will is rationally denominated. For sometimes it is referred to as dianoetic appetite; at other times it is called orectic reason. As an appetite, its proper object is a good apprehended by intellect as something desirable. Just as the cognitions of sense move the sensitive appetites, so the cognitions of intellect move the intellectual appetite. In the sensitive appetites we find both concupiscence and anger; but in the intellectual appetite we find only volition. Because will is an intellectual power, it belongs to the soul alone. Like reason, it can operate independently of any body organ.

xii

The Powers of Man

The powers of man cannot be understood except in relation to the acts which they perform. Only from their effects can we infer to their existence and nature. It follows that, in the order of invention, acts are prior to powers. Moreover, just as powers derive their meaning from correlative acts, so acts are significant in terms of their correlative objects. Broadly speaking, there are three different sorts of things with which the powers of man are exercised: digestible objects, sensible objects, and intelligible objects. Accordingly, we find three orders or hierarchies of powers in man's nature: threptic or vegetative, aesthetic or sensitive, and dianoetic or rational. Within each of these levels, there are numerous species of powers. A species of power is determined by the species of its act, which, in turn, is determined by the kind of object with which it is properly exercised. The accompanying diagram shows us how the powers of man are enumerated according to their species.

DIAGRAM 1. THE POWERS OF MAN (AFTER ARISTOTLE)

threptic	nutritive augmentative reproductive
aesthetic	somesthetic gustatory olfactory auditory visual
	perceptual imaginal memorial prudential
	concupiscible irascible
	locomotive
dianoetic	poietic or energetic receptive or dynamic
	volitional

xiii

The Habits of Man

Habit is a dispositive quality whereby that which is disposed, is disposed well or ill, either in itself or with reference to something else. If the thing so modified is a substance, like the body of man or the soul of man, which are substantial parts of his nature, then the habit is entitative. If the thing modified is an accident, like the powers or properties of man, then the habit is operational. Health is an entitative habit. Science is an operational habit.

Habit is a species of quality. Disposition is also a species of quality. Habit *qua* habit is distinguished from disposition, first, as the more perfect is distinguished from the less perfect; second, as the less alterable is distinguished from the more alterable. Thus, an operational habit is more excellent than an entitative habit, and is less easily lost. This we should expect from its mode of origin, since it is acquired by repeated acts of the same type. One day does not make a spring. So, a short time does not make a man perfectly good. An operational habit is *psychologically* good when it properly disposes the nature of man. It is *morally* good when it conduces to the end of man, which is natural happiness. Moral virtue is a habit that makes its possessor good and his actions good. In a general way, virtue is twofold: dianoetic or intellectual, and ethical or moral. Intellectual habits are qualities of theoretic and practical intellect. Moral habits are qualities of the appetites. The lower appetites are receptacles of moral habits, not because they are rational in themselves, but because they are subject to reason and to that extent participate in rationality.

The habits of theoretic intellect are *understanding, science,* and *wisdom*. The habits of practical intellect are *art* and *prudence*. The habits of theoretic intellect are speculative. They deal with knowledge for its own sake. The habits of practical intellect are actional. They deal with knowledge either for the sake of making things, as in the case of art; or for the sake of doing things, as in the case of prudence. Making is an action that passes into external matter, like building a house or carving a statue. Doing is an action that remains immanent in the agent, like seeing, thinking, willing, and so on. Prudence occupies the same relation to human action that art does to human production. Now, in human action, the last end is the supreme criterion as to how we shall behave; just as, in human speculation, first principles are the supreme standards as to how we shall think. Prudence, therefore, demands that a man be rightly disposed toward his last end.

But in order to be thus properly disposed, one must rectify his appetites; hence the need of certain moral virtues if human nature is to have a secure foundation for the life of happiness. The moral virtues are: *justice*, which is imposed on the will; *temperance*, which moderates the passions of the concupiscible appetite; and *fortitude*, which manages the impulsions of the irascible appetite. Prudence is so immediately related to the moral virtues that its presence always implies their presence. Thus, if the moral virtues make us desire a good end, prudence always dictates the means that appear proper to us for attaining this end. Actually, a man may choose the wrong means and still act prudentially, since prudence requires simply that he calculate well, according to his lights, with a view to some good end. It follows from our analysis that prudence is neither a science nor an art. It is not a science because it deals with concrete performances, about which there can be no science, but only casuistry. It is not an art because art has to do with things to be made, not with things to be done.

xiv

The Person of Man

A solution of the problem of person requires an understanding of the basic doctrines of substance and nature.[i] *Substance* is distinguished, categorically, from *accident*. If it is common to every substance not to be in a subject, it is common to every accident to be in a subject. Loosely and improperly, substance is identified with essence. Properly, substance signifies *something that has existence rightfully in itself, and not in another*. It can be logically divided into first substance and second substance. First substance, which is most properly called substance, is something which is neither predicated of any subject nor said to inhere in any subject. Second substance, on the other hand, is not said to inhere in any subject, yet is predicated of a subject. This difference is obviously founded upon a diversity in modes of being. Second substance signifies a specific or a generic nature. First substance refers to a nature which is individually subsistent. The latter, then, is always singular. The former is always universal. Accordingly, the distinction between the two may be expressed as a distinction between what is predicable and what is nonpredicable. Thus, second substance, as a universal, can be said of something else. First substance, as a singular, cannot be said of something else.[j]

The attributes of substance are: first, not to be inherent in a subject; second, to express "this something," that is, something which exists by itself, thereby indicating its differentiation from accident; third, to be receptive of contraries, since it can be the subject of successive accidents that are mutually opposed; fourth, to be something to which there is no contrary, since contraries expel one another from the same subject, and substance is not in a subject; fifth, not to be susceptible to more or less, since substance cannot become more intense or less intense, more remiss or less remiss, though one substance may be more noble or less noble than another.

Nature originally meant the birth of living things. Because this kind of genesis always demands an intrinsic cause, philosophers gradually extended the first connotation of the term to include any internal principle of movement. We may define nature, therefore, as *anything that has in itself, as such, a settled ground of activity*. Because nature is the principle of operation in substance, natural laws are operational laws. Moreover, actions are always the actions of singular things, that is, of first substances. Nature differs from art in the same manner that what is inborn differs from what is acquired. Thus, nature is in its roots a self-determining source of action. Its determinate character comes from within. Art, on the other hand, places its effects outside of itself. In producing things, it always remains external to what it creates.

xv

The Soul of Man

The *soul* of man appears to be an independent substance and incapable of destruction. If his intellect becomes incapacitated in old age, this is due, not to a corruption of the power of thinking or of the substance of the soul, but to a weakening or disintegration of the body and its senses, whose administrations are objectively necessary to the work of intellection. But intellect itself is divine and impassible. We know this because it can operate without a body organ; and what can act in transcendence of the body is separable from organic life. This fact is true both of poietic intellect, which is active, and of dynamic intellect, which is passive. Now, if intellect is an unmixed and separable power, the soul in which it is lodged must also be unmixed and separable. Thus, the soul of man is distinguished from the soul of the animal as the imperishable from the perishable. It alone, of all living forms, is able to exist in isolation from the matter to which it is conjoined. It alone is not educed from the potentialities of matter or derived from any pre-existent subject. It alone comes into existence *from without*, being divine in its origin. Human reproduction is the occasion, not the cause, of its entering the body. In its making, no material energy is involved. And after its separation from the body, it alone, of all the forms of corporeal substances, appears for what in reality it is—something incapable of corruption and therefore destined to live forever.[k]

The will of man, which is a deliberative faculty, is an instrument of free choice. It is within the power of everyone to be good or bad, worthy or worthless. This is borne out, first, by our inner awareness of an aptitude to do right or wrong; second, by the common testimony of all men; third, by the rewards and punishments of rulers; fourth, by the general employment of praise and blame. Moral acts, which are always particular acts, are in our power, and we are responsible for them. Character or habit is no excuse for immoral conduct. We can shape our own characters, and we can control the beginning of our habits. A man may be sick because of incontinence of life or disobedience of doctor's orders. But he had the option of leading a pure life and of following proper medical advice. As a result, he must be held responsible for the entailments of his disobediences and excesses. You may regret having thrown a stone the moment it has left your hand; but all the regrets in the world will not call it back. The point is, you were not obliged to throw it in the first instance. When the matter is sifted down, the happiness of every man's soul is in his own hands, to preserve and develop, or to cast away.

READINGS FROM ARISTOTLE

De Anima (*Treatise on the Soul*, translated by J. A. Smith), books II–III. Oxford, the Clarendon Press, 1931.

De Sensu et Sensato (*Treatise on Sense and the Object of Sense*, translated by J. I. Beare), Oxford, the Clarendon Press, 1908.

De Memoria et Reminiscentia (*Treatise on Memory and Recollection*, translated by J. I. Beare), Oxford, the Clarendon Press, 1908.

Ethica Nichomachea (*The Nichomachean Ethics*, translated by W. D. Ross), books II–VII. Oxford University Press, 1908.

Categoriae (*The Categories*, translated by E. M. Edghill), chapter 5. Oxford, the Clarendon Press, 1926.

CLARIFICATIONS

(a)

Natural philosophy as distinguished from natural science

The difference between natural philosophy and natural science. as chapter three will abundantly show, is a difference of formalities and techniques. Thus, philosophy and science have the same material object since both deal with the same subject matter, which is corporeal nature. They differ, first, in respect to formal objects; second, in respect to methods. The formal object of science is phenomenal nature; that of philosophy is noumenal nature. The method of science is investigative and grounded on special experience; that of philosophy is noninvestigative and grounded on common experience.

(b)

The transition from physics to metaphysics

The transition from physics to metaphysics is a transition from physical philosophy to metaphysical philosophy, or from the philosophy of becoming to the philosophy of being. The reference here is to the different levels of abstraction on which the human intellect operates in its analysis of reality. The principle involved is the degree of remotion from matter. According to Aquinas, three such degrees are discernible in the abstractive process, corresponding to the three stages of physical, mathematical, and metaphysical analysis, respectively. Before explaining how we reach these different levels, Aquinas makes two important distinctions: first, between sensible and intelligible matter; second, between individual and common matter.

Sensible matter is qualified matter, that is, corporeal matter as subject to various sorts of sensible qualities, such as color, odor, temperature, and so forth. Intelligible matter, on the other hand, is quantified matter, that is, corporeal substance as subject to quantity.

Both sensible and intelligible matter are further divided into individual matter, which is signate, that is, endowed with the singular notes or characters by which it is separated from all other individuals of the same species; and common matter, which is not signate but possessed only of what belongs to the species as such. Thus, this flesh or this bone is individual matter. Flesh or bone, as such, is common matter.

In the first degree of knowledge, intellect abstracts from individual sensible matter and considers only common sensible matter. Here we tear off the identification marks that distinguish singular objects among themselves. The degree of remotion eliminates matter only insofar as it is the source of numerical multiplication, leaving physical nature still subject to the conditions of movement and change. What intellect seeks to know on this level is the universe of sensible being. The area thus circumscribed fixes the limits of inquiry for both the science of nature and the philosophy of nature. It is manifest that the object of such inquiry can neither exist without matter nor be thought of without matter.

In the second degree of knowledge, intellect abstracts from both sensible matter and individual intelligible matter, considering only common intelligible matter. At this point in its explorations, it is dealing with the quantified aspect of things. Matter is no longer viewed as a principle of sensible movement and change, but simply as a basis of extension or dimensional properties. Here we have advanced into the region of mathematics where quantity, with all its special attributes, becomes the goal of our searching efforts. Again, it is manifest that an object of this sort cannot exist without matter, although it can be thought of without matter.

In the third degree of knowledge, intellect abstracts from sensible and intelligible matter altogether. What is left for its consideration is nothing more or less than the substance or being of the thing under analysis. Now we are ushered into the illimitable domain of metaphysics, whose object not only can be thought of without matter, but also can exist without matter. For, by this highest act of abstraction, intellect is exalted above the confines of space and time and isolated from all physical and mathematical context. On such an empyrean plane, even material entities are compelled to yield up the metaphysical elements of their being.

It should be clear now that when we undertake to analyze the acts, powers, and habits of man, we are dealing with the phenomenal side of his nature and therefore with objects that involve the first degree of knowledge. It is the business of both the natural scientist and the natural philosopher to treat of such objects. On the other hand, when we push our analysis beyond the range of phenomena and enter the sanctuary of man's soul, we have sloughed off all his qualitative and quantitative determinations and are dealing with the purely metaphysical aspects of his being. It should also be pointed out that the passage from the first to the third degree of abstraction is immediate. Such a procedure is lawful for the reason that it does not violate any principle of mental continuity. In mathematical analysis, we are operating off the direct line of abstraction, as it were, since mathematics is largely concerned with imaginable entities, whereas physics and metaphysics deal solely with real entities.

Three separate moments, therefore, are discernible in the study of human psychology: first, the investigative physical stage, which is the approach of the natural scientist; second, the noninvestigative physical stage, which is the approach of the philosopher of nature; third, the metaphysical stage, which is the approach of the philosopher of being. The first is essentially a phenomenal study of man as a mobile and sensible being; the second is essentially a noumenal study of man as a mobile and sensible being; the third is essentially a study of the immobile and supersensible nature of man, and, more particularly, of his soul as a separate substance.

In concluding this clarification, a word must be added about the rather perplexing nature of Aquinas's language in describing the three levels of abstraction. Thus, he speaks of common sensible matter as the object of the first degree of knowledge, and of common intelligible matter as the object of the second degree of knowledge. The former is called sensible because it falls directly under the senses. The latter is said to be intelligible, not because it is incorporeal, since it is conjoined to quantity, but because it does not directly affect the senses. As examples of common intelligible matter, the Angelic Doctor uses such quantities as number, dimension, and figure. Yet elsewhere he points to number, dimension, and figure as examples of common sensibles. Indeed, at one place in his writings, he says explicitly that common sensibles are all aspects of quantity, that is, of common intelligible matter. (*Cf.* chapter five, clarification *b*.) This is likely to be very confusing to the mind of the student. Since mathematics is irrelevant to our present study, I would suggest that we go back to our opening remarks in this clarification and simply say that the first level of abstraction is always concerned with an object that is *becoming*, whereas the third level of abstraction deals solely with *being* as such.

(c)

Common sense: a power of animal cognition

The name "common sense" is a literal translation of Aristotle's *koine aisthesis*. We can discover at least four meanings in English for this widely used and much abused phrase: first, the original and proper significance given by Aristotle and explained in the text; second, certain universal convictions which men possess in common, whereby they test the truth of human knowledge and the morality of human actions; third, that kind of intelligence, lacking which, men are accounted mad or foolish; fourth, a feeling of public spirit or of obligation toward the commonweal. Only the first meaning is confined to the level of sensitive powers, as the term "sense" should be confined. The other three meanings are all metaphorical, since they refer to intellectual matters, such as judicial acts, first principles of the speculative order, first principles of the practical order, and so forth. This extended and ambiguous use of the word "sense," to indicate something intellectual, is also found in such phrases as "sense of the beautiful," "poetic sense," "moral sense," "sense of shame," "sense of dignity," and the rest.

(d)

Imaginal power

Aristotle's word for imaginal power is *phantasia* or phantasy. At times, he uses the term loosely to indicate any re-presentative power of the sensitive or rational order. In this meaning, even intellect is an imaginal faculty since it produces an intelligible image or re-presentation of the object which it understands. More strictly, imaginal power signifies an ability of forming sensitive images. In this meaning, imagination, memory, and estimative power are imaginal faculties. Most strictly (and this is the connotation of the present text), imagination is the power of forming sensitive images of absent objects *qua* absent.

(e)

Animal prudence

Aristotle's teaching on animal prudence is only sporadically developed in his writings. It is not touched on at all in his *Treatise on the Soul*, except for vague references to the pursuit and avoidance reactions of animals. Yet the Stagirite very clearly recognized the estimative character of certain forms of sensitive knowledge. The doctrine of estimative power was embryonic in his mind and required the analysis of the later Aristotelians, especially the Jewish and Arabian philosophers, in order to be brought to maturity. By the time it reached Thomas Aquinas, it had become well settled in the Aristotelian psychology. We have already noted how, for Aristotle, the imaginal and memorial powers of man have dianoetic as well as sensitive functions. The same distinction came to be applied to estimative power which, as Aquinas expounds, is cogitative as well as sensitive in man.

(f)

Imperative offices of appetite

When it is said that the function of appetite is to issue commands, the meaning is not to restrict the offices of imperation to appetite alone. The fact is, as Aquinas points out, that sense and intellect, as well as sensitive appetite and intellectual appetite, are able to issue commands. Nevertheless, it remains true that the act of imperation is reserved in a special manner to appetite, since it is by virtue of the impulsions of the appetitive faculties, operating immediately on the locomotive power, that the whole schema of outer behavior is executed.

(g)

Poietic intellect and receptive intellect

No more debated topic is found in Aristotle's psychology than his discussion of the intellects of man. According to the opinion of Aquinas and his followers, the Stagirite admits of three intellects in man: first, *nous poietikos*, which we have translated as poietic intellect or creative intellect, since it transforms the world of sensibility into a world of intelligibility; second, *nous dynamikos*, which is rendered receptive intellect or possible intellect, since it is in potency to actuation by the intelligible form which poietic intellect has abstracted; third, *nous pathetikos*, which literally means pathic intellect or passive intellect. This last-named power, according to Aquinas, is not an intellect at all but a faculty of forming sensitive images.

It will be remembered from clarification (d) that Aristotle sometimes uses imagination to signify an intellectual power. In like manner, he sometimes uses intellect to signify an imaginal power. Aquinas himself does the same thing when he refers to estimative power in man as particular reason. If, then, pathic intellect is really a sensitive power, it follows that, in the Aristotelian analysis, there are only two intellects in man, properly speaking: poietic intellect, which Aquinas calls *intellectus agens* or agent intellect; and receptive intellect, which the Angelic Doctor calls *intellectus possibilis* or possible intellect. I should like to add here that the terms *nous poietikos* and *nous dynamikos* are not actually found in the writings of Aristotle, but the things signified by these two terms are assuredly there: namely, an intellectual power of abstracting and creating, and an intellectual power of receiving the fruit of such creative activity and of being determined by it to understand.

In order to appreciate the truly magnificent contribution which the Stagirite made to the cause of psychology in his theory of a dual intellect, let us see some of the antecedents that led up to the establishment of the theory. In a general way, there were two traditions which the Stagirite had to consider and reconcile: first, that of the atomists, which failed because of its exaggerated views on the material aspects of human knowledge; second, that of the idealists, which was inadequate because it laid too much stress on the immaterial features of ideogenesis. The first tradition, stemming from Democritus, made sensations out of ideas; the second tradition, reaching its full stature with Plato, made ideas completely free of the administrations of sense. Both positions, as Aristotle recognized, had some truth at their basis. The correct solution lay in showing how sensations eventually gave birth to ideas. This meant the necessity of showing how something material is transformed into something immaterial. Sensible objects cannot lift themselves up to the plane of intelligibility. If they are to be made intelligible, it must be through the offices of some power which already exists on an intellectual plane. In addition to understanding intellect, which actually forms the idea, man must therefore possess another intellect whose specific task is to abstract from the sensible datum a form that is connatural with understanding intellect. Such an intellect, precisely, is the poietic power which Aristotle postulates as part of man's intellectual equipment. Now it is no longer necessary to suppose, as did Democritus, that ideas are simply refined sensations, or, as did Plato, that ideas have no connection whatever with sensitive knowledge, being matters of birthright. Both positions were so obviously contrary to experience and psychological insight that Aristotle, very properly, could not tolerate either.

(h)

Speculative and practical intellect

"The speculative and practical intellects are not distinct powers," as Aquinas explains, "since what is accidental to the nature of the object of a power, does not differentiate that power. Thus, it is accidental to a colored object whether it be a man or large or small, since all such things are perceived by the same power of sight. In a similar way, it is accidental to an object apprehended by intellect whether it be directed to operation or not, and according to this the speculative and practical intellects differ. For, it is speculative intellect which directs what it apprehends, not to operation, but to the consideration of truth; while practical intellect is that which directs what it apprehends to operation."

(i)

Aristotle and the concept of person

Aristotle did not formally discuss the meaning of person. Neither was he aware of the basic distinction between person and nature. Yet both these problems are soluble in terms of the Aristotelian concepts of substance, accident, nature, and operation. The Stagirite's distinction between first substance and second substance, or between substance as a singular, existing in an individual, and substance as a universal, existing in a gender or a species, is of prime importance to the analysis of person. Moreover, the concept of nature as substance endowed with a principle of operation is in no wise altered by the fact that substance and nature, or person and nature, are really distinct. Of course, the philosophic notions of substance, accident, person, and nature have been profoundly influenced by theological discussion; but, to repeat: Aristotle's teaching on these points has been confirmed rather than nullified by the advent of Christianity and its ideologies.

(j)

Essence and substance

The primary meaning of substance is that of an ultimate subject. The primary meaning of essence is that of the ultimate constitutive principles of such a subject. The substance of man, if I may use such a phrase, is man. The essence of man, on the other hand, is the matter and form of man. What *is* a being cannot, strictly speaking, be *of* a being. Thus, it is more correct to refer to man the person than to refer to the person of man. Yet, we can scarcely avoid such expressions, especially when the order of exposition and comparison seems to make them desirable, *e.g.* the body of man is not man, the soul of man is not man, but the person of man is man.

I should like to call attention once more to the fact that the distinction between first substance and second substance is a logical one. It is the distinction between singular and universal terms in the category of substance. As such, it must not be converted into an ontological distinction. Aristotle has given us a fourfold difference between terms according as they are: first, both predicable and inherent; second, predicable but not inherent; third, inherent but not predicable; fourth, neither predicable nor inherent. Observe, again, that the logical distinction between "predicable of" and "inherent in" is not a distinction between logical and ontological existence, since "predicable of" is one mode of predication and "inherent in" is another mode of predication. There is, of course, a connection between logical predication and ontological existence, since a thing is said in as many ways as it is. This means that there are as many modes of predication as there are modes of being. In short: the modes of being and predication are the same.

(k)

Aristotle on the soul's immortality

It is not my intention to attribute more to Aristotle than his scattered texts on immortality permit. What he actually says, in his *Treatise on the Soul,* is this: that man's intellect *"appears* to be an independent entity implanted in the soul and incapable of being destroyed"; and again, that "we have no evidence, as yet, about intellect or the power to think, but it *seems* to be [the faculty of] a widely different kind of soul [from the souls of plants and animals], distinguishable as what is eternal [is distinguishable] from what is perishable, it alone being able to exist apart from the body." Among the uncertain and wavering statements of the Stagirite, these two are as close as we can come to a commitment on the problem of immortality. I might also add here that Aristotle's description of the human soul's origin as coming "from without" can hardly be a warrant for attributing to him a creational theory, though it is obviously not adverse to such a theory. The idea of creation, that is, the production of something without any pre-existing material, is neither self-evident nor easy to grasp. If the student should be tempted to think so, let him reflect that it escaped the greatest minds of antiquity and was really developed only in the light of the revealed truth that God created the world in time.

BOOK TWO

AQUINAS

CHAPTER TWO

THE PSYCHOLOGY OF AQUINAS

i

Aristotle's Treatise on the Soul

Aristotle tells us that there are three things in the soul of man that account for all his actions: his powers, his passions, and his habits. Aquinas clarifies the point with some simple examples. Thus, a man acts from habit when he constructs a work of art, from passion when he is angry, and from naked power when he walks or talks or writes or does anything for the first time. These three principles, therefore, represent the mainsprings of human behavior. We may reduce them to even simpler terms, since passions are the acts of appetites, and appetites fall under the category of powers. Accordingly, it is sufficient and adequate to say that all man's actions may be accounted for by his powers and his habits. These are the settled grounds, in the operational dimension, from which we derive our knowledge of his inner nature.

Aristotle's *Treatise on the Soul* is the first well-rounded discussion of the philosophy of mind to be found among the writings of the ancients. Because of this fact, scholars have given to the sage of Stagira the unique title of "father of psychology." Some improvements have been made upon Aristotle's analysis, notably those of Thomas Aquinas; but in the main, the basic doctrines of the *Treatise on the Soul* have remained unchanged. This is explained easily enough, since here, as elsewhere, Aristotle has discovered the truth; and because truth is an enduring thing, so is the philosophic expression of it.

ii

Aquinas's Treatise on Man

It is quite correct to say, then, that for Aristotle psychology is a study of the soul through its acts, powers, and habits. Observe well that the soul about which he is talking is not an isolated or transcendental entity but the principle of life in the organism; that is to say, a principle which, in the deepest reaches of its nature, is designed to inhabit matter. We must not lose sight of this fact; otherwise we cannot understand the real meaning of the acts and powers and habits of the soul. This point impressed Aquinas so much that when he came to write his own matured views on psychology, he incorporated them into his *Treatise on Man*. Now the focal point of analysis becomes man rather than soul. This is an improvement, because it clarifies the fundamental issues in psychology. If we wish to indicate the shift of viewpoint in a word, I believe we can do so by saying that Aristotle's approach to psychology is *animistic;* Aquinas's is *synolistic*. This means that Aquinas is anthropological rather than psychological in his treatment of the philosophy of human nature. Note that there is no opposition between the two modes of approach, since both regard the soul as the form of matter and study it precisely as such. It is the point of reference rather that is different— one assigning the acts of man to the soul as the *ultimate principle by which* he lives, feels, and thinks; the other referring these same acts to man himself as the *ultimate subject* of operation.[a] The Thomistic approach is not only closer to ordinary experience, but emerges all the stronger by comparison with the dominant trends in modern psychology, where synolistic or whole-making views are definitely on the rise.

If we use the term "mind" as a substitute for the term "soul," then we can say that the study of mind has been decidedly impeded by two extreme opinions about its nature: first, the materialistic attitude which regards it as the sum total of properties belonging to cortical substance; second, the angelistic attitude which interprets it as a purely immaterial entity whose whole reason of being consists in thinking processes. Stoutly opposed to these extremes of position is the traditional view of Aristotle and Aquinas, which regards the soul *entitatively* as the first act or substantial form of the body, the root principle of man's very existence; and *operationally* as the fundamental source of all the vegetative, sensitive, and rational acts of man. In the first meaning, the soul accounts for the being of man, since it is an essential part of him and without it man would simply fail to exist; in the second meaning, the soul is responsible for the epiphany of man's being through its possession of powers that enable him to function. But again let me repeat that the soul is not the man, and that the powers of the soul are really the powers of man, which he employs to secure his ends. This brings us back to the anthropological attitude which Aquinas emphasizes so strongly and upon which he founds his psychology. In the synolistic principle, therefore, we have our point of departure for psychological study. It only remains for us to develop it, by reflection upon its implications, by attention to its details, and by logical coordination of the facts of operational analysis that spring from it.

iii

The Meaning of Psychology

To arrive at a correct notion of what psychology is, we must know what its proper subject matter is. On the surface this appears to be an easy task; yet it is difficult to find any two systems of modern psychology (I had almost said any **two** modern psychologists) that agree on the problem. The reason of the difficulty is really not the fault of psychology, but of the psychologists. Before attempting a settlement of the matter, let us go back once more to the philosophic views of Aquinas. Psychology is fundamentally a study of the soul. It is a study of the soul so far forth, precisely, as the soul is the form of matter, the principle of life, sensation, and reason. But it is more than this. Psychology is a study of man or of human nature. While its adequate subject matter is every besouled organism, its proper subject matter is the human organism, or man, who by his nature, or essentially, is an intellectual creature, but by his powers, or virtually, is also a sensitive and vegetative organism. If, then, we are to begin our study of psychology at the proper place, we must start, not with the analysis of man or the soul of man, but with the analysis of the things that manifest both man and his soul to us: namely, his operations. As Aquinas puts it: "We must first analyze the acts of man before we can say anything about his powers; and we must first study his powers before we can say anything about his soul." For Aquinas, then, and for those who follow in his tradition, *psychology is a study of the acts, powers, and habits of man.*

iv

The Distinction of Scientific Psychology and Philosophic Psychology

A. FORMAL OBJECT

Now, it is possible to approach the subject matter of psychology with a twofold object in view, giving us the formal distinction between the *science of psychology* and the *philosophy of psychology*. It is a distinction of capital importance, especially in view of the modern confusions that surround the problem.

Note that, in both cases, science and philosophy treat of the same subject matter—the acts, powers, and habits of man—and both begin with inductions from experience of this same subject matter. The differences arise mainly (though not solely, as we shall see in a moment) from a difference of standpoint or goal which characterizes each discipline. Thus, the science of psychology limits its analysis to acts, powers, and habits—all of which are accidents, belonging to the phenomenal order of man's life. The philosophy of psychology, on the other hand, advances its analysis beyond the facts of induction and does not repose until it has reached some notion of the nature or substance of man. Science is peripheral in its ambitions; philosophy is central. Science, therefore, is interested primarily in laws of operation and their relationships. Philosophy is concerned primarily with laws of being. The science of psychology studies chiefly what a man does. The philosophy of psychology studies chiefly what a man is. But to repeat: both disciplines have the same subject matter and the same starting point, namely, the acts, powers, and habits of man.

B. METHOD

We may further distinguish between scientific and philosophic psychology by reference to the methods appropriate to each. Thus, the philosophy of psychology is grounded on facts of public experience, facts in which all men share by virtue of their possessing the same kind of sensory equipment which is exercised upon the same kind of material. The science of psychology, by contrast, is founded on facts of special experience, exemplified in what is called the experimental procedure, wherein the senses are implemented by tools for making refinements of analysis that would be impossible to the naked powers. Whereas, then, the methods of scientific psychology are investigative, and created to yield special forms of ex-

perience, those of philosophic psychology are simply observa-
tional, designed to produce the reflective forms of experience in
which all men can participate. There is no conflict here, since
special experience does not alter common or public experience,
but merely supplements it with more abundant detail.[b]

v

Empirical Psychology and Rational Psychology

The distinction between scientific and philosophic psychology is sometimes indicated as a distinction between empirical
and rational psychology. This is most unfortunate. The terms
"empirical" and "rational" originated with Christian von
Wolff. The assumption that "empirical" is equivalent to
"scientific" and that "rational" is equivalent to "philosophic"
is wrong on several scores. First of all, the basic distinction
between the science of psychology and the philosophy of psychology is not in terms of what one senses (empirical reaction)
and what one thinks (rational reaction) about a certain thing,
but in terms of formal differences within the same subject
matter and of material differences within the same experience,
as we have already explained. Wolff was entirely ignorant of
the nature and existence of these differences. Second, "empirical" means derived from experience; and, in this sense, both
science and philosophy are derived from inductive facts. True,
philosophy is predominantly speculative, while science is predominantly investigative; yet both are empirical to the extent
that both are emergences from experience. Third, "rational"
properly refers to our human capacity of making inferences;
and since inferential procedures are common to science and
philosophy, then "rational" no more indicates the subject
matter or the method of philosophic psychology than it does
that of scientific psychology. The atmosphere of psychological

discussion would be greatly clarified, and the true nature and distinction of the scientific and philosophic species of psychology would be more clearly apprehended, if the terms "empirical" and "rational" were dropped altogether from our academic vocabularies.[c]

vi

A Generic Definition of Psychology

To sum up: there is a proper subject matter of psychology, which is man. Further, there is a twofold way of studying man: from the scientific point of view, basing our analyses on special experience and striving to express the operational relationships that obtain between the acts, powers, and habits of man; and from the philosophic point of view, grounding our analyses on public experience and striving to determine the entitative relationships of man's acts, powers, and habits to his substance or being or nature. We may define psychology, then, in a generic way, as a *study of the acts, powers, habits, and nature of man.* In this definition we can discern both the scientific and the philosophic goals of psychology, or what is phenomenal and what is noumenal in the analysis of man. Note, however, that the philosophy of psychology is not necessarily dependent upon the science of psychology, since it is possible to create a body of philosophic knowledge without the assistance of science. We have such a philosophic psychology, developed apart from science, in Aristotle's *Treatise on the Soul.* But Aristotle was primarily interested in the soul, as soul. It remained for his most brilliant commentator, Thomas Aquinas, to basically reorientate our psychological studies by focusing analysis on man. This he does in his *Treatise on Man*, where he adopts the synolistic rather than the animistic approach to the problems of human nature.

vii

Difficulties in the Development of Scientific Psychology

A. FAILURE TO DISCERN PROPER SUBJECT MATTER

The science of psychology is a thing of relatively recent invention. To speak of it as an established science is perhaps premature. To have a science of psychology we must have, first of all, a subject matter that is commonly recognized by all investigators. But this is what we do not find. On the contrary, since its establishment as a science, psychology appears to have little more than confusion and conflict to show for all its efforts at development. The most obvious reason for this state of affairs is the fact that the modern systems as a whole are not agreed upon the proper things to study in psychology. Thus, one school constricts the field to consciousness and its immediate data. Another limits its purviews to the area of behavior, leaving out all reference to facts of consciousness. It would appear that, having lost its soul, its mind, and its consciousness, in that order, psychology is now in danger of losing its scientific standing.

In a recent book called *The Logic of Modern Psychology*, Professor Carroll C. Pratt discusses the whole issue. His conclusions are neither hopeful nor flattering for the science of psychology: first, there is no way of showing that mind, or consciousness, as the subject matter of psychology, is any different from the data that all other sciences make use of; second, all psychological explanations must eventually be couched in the language of physiology; third, psychology, as a separate discipline, must ultimately be absorbed into the larger field of biology. Out of the chaos that followed upon the atomistic concept of mind, set in motion by Wundt, came a severe reaction in the other direction—the complete abolition of consciousness from the field of mental science. Thus psychology became totally immersed in physiology. Behaviorism is the modern answer to the content psychology of Wundt and the structural psychology of Titchener. The effects of Cartesian dualism are seen today in two extremes: first, the delimitation of the subject matter of psychology to facts of consciousness—an idealistic trend; second, the inclusion of the subject matter of psychology within the larger area of physiology—a materialistic trend. Fortunately, a more moderate way of looking at the situation is making its appearance in certain quarters. In practice, if not in theory, the research programs of the psychodiagnosticians, the factor psychologists, the personalists, and others, operate upon the basis of a synolistic or whole-making approach to man.

The point about the entire discussion is simply this: in the science of psychology as well as in the philosophy of psychology we must have some general framework of reference on which all investigators are agreed, before we can talk intelligently about the acts, the powers, and the habits of man, or even about his soul. We must recognize that the subject matter which is common to all approaches, whether scientific or philosophic, is man himself.

The very existence of different and often opposed schools of psychology today is proof of the fact that each system has developed in academic neglect of the true concept of man as a whole, that is, of man *as man*, whose conscious and unconscious life, whose behavior and overt modes of response, are made manifest and amenable to scientific investigation by his acts, his powers, and his habits. If the materialists are correct in their surmise that the mind of man is merely a piece of physiological mechanism, it follows that psychology is not a separate science, but merely an aspect of biological knowledge. If, on the other hand, the formalists are correct in their description of mind as an autonomous substance, existing in complete independence of the body, it follows that a science of psychology, based on methods of controlled observation, is impossible. But if, finally, we hold to the view of Aristotle and Thomas Aquinas that man is a composite substance, made up of matter and mind, the one without physical dimensions, the other possessing all the characters of extended matter; if, further, we hold that no single intellectual operation is to be found without its material correlate, no thought without an image, no volition without feeling of some sort—at once the concrete phenomena of man's mental life are seen in their true context, which is both psychological and physiological.

B. FAILURE TO DISCERN THE SCIENTIFICO-PHILOSOPHIC NATURE OF PSYCHOLOGY

The persistent polemic that has marred the story of psychology since its birth as a science may be traced to another defect: the inability of the modern investigator to recognize that psychology is a unique branch of knowledge, appropriating to itself a subject matter that is at once a subject of scientific investigation and of philosophic speculation. This means, of course, that the strictest caution must be exercised to keep the scientific and philosophic problems apart, at the same time that we recognize the validity of the methods of each.

Where we have a commonly shared subject matter, it is easy to see how the methods and objectives of science and of philosophy should be confused. Yet the two parts of psychology are not for that reason antagonistic to each other. On the contrary, observing the proper distinctions, it is quite easy to correlate them. The need of philosophic guidance for the scientist, it may be pointed out at once, is much greater than the need of scientific analysis for the philosopher. Irrespective of its advances, the most that science can contribute to philosophy is a new refinement of experience or a new illustrating of principles that were formulated centuries ago. To imagine, as some have imagined, that the basic doctrines of psychology must be transformed to meet the changing results of scientific research is as absurd as to imagine that the soul of man is transformed according to the different sorts of opinion that he entertains or the different kinds of food that he eats. Science progresses by a transition to new and better knowledge, often discarding the old as false or unsatisfactory. Philosophy progresses by a deeper and richer understanding of principles that are already known.

To repeat: the propositions of philosophic psychology are not founded on scientific fact. They cannot, therefore, be either established or repudiated by appeal to such facts. The relation of the science of mind to the philosophy of mind is a purely material relation, so far forth as science refines our public experience of things and supplies example and clarification of philosophic principles. The relation of the philosophy of mind to the science of mind, on the other hand, is both formal, to the extent that it provides the latter with principles of interpretation; and material, inasmuch as it restricts the investigation of science to the analysis of phenomenal problems. And so we reach the important position that psychology unites both philosophic analysis and scientific research in one continuous doctrine, in which philosophy answers the fundamental questions about the nature of man, and science resolves in detail the problems of his acts, powers, and habits. This is the only basis upon which the science and philosophy of mind can be related into the whole of psychological knowledge.[d]

viii

Introspection

We have said that, among the natural sciences, psychology is peculiar in having a particular subject matter: man. This fact in turn gives rise to another peculiarity within the field of methods, since man is simultaneously both the subject and the object of psychological analysis. Accordingly, it is possible and legitimate for him to employ the technique of what is called introspection (*introspicere:* to look within) in gathering the material from which his knowledge of man is structuralized. In no other branch of science does such a situation obtain. Introspection, of course, is not confined to the scientific side of psychology. It is equally valid in the philosophic dimension. This means that both the special experience which characterizes the science of psychology and the public experience on which the philosophy of psychology is founded may be drawn from facts of introspection. The differences between the two sorts of self-analysis have already been indicated in our discussion of special and common experience.

A. IN SCIENTIFIC PSYCHOLOGY

As a scientific tool, introspection has been developed only after careful and laborious efforts at precision. In Wundt's time, it meant simply having an experience and later describing it. In Titchener's time, it meant having an experience so refined and special that apparently only Titchener and his students could achieve it. A reaction was bound to set in. It was the disgust of Watson, chiefly at the overspecialized and artificial methods of the structuralists, that led the behavioristic school to reject not only introspection and all its works and pomps, but also the object of introspection, which is consciousness or the data of consciousness. This, as one observer remarks, is like throwing out the baby with the bath. Of course, the position of both the structuralists and the behaviorists is extreme, and the correct attitude towards the methods of self-observation lies somewhere in between.

The credit is usually given to Külpe and his Würzburg

school for having perfected the introspective technique and made it a scientific tool for special experience. Now, introspection means a particular kind of attitude, the adoption of which enables the investigator to observe his experience in detail, as though under a microscope. The whole conscious reaction is recorded methodically and broken up, for analysis, into fractionized periods. The same tasks are repeated over and over again, so that the account may be corrected and amplified. In the laboratories of men like Külpe, Lindworsky, and Ach, introspective analysis has reached a high degree of perfection.

B. IN PHILOSOPHIC PSYCHOLOGY

As a method of philosophic study, introspection is more naïve, since it derives immediately from the public experience of all men. It requires simply that the powers of sense be in a normal condition, and operating within the normal dimensions of space and time. Because common experience is shared by the brotherhood of men, the possibility of its being in error is reduced to a minimum. Its observations take on the character of universal pronouncements, since they do not depend on any single individual—though any single individual, with his five wits about him, can report such observations. To grasp the matters with which they deal, no education is required, no scientific or philosophic training is necessary. They are the spontaneous utterances, so to speak, of everybody's sense of reality. And so, what was true for Aristotle and Aquinas is verified by the living experience of all of us, since neither man, nor the powers of men, nor the cosmic environment in which humanity lives, nor the cosmic data on which the sense organs are commonly exercised have changed in their essential natures. Because the facts of philosophic introspection are public property and are verifiable by the experience of all men, they may be said to have the validity of objective certitude.

C. INTROSPECTION AND REALITY

Introspection means observing what is in consciousness. But, strictly speaking, what is in consciousness is not primarily an object of knowledge. Rather, it is a means of knowing or an instrument of knowledge, as we shall see in a later chapter. Moreover, the objects present to consciousness are objects either of the senses or of intellect. Some of them are capable of being apprehended by all men; and these are the objects of philosophic observation. Others can be discovered only by certain men, who are specially equipped with implements or other techniques for their detection; and these are the objects of scientific observation. But, whatever the type of cognition involved, there is no content of consciousness different from the *known* world. If the sensible in act is identical with the sense in act, and if the intelligible in act is identical with the intellect in act, then the datum of consciousness which is both known and introspected is in no wise different from the datum which is known but not introspected. The content psychology of Wundt and the structural psychology of Titchener were both wrong on the score that they made the data of consciousness, rather than the data of reality, the primary objects of their analyses. These workers failed to see that introspection is valueless unless the datum of consciousness, which is introspected, is interpreted, first and foremost, in terms of the thing which causes the conscious datum, namely, the objective world.

READINGS

Adler, M. J., *What Man Has Made of Man*, pages 124–203, New York, Longmans, 1937.

Maritain, J., *The Degrees of Knowledge*, chapter I: Philosophy and Experimental Science; chapter III: Our Knowledge of the Sensible World. New York, Scribner, 1938.

Pratt, C. C., *The Logic of Modern Psychology*. New York, Macmillan, 1939.

CLARIFICATIONS

(a)

Difference of quod and quo in principles of operation

In the operation of every corporeal substance, two principles are involved: that which acts, and this is the substance itself; and that by which it acts, and this is the first form of the substance. Moreover, the first form of a substance, as the principle by which it acts ultimately, is distinguished from the powers of a substance, as the principles by which it acts proximately. Translating these distinctions into terms of human psychology: man is the ultimate principle which acts; the soul of man is the ultimate principle by which he acts; the powers of man are the proximate principles by which he acts. Every individual substance, which is complete and perfect after its kind, is a supposit. When a supposit is endowed with rational powers, it is a human supposit or a human person. To say, then, that acts are always of a supposit simply means that the substance in question is the ultimate subject of such acts or the ultimate principle which produces such acts.

(b)

Further distinction between scientific and philosophic psychology

Philosophic psychology, as we have noted in the text, studies the nature or essence of man, whereas scientific psychology is confined to an analysis of the acts, powers, and habits of this essence. There is another distinction between the two disciplines which may be added: namely, that philosophic psychology studies the essence of man's acts, powers, and habits; whereas scientific psychology analyzes the accidental modes and quantified correlations of these acts, powers, and habits.

The relation of scientific psychology to philosophic psychology is simply a concrete instance of the broader relations that obtain between natural science as a whole and the philosophy of nature as a whole. In this connection, I should like to make reference to Professor Maritain's distinction between the empiriological character of natural science and the ontological character of natural philosophy. Both disciplines have the same subject matter, wh:ch is mobile sensible being; and so both are ultimately orientated toward the same goal, which is a knowledge of the substance of corporeal reality. But, whereas the former confines itself to the periphery of substance, investigating the accidents that manifest corporeal reality in a mobile and sensible manner, the latter plunges through to the substance itself. We might put the matter more simply by saying that while the scientist is primarily interested in the *mobility* of corporeal substance, the philosopher is chiefly concerned with the *being* of corporeal substance. Because scientific knowledge leaves us at the surface, so to speak, of corporeal reality (since its function is to study the phenomenal and changing dimensions of mobile being) it is very properly called *perinoetic*. Because philosophic knowledge leads us to the essence of corporeal reality (since its function is to analyze the nature, origin, and destiny of mobile being) it is very properly referred to as *dianoetic*.

(c)

Empirical and rational psychology

As Professor Adler points out, there is one meaning in which the Wolffian distinction between empirical and rational psychology is legitimate. Thus, empirical psychology is that body of psychological knowledge which deals with purely physical questions, that is, questions which fall within the fields of natural science or natural philosophy and have the composite man as their proper object. Rational psychology, on the other hand, is that body of psychological knowledge which is concerned with purely metaphysical questions, that is, questions which have the soul alone as their proper object.

(d)

The philosopher and the scientist

If the scientist has attempted to solve problems that rightfully belong to the philosopher, the philosopher, in turn, has been overly resistant to information that rightfully comes from the scientist. It is altogether wrong to suppose that, because a man is a great scientist, he cannot therefore be a great philosopher. The fact is, of course, that both scientific and philosophic knowledge may belong to one and the same mind. Both are habits of the intellectual order. Both are naturally complementary to each other. Both can be the achievement and possession of the same reasoning ability which is employed differently according as the objects and methods of science and philosophy differ.

CHAPTER THREE

MAN: THE INTEGER

i

Introduction

Man, the proper object of study in psychology, is a creature composed of body and soul.[a] That he has a body is self-evident. That he has a soul is concluded from the fact that he manifests vegetative, sensitive, and rational acts which cannot be explained in terms of the body alone. For, if the body of man, *qua* body, were the principle of his vital operations, then, as Aquinas observes, there is no reason why any and every body should not be living. The problem which confronts us here is the relation that obtains between the body and the soul of man. It is the most fundamental issue in psychology, since all our knowledge of the acts, powers, and habits of man is modified by the views that we take of the soul which is the root principle of these things, and of the body which is their material coefficient. Thus it makes a great deal of difference whether we consider the acts of man as acts of his soul alone, or of his body alone, or of his soul as the form of his body. Properly speaking, the problem here involved is not one of the relation of soul to body, but of soul to the material substrate which it informs. To understand this relation it is necessary to go back, briefly, to the hylomorphic doctrine of Aristotle—a doctrine founded on empirical observation and designed to explain the nature of all corporeal substances. Man is such a substance since he is made of spirit and matter; and the special position that he holds in the hierarchy of created being is due precisely to his hylomorphic constitution.

ii

The Hylomorphic Teaching of Aristotle

A. SUBSTANTIAL CHANGE

Let us start, first of all, with the broad notion of corporeal substance as anything that has matter in its nature. For the sake of clearness, we may distinguish four species of such substances, representing the four hierarchical orders of being in cosmic creation: nonliving bodies, plants, animals, men. The hylomorphic doctrine states that every individual substance included within any one of these species is composed of two principles: *hyle* or matter, and *morphe* or form.[b] Aristotle bases his philosophic interpretation on something that public experience regards as certain, namely, that in the course of the changes in nature, one substance is transformed into another. To illustrate: carbohydrates, fats, and proteins are made over into living tissues. Now, in every transformation of this sort, something remains and something is changed. To say that nothing remains would be tantamount to saying that corporeal substances are annihilated. But this is manifestly false because the chemicals that enter into a protoplasmic system can be recaptured. Again, to say that nothing is changed would signify that an organism is no different from the food that it eats. But, this, too, is wrong because living and nonliving bodies exhibit specifically different kinds of properties. We are brought back, then, to our original view: that in every conversion of substance, there must be a principle of permanence and a principle of change at the roots of such a conversion. Now, in the language of hylomorphism, the principle of permanence is known as *first matter*, and the principle of change is referred to as *first form*.

Further: if first matter is a principle of permanence, it must lie, as an abiding substrate, at the bottom of all corporeal being. Similarly, if first form is a principle of change, it must be united with first matter in such a way that, actually existing, it causes a particular corporeal substance to exist; but actually ceasing to exist, it causes a particular corporeal substance to disappear out of existence. Thus, when food is converted into protoplasm, the first matter of the food, as a principle of permanence, continues to exist as the material substrate of the living organism. The first form of food, on the other hand, as a principle of change, is lost to actual existence. And so the conditions of a true change of substance are verified, since the first matter of the food is deprived of its first form, yet, in the very instant of its loss, becomes possessed of a new determining principle which is the first form of the organism.

B. THE NATURE OF FIRST MATTER AND FIRST FORM

From an analysis of substantial change, then, we are led to infer to the existence of two basic constituents in every corporeal being: first matter, the indeterminate but determinable principle which makes possible the transformation of one substance into another; and first form, the determining principle which accounts for the fact that a given substance is the particular thing that it is and not something else. Each of these constituents, let it be noted, is real, though its reality is arrived at by an inferential process. Each, moreover, is first in its respective order of being, since nothing can be presupposed to it, nothing can be more fundamental than it. Each, too, is substantial in nature, though neither, in itself, is a complete substance. To be a complete substance or a synolon, first matter must be compounded with first form. Because it is substantial, first matter may be referred to as substantial matter. For the same reason, first form may be referred to as substantial form. If first matter represents what a thing can

be, first form represents what a thing is. Because of this opponency, first matter is separable from first form in thought,
though never in fact. There is no such thing as first matter
without first form, since there is no such thing as half a being
or an entity intermediate between being and nonbeing.

First matter has no character in itself. It is absolutely
featureless, formless, indefinite, without quality, without
quantity. To acquire definiteness and quality, to be earmarked with quantity, it must have first form. It is potentially everything, though it is actually nothing. The abundance of its thirst for form is without limit. But it exists in
reality only when conjoined to form. Consequently, there are
no differences within first matter. By nature, it is the same
wherever found: in nonliving substances, plants, animals,
men. All these things are different specifically from each other
because the material substrate of each is possessed of a specifically different substantial form. Precisely for this reason,
Aristotle calls the first form of anything its first actuality or
its first perfection: since it explains the fact that a thing is,
and that it is a particular thing, distinguishable in nature from
other species of things.[c]

C. IMPORTANCE OF THE HYLOMORPHIC DOCTRINE

It is difficult to overestimate the value of the hylomorphic
concept of substance. Beginning with corporeal reality, both
nonliving and living, wherein he finds a dual principle of
matter and form, Aristotle progresses to a higher level of
abstraction, wherein the hylomorphic doctrine is metaphys-
ically refined into the principles of potency and act, thus
supplying the analytical mind with the primary determinations of all created being. Before his time, both Democritus
and Plato had made the mistake of conferring upon matter an
existence apart from form. Indeed, form was regarded simply

as an adjunct or accidental determination of matter. Aristotle gave entitative value to each principle. For him substance meant a union of matter and form in furdamental proportions. From the Aristotelian concept of substance comes the further distinction of what is essential to a thing, such as its active and passive principles of being, from what is accidental, such as its powers and operations. It is this concept of substance that furnishes the philosopher with the focal point of his analyses. The scientist, however, may ignore it with no detrimental results, so long as he does not falsify or negate it. He can ignore it for the reason that it does not properly fall within range of scientific investigation. The only way he can employ it is through its structural or operational implications.

iii

Man a Hylomorphic Creature

Applied to man, the hylomorphic doctrine states that between the first matter and the first form of every human being there is a bond of perfect substantial union. This means, more concretely, that the body of man, as first matter, is an incomplete substance; that the soul of man, as first form, is likewise an incomplete substance; that body and soul together, in a bond of mutual complementation, make one complete substance which is man. We may remark again in passing that the problem of a substantial union between the material and formal elements of man's being was so obvious to the mind of Aristotle as to require no special discussion. Thus, in his *Treatise on the Soul*, he says: "We can dismiss as wholly unnecessary the question whether the body and soul are one [complete substance]. It is a question as meaningless as to ask whether the wax and the shape given to it by the stamp are one. . . . Oneness has many meanings . . . but the most proper and fundamental meaning . . . is the relation of an actuality to that of which it is the actuality." Aquinas, however, visualizing the subject matter of psychology as man rather than the soul of man, was obliged, by the very terms of his anthropological position, to make an issue of the body-soul problem; and he adduces several reasons to show that the union between the two is a substantial one.

iv

Proofs of Man's Hylomorphic Nature

A. SOUL THE FIRST FORM OF MATTER

The first argument of the Angelic Doctor is simply a demonstration of the fact that the soul of man is the first form or first actuality of his material substrate. For obviously, if such is the case, then between first matter and first form, or between body and soul, there must be a substantial union. "That by which any organism lives," says Aquinas, "is its soul. Now, life is exhibited in different kinds of substances by different sorts of operations. It follows, therefore, that the source of all man's vital acts is, in the last analysis, his soul. For, the soul is the first principle by which we live, and feel, and move about; and likewise the first principle by which we understand. And so this basic source of our intellectual achievements, whether it be called mind or rational soul, must be the form of the body."

Thus, from the beginning of his psychological analysis, Aquinas is stoutly opposed to the notion of soul as some mysterious entity that, by miracle or trickery, has to be fitted into a body. Rather, it is the operational concept which interests him first; and, from his study of human activities, he concludes to the existence, within man, of a principle of organ-

ization and unity which alone can give meaning to the pattern
of human behavior. This principle, of course, is the soul.
Now, it is in the very nature of the soul to be united with
matter, since only on this condition is it able to expand and
perfect its powers. Together with matter, it constitutes the
integral being which is man. Just as the hand or the foot is
not called a body but only the member of a body, so the
human body or the human soul, considered separately, is not
called a person but only the entitative part of a person. The
complete being or synolon is man, since only man possesses
the entire nature of a species. Yet, to be a person, man must
have a body and a soul, combined in a substantial union.[d]

B. SENSATION AND EMOTION

The same inference is reached from a study of the facts of
sensational and emotional experience. Thus, certain of the
acts of man are common to his *psyche* or soul and his *soma* or
body. Such operations have a formal as well as a material
principle of origin and are, therefore, very properly described
as psychosomatic in character. In the words of Aquinas:
"Although the soul of man has functions which are peculiar
to itself and in which the body does not communicate, for
instance, the acts of his intellect, there are, nevertheless, other
functions that are shared by the soul and body conjointly,
such as his sensations and his emotions of fear and anger.
Phenomena of this kind originate as a result of certain changes
in definite areas of the body; from which it is manifest that
they are acts of the soul and body working together." Now,
a sensation or an emotion is a unit experience. It possesses a
synthetic quality and a character of oneness that would be
impossible to explain except on the grounds that its psychic
and somatic features proceed ultimately from a single substance, which is man.

C. MUTUAL INFLUX OF HIGHER AND LOWER FUNCTIONS

Further, were this not so, it would be impossible to explain why intense acts within the psychosomatic field, such as our emotional disturbances, very often constitute impediments to our purely intellectual functions; just as, in the other direction, deep abstract study frequently slows down the body processes, makes us impervious to the effects of external stimulation, and even impedes altogether the operation of the senses. The whole matter is described very clearly by Aquinas. "Because all the powers of the soul are rooted in one essence, and because body and soul together form a single composite being, it is quite natural to find that body and soul are mutually interactive, and that the higher and lower powers of the soul influence each other. To give a few instances: the apprehensions of the soul may be so violent as to make the body change its temperature, even to the point of producing illness and death. Men have been known to die because of the excess of their joys or sorrows or loves. On the other hand, the changes that take place in the body react upon the soul, and the material complexions of the one are frequently reproduced immaterially in the other, as in the case where somatic disease produces psychic abnormalities. Similarly, the intensity of acts produced by the higher powers often has a direct and immediate effect upon the lower powers. For example: acts of strong volition may produce emotions in the sensitive appetites; just as acts of deep contemplation slow down or stop altogether the movements that are proper to our animal nature. On the other hand, the intensity of acts produced by the lower powers may have a positive influence upon the higher powers. A man's reason, for instance, may be so befogged by the violence of his passions that he cannot think properly. Under such conditions, he may even go to the lengths of concluding that the satisfaction of his appetites is the only thing worth-while."

D. UNITY OF THE EGO

Again, if anyone should say that the soul of man is not the form of his body, he must explain how it is that a particular act of man, such as his thinking, is an act of man himself. For, as Aquinas says: "A man is always conscious of the fact that it is he himself who understands." The evidences are plain enough. Thus, men commonly attribute all their actions to a single subject which is the ego, as when they say: "I know, I feel, I live." But it would be patent nonsense to assert that a man's highly diversified modes of response, his intellectual apprehensions and intellectual loves, his sense knowledge, emotions, and animal movements, his eating, drinking, sleeping, and begetting, are really his own actions and unified by reference to himself, unless he is a single substance. It would be just as nonsensical to identify himself today with the person that he was yesterday, a year ago, or a decade ago, as he most certainly does, unless there were a permanent basis for his existence and actions as an individual. Public experience testifies to the fact that there is such a basis for all that he thinks and says and does, something that endures throughout the multitudinous changes to which every human being is liable. This is what we mean by the *person* of man, the perfect and complete substance which is the ultimate subject of all his actions—a substance made up of body and soul joined together by nature in a most intimate substantial union.

E. REPUGNANCE TO SUFFERING AND DEATH

Man's life and health, as Aquinas observes, depend on the subjection of his body to his soul. His suffering and death, on the other hand, are due to a failure of such subjection. Now, life is being, and health is well-being. When, therefore, the body of man is conjoined to the soul of man, we refer this fact to his being. When, in addition, the body of man is perfectly united with the soul of man, we refer this fact to his well-being. Just as what is capable of being made perfect is subject to what is actually perfect, or, more generally, what is potential is subject to what is actual, so the body of man is subject to his soul. As Aristotle pointed out, the body of man corresponds to what exists in potentiality, since it is the material part of his nature. The soul of man corresponds to what exists in actuality, since it is the formal part of his nature.

The body of man, therefore, is disposed and perfected precisely to the extent that it falls under the domination of the soul. But, sickness and death are failures of the soul to achieve such domination. For, sickness is a partial conquest of matter over spirit; death is a complete victory. While on earth, man naturally desires, first, the things that contribute to his being; then, the things that make for his well-being. Now, as we have already said, life is the good of being, and health is the good of well-being. For this reason, man naturally shrinks from what endangers either his life or his health. But the instinctive character of this aversion cannot be accounted for except on the grounds that nature has wedded the flesh and spirit of man in a bond of the closest intimacy. Such a bond is found only in a substantial union. So we conclude, once more, that man is a creature substantially composed of body and soul.

v

Oneness of Man's Substantial Form

If man is one, concludes Aquinas, then so is his soul one. "There is no other substantial form in man besides his intellectual soul, a soul that virtually contains a sensitive and vegetative form, just as it virtually contains all other inferior forms, since it alone can do whatever forms less perfect than itself can do." And again: "By his substantial form, which is human, man is not only a man, but also an animal, a plant, a body, a substance, and a being." In these passages, Aquinas clearly indicates his position regarding the erroneous doctrine of plurality of forms which was quite the common teaching of his day. Note that an inferior form, which is virtually contained in a superior one, is not actually present as a form, but is operationally included in the hierarchy of powers which the superior form exhibits. Every substance has an ordered arrangement and sequence of powers, though it has no ordered scale of forms. As Aquinas points out: "There is but one substantial being in every single substance. Now, it is substantial form that endows a thing with substantial being. Consequently, one thing possesses but one substantial form; and since the soul is the substantial form of man, it follows that there can be no substantial form in him except the intellectual soul."

Moreover: "If a man were vegetatively alive because of a plant form, sensitively alive because of an animal form, and intellectually alive because of a rational form, then he would not be simply one." We may illustrate the point, as Aristotle did, by reference to a mathematical figure. A pentagon virtually contains a quadrangle, which in turn virtually contains a triangle. To reveal the actual presence of the quadrangle and the triangle, it is necessary only to draw diagonal lines. We may go even further and say that, although the properties of a pentagon are not the same as those of a quadrangle, yet they include the properties of the latter figure, just as the properties of a quadrangle include those of a triangle. Note, however, that *potential* quadrangular or triangular properties, as they lie in a pentagon, are not the same as *actual* quadrangular or triangular properties, as they lie in a quadrangle or triangle.

This leads to a further important observation on the powers of man. For, although the human soul contains all the powers of the animal and plant soul, these powers are only virtually identical with those of the lower forms. Thus, man is only virtually an animal and a plant, because his sensitive and vegetative powers are subordinate to his higher powers, which are intellect and will. This means, in effect, that the abilities of man are comparable to the powers of animal and plant life only in an analogical way.

vi

Nonhylomorphic Explanations of Human Nature

In the history of philosophic thought, there have been many attempts to solve the body-soul problem in a manner quite different from that of Aristotle and Aquinas; yet, in the last analysis, we find but one alternative to the hylomorphic solution. For, if the body and soul of man are not substantially conjoined, then the union between them must be a merely accidental one. Two types of explication have been advanced, under which all nonhylomorphic accounts may be grouped: first, theories of interactionism, which began with Plato and were repeated by Descartes and the later Cartesians; second, theories of parallelism, which were first expounded in scientific language by Fechner and Wundt and afterwards developed with incidental variations by succeeding psychologists.

To see that all these accounts are ultimately the same, one need but reflect that, historically, parallelism stems from the teaching of Descartes, through Leibniz's theory of pre-established harmony and Geulincx's occasionalism; while, philosophically, parallelism is simply an attempt to show how body and soul can operate side by side without being causally related. It makes little difference that the Platonists were less concerned about the body and more about the soul and its spiritual integrity; and that the parallelists are less concerned about the soul and more about the body and the law of physical conservation. Fundamentally, the two positions come to the same thing: that body and soul have only incidental relationships with each other.

vii

Theories of Interactionism

A. STATEMENT OF DOCTRINE

It is relatively easy to set forth the case of the Platonist and the Cartesian. For Plato and his school, the soul is a substance complete in itself and of such pure spiritual texture that it is repulsive to think of it as substantially united with matter. Aquinas describes the position of Plato and his followers by saying that body and soul are linked together as a pilot is attached to his ship or as a person is attached to his clothing. It is wrong, therefore, to maintain that man is composed of soul and body. Rather, one should say that man is a soul, wrapped up in a body. Peter, for example, is a human being dressed in a dinner jacket. So, man is a soul clothed in a body. There is no more intimacy of contact between the soul and body of man than between Peter and his dinner jacket.

Similarly, for Descartes and his disciples, man is not one substance, but two different and widely opposed substances: mind, something that thinks, whose very essence, in fact, is thought; and matter, something that mechanizes, whose very essence is extension. In the Cartesian picture of man, therefore, the dichotomy of soul and body, or of mind and matter, is complete and absolute, since Descartes's unextended mind cannot communicate with his extended body—except, of course, in a purely mechanical or accidental way.

B. REJECTION OF DOCTRINE

Set squarely against all such views are the facts of ordinary experience already recounted, which Aquinas adduces in disproof of the Platonic position. Thus, it is impossible to account for sensations and emotions—acts that are essentially psychosomatic in character—except on the grounds that soul and body are entitative parts of the total substance which is man. Again, the interchange of effects between the rational and sensitive levels of operation, the influence of strong acts of the will on the passions, for example, and of vehement passions on the intellect, are also inexplicable except on a basis of a substantial union between soul and body. The conclusion which Aquinas draws from these factual data is inevitable: that the principle by which the body of man exercises any of its living functions is the soul. But, to live is the essence of living things. Consequently, the soul of man must be the principle from which his body derives its life and very being. This is equivalent to saying that the soul is the substantial form of the body.

viii

Theories of Parallelism

A. STATEMENT OF DOCTRINE

The case of the parallelists is more difficult to expose because of the obscurity that attaches to their meaning of the word "mind." For Aquinas, mind is synonymous with intellectual power or intellectual essence.[e] For the moderns, on the other hand, mind is synonymous with a state of consciousness or a series of such states. At any rate, consciousness appears to be the only thing left of Descartes's original thinking substance; and even consciousness is not admitted on all sides. The whole situation is confusing, paradoxical, and full of contradictions. Thus, while most parallelists would deny the reality of the soul, all of them seem ready to grant at least a theoretical existence to psychic as well as physical activities in the life of man. To be sure, these psychic activities may be nothing more than aspects of physical activities, just as thinking may be nothing more than an aspect of cortical function; yet the problem is always posed by the parallelists as a psychophysical one, and the end result of all their speculative efforts is ever the same: a puzzle that simply cannot be put together; an enigma that will not yield up its secret; an insoluble issue. This is hardly to be wondered at when the problem is neither properly understood nor properly stated.

Let us try to outline the basic features of the parallelist position, as set down by Wundt and Fechner. According to its most general terms, for every variation in neural processes, there is a concomitant variation in conscious processes. The neural processes are physical; the conscious processes are psychic. The account, therefore, is commonly referred to as the theory of psychophysical parallelism. According to Wundt, the two realms of actions here indicated are separate, in the sense that they are not related by any causal link. According to Fechner, there is no mental event without its physical counterpart, and no physical event without its mental counterpart. Indeed, the two are really not separate things at all, but merely two phases or moments of one and the same thing.

B. REJECTION OF DOCTRINE

To illustrate Wundt's parallelism we may use the double-clock figure. It helps to explain (so the Wundtians say) how psychic energy, manifest in all vital operations and especially in the volitional dimension, can be reconciled with the law of conservation. The two clocks synchronize exactly, although they run in complete independence of each other. One clock represents the conscious processes, the other the neural processes. The account, however, does not tell us how the two timepieces are kept going and why they synchronize so perfectly. Neither does it indicate on what grounds neural events are identified with purely physical events.

To illustrate Fechner's parallelism, we may use the example of a concave-convex lens. Thus, if we look at the psychophysical process from the inside it is concave, that is, conscious or psychic; if we regard it from the outside it is convex, that is, neural or physical. What is a complicated process in light transmissions and in the ganglion cells of the nervous system from a physical point of view, is a sensation of color from a mental standpoint. Two monistic alternatives present themselves to such an explanation: either the neural process is simply an aspect of the psychic, and then we have panpsychism, which is pure formalism; or, the psychic process is simply an aspect of the physical process, and then we have panhylism, which is pure materialism. In neither case can we have a true mind-matter problem.*

If mind is simply a series of psychic or physical processes, then we should have as many minds as we have conscious experiences or changes in metabolism. Further, if thinking is the thinker and eating is the eater, then one should become a different person every time he alters his point of view or changes his habits of feeding. All of which is utterly absurd, as common sense tells us! The fact is, of course, that a man does change his opinion, just as he changes his diet. But beneath the succession of vegetative, sensitive, and rational acts that comprise his daily life, there is a permanent substance which remains throughout these mutations of consciousness and organic life, and supplies the foundation for them.

No man, in his right reason, can deny the permanency of his ego. The facts of recall and personal identity are unintelligible except on the condition that man is fundamentally an enduring substance, not a series of psychic or physical processes. What the parallelist refuses to admit is that, apart from the complete identification or the complete separation of psychic and physical events, there is another way of explaining the mental life of man within the system of mechanical energies. He fails to see that mind is primarily, not an operation, but a substance; that as a substance its nature is incomplete; that it constitutes a perfect being only when it informs the body; and that where material energies are concerned (as in vegetable movements, like metabolism, or in sensitive movements, like emotion), the functions of mind or soul are directional, not causative. To picture mind as a stream of consciousness or as a force within a force is meaningless. It gets us nowhere. But to picture it as the form of the body and the ultimate reason of man's existence and ability to act is to give the only account of it that can satisfactorily explain both the findings of experimental science and the data of public experience.

READINGS FROM AQUINAS

Summa Theologica, part I, questions 75–76.
Contra Gentiles,　　book II, chapters 56–72.

NOTE: for all readings from Aquinas, the student is referred to the translation made by the English Dominican Fathers and published by Burns, Oates & Washbourne, Ltd., London. This translation includes the *Summa Theologica* in 22 volumes; the *Contra Gentiles* in four volumes; and the *De Potentia Dei* in three volumes. All the suggested readings in the text are confined to these three works of Aquinas.

CLARIFICATIONS

(a)

Body and soul

I should like to make it clear from the outset that when the term "body" is used in conjunction with the term "soul" as in the phrases "the body-soul relationship," "man is a creature composed of body and soul," "the soul requires a body for its perfection," and so on, "body" always refers to first matter. Actually, the human soul confers on first matter all the perfections that we witness in the human body. In other words, the soul is united directly and immediately to first matter, as to its co-principle in the constitution of man. Strictly speaking, a body or corporeal substance is something that has already been perfected by union with a substantial form. To be precise, therefore, one should always say that the constitutive principles of man's essence are first matter and rational soul. This is the way in which the "body-soul" phraseology is to be understood in the text.

(b)

Etymology of hylomorphism

In the classical Greek, both *morphe* and *eidos* are used to signify "form," but with certain differences. Thus, *morphe* means (a) the shape of an object; (b) the appearance of a thing as opposed to its reality; (c) accidental form as opposed to substantial form. *Eidos* means (a) the shape of an object; (b) predicable form or predicable species as contrasted with predicable gender, predicable difference, and so forth; (c) intentional form or the medium by which subject and object are united in the act of knowledge, as opposed to real form or substantial form; (d) first form as opposed to first matter. From this comparison of meanings it appears that, as a means of indicating the basic constituents of corporeal substance, the combination of *eidos* with *hyle* would be more accurate than the combination of *morphe* with *hyle* which is the one in current use.

(c)

First matter and first form

First matter is distinguished from second matter in the same way that the constituent part of an entity is distinguished from the whole entity. Thus, first matter is united with first form to produce a complete corporeal substance. Second matter is united with nothing else substantial since it is already complete, having its first matter and first form combined in basic proportions, so that it is able to exhibit itself to the observer in all its sensible properties.

The distinction of first form from second form, on the other hand, is a distinction of what is substantial from what is accidental. Thus, a corporeal being must have substantial form before it can have accidental form. Moreover, from the nature of the case, a corporeal being can have only one substantial form, though it can, and does, possess several accidental forms.

(d)

Complete and incomplete substances

"For one thing to be the substantial form of another thing," says Aquinas, "two conditions must be fulfilled. The first is that the form be the principle of substantial being for the thing of which it is the form. . . . The second is that the form and matter combine together in one being."

The soul of man satisfies both these conditions, and so it is a substantial form. Yet it is like no other substantial form. On the one hand, it is not so independent of matter that, without a body, it can attain its operational perfection. On the other hand, it is not so dependent on matter that, without a body, it ceases actually to exist. It cannot, therefore, be a complete substance in the sense that it is a complete essence or complete species, since it needs to be united with matter before its own nature is perfected and before, in conjunction with matter, it establishes the complete essence which is man. Nevertheless, there is a meaning in which it is complete, namely, from the point of view of its substantiality, since it is able to continue existing after its separation from matter.

I should like to point out further, with Aquinas, that "although matter and form have one being, it does not follow that matter always equals the being of the form. In fact, the more noble the form, the more it surpasses matter in its being. This is clear to anyone who studies the operations of form, from the analysis of which we conclude as to the nature [of the form], since a thing operates according as it is. Consequently, a form whose operation surpasses the condition of matter, itself also surpasses matter in the excellence of its being." To this we may add the further consideration that a form whose operation surpasses the condition of matter also surpasses, in the excellence of its being, other forms whose operations are wholly immersed in matter. Of the latter species are the forms of all corporeal substances below man in the hierarchical scale.

(e)

Mind: intellectual power or intellectual soul

Aquinas uses the word "mind" in two meanings: first, to signify an intellectual power, as when he says: "Mind may be understood to embrace . . . those powers which, in their operations, are altogether removed from matter and material conditions"; second, to signify an intellectual soul, as when he says: "The soul of man, which is also called his mind or intellect, is something incorporeal and subsistent."

I agree with Professor Pegis when he says that, in its modern meaning, "mind" is a most misleading term, because of its mystic or quasi supernatural connotations, and because its definition has been so enucleated as to correspond with nothing real. Certainly it is not a term in frequent use by Aquinas. I should like to emphasize once more the fact that, for the majority of our contemporary psychologists, mind means nothing more than a state of consciousness or a series of such states. In this diluted significance, it is applied to sensitive as well as rational forms of awareness, for example: the mind of the animal, the mental life of the animal, and so forth. This "denatured mind of the modern," as Professor Pegis characterizes it, has little or no connection with the *mens* of Aquinas, which, as indicated above, is either an intellectual power or an intellectual soul.

(f)

Philosophic approaches to the body-soul problem

Reference is made in the text to the monistic explanations of human nature. Applied to man, the doctrine of monism holds that only matter or only spirit is real. The first position is materialistic, the second, idealistic. Obviously, there can be no problem of psychosomatic relationship for the monist if body alone or soul alone is real. In the following diagram, I have indicated the various philosophic attitudes that have been assumed toward the body-soul problem, the proper solution of which is critical for all psychology.

DIAGRAM 2. THE BODY-SOUL PROBLEM

Monism	soma the only existent	materialism
	psyche the only existent	idealism
Dualism	soma and psyche accidentally related	interactionism
		parallelism, etc.
	soma and psyche substantially related	hylomorphism

CHAPTER FOUR

THE VEGETATIVE LIFE OF MAN

i

The Body of Man

Speaking of the idealists and their attitude toward the mind-body problem, Aquinas remarks rather sharply: "In focusing their attention on the nature of the soul alone, Plato and the other philosophers like him overlooked the equally necessary task of discussing the nature of the body; why a body is appropriate for the soul; what sort of body is united with the soul; how the union of body and soul is actually accomplished." It was quite inevitable, in fact, that the Platonists should fail to grasp the true nature of the soul when they so studiously neglected to consider the body which is the material coefficient of man's being. I dare say that if the Angelic Doctor were alive today, he would make it his business to learn all there is to be known about the human body.

As a part of creation, man stands on the fringe of two universes: one, the world of matter and material dimensions; the other, the world of spirit, which has neither length, nor breadth, nor weight, nor any other tangible property. If, on one side, he is akin to the animal, plant, and mineral, on the other, he is neighbor to the angels. Truly, he is a denizen of two worlds, a horizon and a meeting place. Though angelic by his intelligence, yet he is not a pure spirit; though sensitive and passionate by his brute powers, yet he is not entirely material. He is placed between beast and angel, sharing something of the destiny of both. Many philosophers since the time of Plato have been inclined to look upon the body as a hindrance and

85

an evil. Many have advocated a Platonic flight into the world
of fancy. Not so Aquinas! Of the Angelic Doctor it cannot be
said, as it was said of Plotinus, that he hated to be a man.

As a hylomorphist and a follower of the Aristotelian tradition, Thomas was compelled to defend the rights of the body
against the doctrines of a false angelicism, and to claim for it
a substantial share in the composition of human nature and
in the economy of human action. Man is bound by a natural
debt to live with others in a spirit of true conviviality, to share
his material pleasures with others, to give his body the care,
attentions, and recreations that befit it as an essential part of
his person.[a] In the final analysis, the soul is not a complete
and independent substance as far as man's specific nature is
concerned. It requires a body in order to reach the level of
perfection that is possible to it, since actually it can perform
no single operation until it has been immersed in matter. Because he has matter as well as spirit in his make-up, and because all the attributes of created reality are somehow tele-
scoped within his being, man is very properly referred to as a
microcosmos.

ii

The Plastic Medium of the Soul

The human body occupies a place, on the scale of magni-
tudes, halfway between the atomic and stellar worlds. It is
truly gigantic by comparison with the atom, but dwarfed and
insignificant when measured by the stars. To outward appearances it is a thing of simplicity; yet the actual character of
its arrangements and functions is so complex as to bewilder
the imagination. Because his being has a material texture,
man is able to express himself to the world. His figure and
posture, his carriage and lineaments, are all so many sacramental forms that reveal the powers and habits of his soul. In

the open book that we call a man's visage, it is possible, very often, to discover his virtues and his vices, his insights and his stupidities, his feelings and attitudes, and the whole cultural background against which his life has been projected. Even his temperament and disposition, his state of health and proneness to disease, are written, as plainly as symbols can convey meaning, across the lines and features of his face. And so the body of man, and particularly the countenance of man, is a mask of inner realities, but a mask that is sometimes pierced by the living light which shines out from his soul.[b]

iii

The Outside of Man's Body

Man's body may be likened to a cylindrical mass of matter, perforated by several tracts or cavities that open upon the outside world. One of these, the alimentary tract, runs through the body from end to end. Another, the respiratory tract, starts at the top and extends downward. A third and fourth, the urinary and uterine tracts, start from the bottom and reach upward. Whatever is in these spaces, as food in the stomach, air in the lungs, urine in the bladder, the growing child in its mother's womb, is not, strictly speaking, inside the body. This means that there are two surfaces to the human body: an outside surface, covered by skin; and an inside surface, covered by mucosae.

The skin is relatively impervious to the action of water, gases, and foods, but the mucous membranes allow these substances to pass through with ease. The skin is exposed to the elemental forces of nature: light, heat and cold, wind and rain, dryness and humidity; yet it effectively protects us against the unceasing variations in our environment, at the same time that it regulates the temperature of the body by the evaporation of moisture over its surface. It is supple, elastic, and durable, permitting the delicate underlying tissues to act in their proper fluid media without wear and tear, without friction and excessive heat. Its durability is due to the manner in which it is constructed, with layer upon layer of cells that slowly and endlessly multiply and die as they push toward the outer surface of the body, to be sloughed off eventually and replaced by other cells.

Through both its external and its internal faces, or through modifications of its surface areas, the body comes in contact with the objects of sense. The skin and mucosae are the dwelling places of numerous receptors that admit lights and sounds, odors and flavors, pressures, painful and thermal stimuli, as food for the mind of man; just as the membranous linings of the intestines permit the passage of nutritive material, as food for the body of man.

iv

The Inside of Man's Body

On the inside, the human body is structuralized out of cells, tissues, organs, and fluids, protected by serous membranes, and supported by bones and muscles. In its general form, it is molded upon the outlines of the skeletal system. The bones that comprise it are of varying sizes and shapes, and are designed by their patterning to supply attachments for muscles, tendons, and ligaments, and to provide scaffolding and enclosures for the vital organs. The brain and spinal cord are the most fragile of all man's anatomical instruments. To secure them against injury, therefore, nature has provided the hard osseous boxes known as the cranium and the spinal vertebrae. At the same time, she shields them from internal friction by lodging them in the folds of a system of membranes and surrounding the whole delicate mass with a cushion of liquid.

The heart and lungs, also so necessary to life, are suspended in a framework built of the sternum, ribs, and spinal column. Finally, in the large cavity formed by the pelvis, abdominal muscles, and diaphragm, we find all the organs that go under the name of viscera: the stomach, intestines, liver, kidneys, spleen, pancreas, adrenal and reproductive glands. In addition to their supportive offices, the ends of long bones, like the humerus, femur, and tibia, also contribute toward the production of red blood corpuscles, by supplying from their marrow the elements out of which these tiny but indispensable bodies are created.

v

The Biological Unit of Man's Body

A. THE CELL

The unit of all living matter is the cell. Some organisms are simply one cell. Others are multicellular. Man's body is of the latter sort. It is composed, in fact, of billions of cells, built into various kinds of tissues and organs. Despite their minuteness, cells are very complex things. When we isolate one of them and magnify it on a screen, it appears larger than man himself. All its parts are then visible. In the middle of the cell body floats an ovoid and elastic structure known as the nucleus. Around it, we notice a great agitation of small particles, clustered together in vesicles, and identified by the biologist as the apparatus of Golgi. Other small granules congregate near one end of the nucleus to form a centrosphere whose function, along with that of the nucleus, is connected somehow with the reproductive acts of the cell. Other important organs are the chondriosomes, resembling short bent pieces of thread. They are quite constant in the various kinds of cells, and, along with the apparatus of Golgi, are involved in nutritional and growth activities. Plastids are modified portions of cellular substance, presumed to function as storehouses of physiological energy, which they radiate out in all directions for the lifework of the organism. All these elements, appearing in our picture on the screen, are seen to glide and dance and undulate perpetually in the extranuclear spaces of the cell body.

The nucleus, through the magnifying lens, looks like an inert transparent jelly. In it we may discern other smaller ovoid bodies known as nucleoli which, because they disappear when the cell is dividing, are thought to hold metabolic reserves for the reproductive procedure. But most vital and significant of all, the nucleus contains chromatin, the physical basis of heredity. When the cell is in a resting stage, the chromatin is scattered in granular form throughout the whole nuclear area. With the onset of the reproductive process, however, it loses its granular appearance and assumes the shape of a string of beads. Each bead is known as a chromosome; and the number of chromosomes for the various species of plants and animals is always fixed—forty-eight, for example, in the case of man. Actually, each chromosome is a packet of submicroscopic entities called genes; and it is by the genes that the traits of a family are handed down from one generation to another. When the cell is about to reproduce, the entire chromatinic thread is split lengthwise, giving rise to two fairly well-defined groups of halved chromosomes. At the same time, the whole cell shakes violently, tosses its contents about in all directions, and divides into separate parts. Now we have two daughter cells, resultant upon the mitosis of the original mother cell. By reproductive acts of this sort, the tissues, organs, and systems of man's body are built up from a single cell, the original fertilized ovum, or zygote.

B. KINDS OF CELLS

Cells, like plants, animals, and men, belong to different races. Some of them are fixed, forming the tissues and organs of the body. Others are mobile, able to travel throughout the organism. Of the first category, the epithelial and connective cells are the most important because they supply the building stones of the tissues and organs, as well as the solid protection and elasticity which these parts of the body demand, according to their respective functions. Of the second category, the white and red blood corpuscles are the chief representatives. The whole body of man is a compact unit, in which all the cell communities are integrated. The spatial arrangement of these cell communities is dependent upon their food requirements. Thus, the architecture and healthy functioning of each organ always calls for its immersion in a medium that is rich in nutritive materials and not too much encumbered by waste products. The blood, of course, is the most widespread of all organic media, since it penetrates to every part of the body. But besides the blood, there are several local media, composed of the lymphatic fluids that filter through the walls of the capillary vessels surrounding each organ. Not a great deal is known about the characteristics of these local media except that the tissues and organs of the body create them at the expense of the blood plasma.

C. BLOOD PLASMA AND ITS CELLS

Blood plasma is a solution of bases, acids, salts, and proteins, so perfectly balanced that it is able to furnish the cells of the body with a medium which is neither too sour nor too alkaline. Blood plasma also contains sugars, fats, enzymes, metals in small quantities, and the secretions of all the glands. It is an enormously complex thing, whose chemical nature is still imperfectly known. What we do know, however, is that every cell of the whole body finds in it the nutriment that is necessary to life. In addition, blood plasma contains a number of antibodies which act to prevent the multiplication of harmful bacteria; as well as fibrinogen, mother of fibrin—a substance that spontaneously adheres to the wounds of blood vessels and tends to stop excessive bleeding.

Suspended in the blood plasma is an immense population of red and white corpuscles, the mobile units of man's body. Red corpuscles are not living entities, but enucleated cells. They contain a pigment known as hemoglobin, which gives them their distinctive color. During the passage of blood through the lungs, each sac of hemoglobin takes on a load of oxygen, to be handed over, a few minutes later, to the greedy tissues. At the same time the tissues take delivery of the vital oxygen, they get rid of their waste products by passing them off into the blood stream. White corpuscles, on the other hand, are living cells. Sometimes they float in the blood stream; sometimes they escape through the walls of the capillary vessels into the lymphatic fluids and creep onto the surfaces of tissues and organs. Some of them are phagocytes, ingesting and destroying waste matter and bacteria that would harm the body, and rushing to the surface of a wound where they fight the agencies of infection. So versatile is their power that they can actually metamorphose into fixed cells and become connective tissue when nature is healing an injury.

vi

The Vegetative Acts of Man

A. NUTRITION

Nutrition is synonymous with life itself. Three sorts of nutritive material contribute to the sustenance of man's body: oxygen; the food that he eats; and the chemicals that are secreted by his internal glands. All of these substances, it should be noted, are distributed throughout the body by the blood stream. Oxygen is vital for the combustion of tissues and the consequent release of energies that enable the body to work. It is absorbed out of the atmosphere by the lungs. The foods that we eat are treated in turn by the saliva, the gastric juices, and the secretions of the pancreas, liver, and intestinal mucosae. Sugars, fats, proteins, and inorganic salts are the main constituents of our diet. The digestive ferments work on these substances until they are molecularly dispersed and able to traverse the mucous membranes of the intestines. Of course, we do not digest and absorb all the things that we eat. What remains is waste, as far as the body is concerned; and so it passes along the intestines and is cast out in the alvine discharge.

The secretions of the internal glands are true nutritive elements for the organism. They not only supply food to certain tissues, but also furnish the necessary stimulus for many of our vital functions. The thyroid, for example, manufactures thyroxin, the adrenal glands and the islands of Langerhans in the pancreas synthesize adrenalin and insulin—chemicals that are indispensable for the nutrition of cells and organs. The whole endocrine system, in fact, has specific services to perform without which metabolism and growth would be seriously impaired. Moreover, excess or defect in the action of these important somatic structures often means stunted psychic development, lack of emotional balance, and even idiocy.

But metabolism is not complete with the absorption of oxygen, digested foodstuffs, and glandular secretions into the blood. These substances must be distributed throughout the body. Further, all the waste products resultant upon constructive metabolism must be safely and adequately eliminated. Accordingly, nature has provided the body with the circulatory system. The speed with which the blood flows through the organism is sufficiently moderate to ensure that the cells and tissues are properly supplied with nutriment. At the same time, it is rapid enough to prevent its composition from being modified by the lactic and carbonic acids and other useless products that are created when cells and tissues are oxidized. When circulation slackens or stops, the acid content of the blood plasma and interstitial lymph becomes high and injurious effects may result. Interference with the blood supply of the brain, for example, ends in death if the anemia is extended beyond a few minutes. Even the briefest stoppage of bloodflow through cortical areas is always attendant with disorders of one kind or another. Lowering of blood pressure is also dangerous, since the brain and other organs of the body require a certain tension in their fluid media. Quite obviously, therefore, the conscious life of man is conditioned in large measure by the soundness of his circulatory mechanisms.

To purify itself, and maintain its composition in proper balance, the blood passes through certain systems that are able to extract all the waste matter with which it is laden. When venous blood returns from the muscles and organs, it is surcharged with acids and other catabolites of nutrition. The pulsating movements of the heart then drive it into the immense network of the lung capillaries, where its carbonic acid is discharged into the bronchial cavities as carbon dioxide and exhaled in the act of breathing. But the blood still contains a number of acids that are nonvolatile and must be eliminated in some other way. Its purification is completed during its passage through the kidneys, where all the remaining by-products of metabolism are effectively removed, passed on through the renal tubules and ureters into the bladder, and eliminated finally in the urine.

Such are the main features of man's metabolic acts. In

their fundamental philosophic aspects, they bear witness to
the fact that he is a creature fashioned out of the dust of the
earth, into whose ample bosom his body must finally sink.
Matter is perpetually flowing through the cells of his organism.
From it he derives the energy necessary to perform his vegetative functions and to execute his animal movements. Yet,
strange to say, his highest and noblest operations, the acts of
his intellect and will, have scarcely any measurable connection with the processes of metabolism. Such acts apparently
require another sort of energy which the techniques of physics
and chemistry cannot determine.

It is indeed astonishing that human thought and human volition, which have transformed the face of the earth, founded
civilizations, developed the arts and sciences, worked out a
natural morality, and created natural religions, should be
brought into existence without demanding any appreciable
amount of the energies of the physical universe. On the other
hand, because the body of man is so intimately united with
his soul, his intellectual activities have sometimes been deeply
influenced by the character of the land on which he lives, the
air that he breathes, the plants and animals that make up
his diet. The strength and weakness of races, their mental
aptitudes and their moral habits, their cultural rise and de-
cline, have all been connected in some way or other with the
various kinds of chemical substances on which they have had
to depend for bodily sustenance.

B. GROWTH

Growth is the progressive development of an organism from
its earliest stages. It is based squarely on the nutritive function since, obviously, food must be absorbed into the protoplasmic system before increase in mass can result. The final
purpose of growth is to bring the organism to a state of matu-

rity and, by further implication, to prepare it for the all-important task of reproduction. Being a true development, therefore, growth involves specializing activities as well as quantitative changes. Man begins his biological life as a single cell, as we shall see in a moment. In this cell there are no traces whatever of the highly complex arrangement of cells, tissues, and organs that his body will eventually exhibit. By the time he is born, however, he is equipped with everything that is needful to his life as a plant and an animal. This means that all the developmental aspects of his body have been substantially perfected during the period of gestation.

Like his nutritional procedure, the growth of man is a living activity because it is intus-susceptive. The new particles of chemical substance that are deposited in the cells of his body actually become protoplasm, and are not mere mechanical accretions to it. When man is young, the anabolic or building-up phase of nutrition is greater than the katabolic or breaking-down phase. An increase in weight and stature follows. In the mature man, there is more or less equilibrium between the two phases, and the mass of his body remains at a relative standstill. In old age, however, the breaking-down process overtakes and exceeds the building-up process, with the result that the physical mass of the body decreases. Natural death simply means the slowing down of somatic activities beyond the point where new nutritive matter can be incorporated and old waste matter eliminated.

C. REPRODUCTION

The reproductive acts of man perpetuate the race. In their basic features, they are vegetative in nature, since their term, the nuclear conjunction of two gametic cells, is a function of vegetative life. They are designed simply to produce the body or material coefficient of man's being. But physical propagation cannot be separated from higher conscious phenomena in the total scheme of human life. It colors and intensifies the mental and spiritual achievements of the individual; it is intimately associated with his desires, ambitions, hopes, frustrations, ideals, and even his final salvation.

Testes and ovaries possess functions of an overwhelming import for the sexes. They not only generate spermatozoa and ova—the immediate instruments of reproduction—but also secrete substances that impress male and female characteristics on all the tissues of the body and give to human behavior the peculiar intensities by which the sexes are differentiated. Thus, the testes engender manliness, courage, enterprise—masculine characters at their best; and violence, brutality, callousness—masculine characters at their worst. The ovaries engender womanliness, domesticity, tenderness—feminine characters at their best; and instability, emotionalism, vacillation—feminine characters at their worst. The point is that the differences between man and woman are more fundamental than the differences between their bodies, or the construction of their sexual organs, or the rôle that these organs play in the reproductive process. The differences are also more basic than the environment in which male and female are reared, or the education that they receive. Every cell of the human body bears the stamp of its respective gender. The physiological laws that govern the creation of sex hormones, and the impregnation of blood stream, tissues, organs, and nervous system by fluids that derive from the reproductive glands, are just as inexorable as the laws that govern the material universe. We cannot equate man with woman by giving both the same training, the same offices to perform, the same responsibilities to discharge.

In the act of human generation, the conjugating cells are the spermatozoon and the ovum, which germinate from the tissues of the testes and the ovaries. Before fertilization takes place, each gamete must go through a process of maturation in which the original number of chromosomes is reduced to one-half. By comparison, the ovum is large, abounding in food material, and relatively immobile; the spermatozoon is diminutive, but gifted with extraordinary powers of locomotion. The number of eggs produced by the ovaries is incomparably smaller than the number of spermatozoa produced by the testes. After undergoing cyclic changes in the ovarian tissue, the cyst containing the matured ovum bursts. This phenomenon occurs some twelve to sixteen days before menstruation. The egg is caught at the funnel-shaped opening of the Fallopian tube whose vibratory cilia project it towards the uterus. Somewhere in its journey from ovary to womb it is met by a spermatozoon. Penetration of the relatively large mass of the egg by the smaller body of the male gamete results in the fusion of the nuclei of each cell. With the act of fertilization a man is conceived, and the essential part of the reproductive process is over. The newly formed organism moves into the uterus, where it lives and grows and develops until the period of gestation is over.

In the genesis of the primitive organism, therefore, the gifts of each parent are equal since each contributes a cell to the formation of the zygote. This means, of course, that father and mother alike are reproduced in their offspring, and that family traits are impartially divided between two lines of ancestry. Man's share in the work of propagation is in reality very short; woman's endures over a course of months. During this space of time, the growing embryo is nourished by chemicals that filter through the membranes of the placenta from the maternal blood. While the mother supplies her child with the elements from which its tissues and organs are constructed, she receives in return certain substances secreted by the organism which she is carrying. Her physiological and mental conditions are always modified by the presence of the child in her womb.

vii

Integration of Man's Vegetative Acts

A. THE NERVOUS SYSTEM

In the execution of its various metabolic and reproductive tasks, the human body employs a wide range of organs whose functions must be adequately harmonized if they are to attain their proper goals in the division of physiological labor. By his nervous system man is able to coordinate all his vegetative acts in such a way as to achieve unity of operation on the inside, and successful adaptation to his cosmic environment on the outside. One part of this integrative system is set aside for the sole purpose of controlling and orchestrating his vegetative functions. This is the autonomic sector. Another part supplies him with the physiological foundations of his sensitive acts. This is the cerebro-spinal sector.

Nerve impulses in the autonomic system do not ordinarily result in consciousness. They have no intrinsic connection with mental life. Nerve impulses in the cerebro-spinal system, and, more particularly, in the cortex of the brain, have an intimate causal relation with conscious phenomena. They not only furnish a direct somatic basis for sensations, emotions, and animal movements, but also contribute indirectly to the genesis of thought and volition. In all cases, it should be observed, nerve impulses are identical in nature, since they are purely vegetative types of function. As such, they are not conscious, though some of them result in consciousness. It is solely a matter of topography, or of position in the nervous system. Thus the nerve impulses of the autonomic sector are fundamental to the plant life of man, just as those of the cerebro-spinal sector are essential to his animal life. But in both cases, the energizing of the nervous system is an act of vegetation.

B. UNIT OF THE NERVOUS SYSTEM

The unit of the nervous system is called a neurone. It is very easy to picture each neurone as a whole nervous system in miniature. Like other cells, a neurone has a central body containing a nucleus. But, unlike other cells, it also has special processes that spread out from opposite sides of the central body, giving it a fibrous appearance. Of these special processes, some are short and many-branched, like a tree. They are called dendrites, and their function is to carry impulses to the central body of the neurone. Others are long and terminate in filaments that are relatively distant from the cell body. They are known as axones, and their task is to carry impulses away from the center of the neurone. The threadlike endings of dendrites and axones mesh with the processes of other neurones, the point of connection being referred to as a synapse. Thus, the diffusion of nerve currents in several directions is made possible by the numerous synaptic networks that integrate the whole nervous system. A neurone may be microscopic in size, but often its axone extends for several feet in length. What we commonly call nerves are in reality large aggregations of axones bound together with connective tissue. Most cell bodies of the nervous system are located in its central axis, that is, in the brain and cord. But some exist in groups apart from this central area. They are known as ganglia, and their function is to act as regional coordinating centers for both the cerebro-spinal and the autonomic systems.

C. KINDS OF NEURONES

Neurones are divided into three categories, relative to the position and direction of the nerve current which they carry.

Thus, afferent neurones convey impulses from peripheral areas in the nervous system, such as the organs of sense, to central areas in the brain or cord. Efferent neurones transport impulses from central areas to outlying regions such as muscles and glands. Finally, intermediate neurones, which lie in the central areas, connect afferent and efferent neurones in such a way that incoming impulses become outgoing impulses by a change of pathways. Because afferent neurones and their impulses are involved in conscious life, they are often referred to as *sensory;* just as efferent neurones and their impulses are frequently called *motor* because of their immediate connection with movements of various sorts.

D. PROPERTIES OF NERVE PLASM

Nerve substance is highly excitable. In this respect it is much more responsive to the action of physical and chemical agencies than are other kinds of living substance. Heat, cold, pressures, sounds, lights, all have the power of creating impulses in it. When a stimulus impinges upon some part of the nervous system, it releases energy that is stored up in the nerve tissue. The impulse thus aroused is propagated throughout the whole area of the particular unit involved. The procedure may be illustrated by a trail of burning gunpowder. The gradual release of energy, as particle ignites particle, is obviously determined, not by the flame of the match, but by the successive combustion of each particle. In the same way, the impulse created by the action of the stimulus on the nervous system is propagated by the successive consumption of nerve substance. We might extend the analogy even further and say that, just as there can be no further combustion of powder until a new trail is laid, so there can be no new arousal of impulses until the nerve plasm is recuperated. The passage of an impulse from one neurone to another is subject to certain temporal conditions since both units through which the nerve current travels must have isochronic rates of impulsation before their synaptic connections can be crossed. This is significant because it implies that the temporal relations of the different parts of the nervous system are just as important as their spatial connections. Stated more briefly: the nervous system integrates in time, as well as in space.

viii
The Autonomic System

A. INTEGRATION OF VEGETATIVE ACTS

The autonomic nervous system has been given to man as an instrument for integrating his vegetative acts. Like plants and animals, he must eat, digest and absorb food, aërate his body, and throw off waste matter, if he is to survive as an individual. Further, he must develop from his own living substance the necessary reproductive elements that will ensure the continuance of the species. And thus the autonomic system has offices of profound importance for him. It must adjust the functions of his vital organs and fluids, the calibration of his arteries, the rhythm of his heart beat, the peristalsis of his intestines, the expansion and contraction of his diaphragm, the secretions of his glands. He could not possibly take care of all these vegetative acts by exercises of conscious control. Nature has made them relatively free of the domination of mind by providing a special sector in the nervous system which deals exclusively with vegetative operations.

B. REFLEX ACTIVITY

The autonomic character of this sector is due to the presence of reflex arcs which work spontaneously in all the areas under its government. The autonomic system comprises a large number of ganglia or nerve centers which lie in front of the spinal vertebrae. A ganglion is formed by the massing of nerve cells at one spot. The ganglia of the autonomic system are connected by preganglionic fibers with the cerebro-spinal system, and by postganglionic fibers with the organs, involuntary muscles, and glands of the body. The preganglionic fibers derive from three different regions in the cerebro-spinal axis. Accordingly, we find three kinds of nerves in the autonomic system: cranial, dorsal, and sacral. The cranial and sacral nerves constitute the parasympathetic part of the autonomic system. The dorsal nerves make up its sympathetic portion.

The two sections have antagonistic functions. For example, if the parasympathetic slows down the heart beat, the sympathetic speeds it up; if the parasympathetic accelerates the secretions of the digestive and reproductive glands, the sympathetic retards them. The effects of the sympathetic are diffuse and general; those of the parasympathetic are localized and particular. The action of the sympathetic is analogous to that of a pedal on a piano which liberates the entire keyboard so that the sounding notes may be sustained and heard together. The action of the parasympathetic is like that of the individual keys when the pedal is not pressed.

C. TYPES OF REFLEX ACTIVITY

The autonomic system works reflexly, as we have just noted. Let us briefly indicate some of these reflexes. The heart has its own fundamental beat, but its action must be adjusted to fit the tempo of body movements. This is done by reflex action. In the same manner, the pressure of the blood is properly regulated. Arteries and veins are provided with tiny muscles that contract and expand according to the demands of the body. Equally important are the reflexes of the respiratory apparatus, such as breathing, yawning, coughing, sneezing, laughing, and crying. Associated with the alimentary system are several reflexes controlling salivation, swallowing, contraction of the stomach walls, opening and closing of the pyloric and cardiac sphincters, secretion of gastric juices, peristalsis, and vomiting. Among the eliminative reflexes, the commonest are defecation and urination. The reflexes of the reproductive system comprise a whole series of muscular and glandular reactions that induce tumescence in the external genitalia; peristalsis in the vasa deferentia and vagina with their ensuing discharges; and, to a partial extent, parturition. From all this it is obvious that the organs, tissues, glands, and muscles that mediate our vegetative life are marvellously balanced and controlled in their functions. Each system of the body may have its own individuality, its special structures and peculiar mode of operating; yet all systems are orchestrated in a perfect symphony of movement that gives unity and effectiveness to the total organism.

ix

The Cerebro-Spinal System

A. PHYSIOLOGICAL BASIS OF SENSITIVE ACTS

The physiological foundation of man's sensitive life is supplied in the cerebro-spinal system. Its central part consists of the brain and cord. Its peripheral part is made up of cranial and spinal nerves that connect the central axis with all the numerous sense receptors and voluntary muscles of the human body. The brain, of course, represents the most important area for conscious life. Without it, sensations, feelings, and locomotive movements—the acts of man's animal nature—would be impossible. The brain is divided into two sections: a large one, called the cerebrum; and a smaller one, known as the cerebellum. The outer layer of each of these sections is referred to as the cortex. The cerebral cortex is the most vital part of the brain for conscious processes. In man it measures from three to five millimeters in depth.

From top to bottom throughout the cerebro-spinal axis we can discern two distinctive kinds of substance: gray matter, made up of masses of neurones; and white matter, which forms the sheaths of nerve fibers. There is a regular arrangement of the neurones in the cerebral cortex; so that a rough estimate of their number reaches the almost incredible total of twelve billion. This becomes all the more astonishing when we reflect that the nervous system, with all the other systems of the body, develops from a single fertilized ovum. To repeat: the cubic inch of protoplasm which composes the cortex of man's brain represents the immediate physiological and somatic foundation of all his sensitive acts—his percepts, images, memories, estimative judgments, emotions, and animal behavior. Further: since intellectual knowledge is dependent extrinsically upon the operations of the senses, we may very properly speak of this important cortical substance as the indirect material basis of man's thoughts and volitions.

B. COORDINATION OF LOCOMOTIVE ACTS

The nerves that link up the central with the peripheral parts of the cerebro-spinal system not only convey impulses from the sense receptors to the cortex, but also transport impulses from the cortex to muscle effectors. We might think of man's voluntary muscles, therefore, as extensions of his brain; just as his involuntary muscles are extensions of his autonomic ganglia. Through his centrally controlled organs of locomotion, man has been able to manipulate matter and set the imprint of his mind on it. Hand, foot, and tongue are all designed to follow the lead of his intellect and the command of his will.

The hand of man is a masterpiece of mobile dexterity. It

can move in all directions, bend and twist and shape itself to the form of almost any kind of object. It can wield the scalpel and the sword with equal ease. It can manufacture tools and implements, for the welfare of humanity or its undoing. Its fingers may be raised in blessing, extended to bestow a caress, or doubled to strike with violence.

So, too, the foot is elastic, strong, and capable of adjusting itself to the earth that it treads, to rough stone walks, to smooth pavements, to icefields and ballrooms. Like the hand, it is attached to a system of levers that give grace and ease and assurance to its movements. Man walks, runs, sits, dances, swims, climbs, and so wanders over the face of the globe, probing, investigating, exercising his powers of observation in new climates and new places and on new objects of experience.

Finally, and perhaps most important of all, nature has given to his lips, teeth, tongue, and larynx an arrangement and coordination that enables him to talk. Of all the material instruments of intelligence, the spoken word is the most expressive. It is closest to the mind of man since it is the garment in which his ideas are immediately clothed. No medium is more intimate, more natural, more primitive for the transmission of human culture, morals, and religion. Without the gift of speech, it is difficult to see how the magnificent story of humanity could ever have been told.

x

The Philosophic Concept of Man's Vegetative Acts

A. IMMANENCE OF OPERATION

Modern science, as we have just seen, has given us a very detailed analysis of man's vegetative functions and of the manner in which they are divided among the systems of his body. Thomas Aquinas did not possess such refinements of knowledge; yet his observations were ample and accurate enough to yield an idea of the fundamental meaning of life in its vegetative aspects. His point of view is a development from the kind of knowledge that we have called common or public experience; and his interests in the problem extend far beyond the limits of plant life. What fundamental property, he asks, must any living substance have if it is to be distinguished from nonliving substance? And the reply is: *immanence of operation*. To show this, he analyzes corporeal life in one of its most patent features: self-nutrition.

B. IMMANENCE OF THE NUTRITIVE OPERATION

We note, first of all, that nutrition is a kind of *movement*, since it involves a change or alteration in the organism wherein lifeless matter is built up into living tissue. Second, it *proceeds from within*. This means that the root and source of the nutritive phenomenon is lodged in the organism itself. Certainly there is nothing in the food that we eat which would account for the fact that it is broken down, digested, and absorbed into the cells of the body. In fact, as Aquinas points out, living matter is distinguished from nonliving matter precisely because it moves itself to act. Lastly, the ultimate design of the nutritive function is *to perfect the organism from which it proceeds*. Only when the body has secured and utilized the foods that are necessary to its own life is it able to transmit energy to other bodies. And so the act of nutrition is expressed in the language of Aquinas as a form of immanent movement. This differentiates it at once from all the categories of transient movement, since the term of the movement in living processes is primarily intrinsic, not extrinsic, to the organism.

C. IMMANENCE OF ALL LIVING OPERATIONS

The immanence detected in vegetative life, however, is only a beginning and a promise of higher things to come. The nutritive act, as Aquinas points out, starts from within but really ends in something that is extrinsic to the organism, since its final purpose is to enable the body to propagate itself by producing another body. But over and above the vegetative functions that he shares with the world of plants, man also possesses a sensitive mode of life which establishes his community of being with the animals. Sensation is more perfect than nutrition because it is accomplished by forms detached from matter. The emanations that are proper to it arise from stimuli on the outside and proceed within, through the organs of sense, to the imaginal, memorial, and cogitative powers. They are more perfect than the emanations of vegetative life because of their greater remotion from the contingencies of matter.

Yet, they do not represent man's highest accomplishments, because they are still immersed in a material context. The most perfect form of human life, of course, is the life of reason, wherein mind reflects upon itself and understands itself. Acts of this sort are utterly impossible to the senses. Towering above the human intellect is the angel's power of understanding, a power that, unlike man's, needs no phantasm or other extrinsic help in order to be determined, but knows itself entirely by itself. Still we have not reached the peak of immanence, because the mental image wherein the angel beholds itself and all reality is not the angelic substance. Were this so, its knowing would be its very being. We come, then, at last, to the Creator in Whom knowledge and substance are one; Whose act of understanding is supreme and identical with His very being; Who therefore has life in the highest degree, because His action is immanent in the highest degree.

READINGS FROM AQUINAS

Summary Theologica, part I, question 18, article 1.
———   part I, question 75, article 1; question 78, article 2.
Contra Gentiles,   book IV, chapter 11.

CLARIFICATIONS

(a)

The material side of man's nature

Man's soul is immersed in matter; and man himself is immersed in a material environment. The first objects he knows and loves are the things that appeal immediately to his senses. It is exceedingly difficult for him to maintain a proper balance between the lawful pleasures of the body and the lawful demands of the soul. He is easily led to overlook what is advantageous to his spiritual nature. This is a real obstacle in the way to his total development as a man. He has cultivated his material well-being to the point where he is in danger of being swallowed up in its luxuries. The more he feeds his senses, the less inclined he is to nourish his mind. The more he gives rein to his passions, the less inclined he is to discipline his will. This means that, by some strange law of his being, progression in the things that pertain to his body brings on retrogression in the things that pertain to his soul. The conquest of inanimate nature, which should so greatly profit the races of humanity, is more easily employed for the destruction than the development of human nature. The point about our whole observation is this: not that matter and spirit are incompatible, since they are actually wedded together in man's hylomorphic being; but that the legitimate privileges of the one must not be emphasized at the expense of the rightful claims of the other. Otherwise, there will be a negation of the human person and a failure of human nature to attain its proper goal.

(b)

The sacramental character of matter

Matter is the creature of an all-good Being, and is, therefore, in itself "very good." But matter, as well as spirit, became corrupt with the disobedience of our first parents. The doctrine of original sin, which can be established on purely philosophic grounds, has an immediate bearing on the study of human nature. Thus, while it is possible to make a relatively complete analysis of man in his phenomenal and noumenal aspects, proceeding as though each of his acts, powers, and habits were perfect after its kind, the fact is that no human being exhibits the excellencies which we theoretically attribute to human nature. Neither are the acts, powers, and habits of man subordinated in proper rule and measure, as we speculatively picture them in their relationships. The doctrine that matter, as the coprinciple of man's form, has a sacramental office to discharge in reference to that form, is a point of offense and scorn to materialist and idealist alike. The Christian philosopher who follows the teaching of Aristotle is not only convinced of the truth that man is composed of matter and form; he is also aware of the fact—which Aristotle did not know, though it accords well with his teaching—that matter is susceptible of grace, and, most important and awe-inspiring of all, that matter is capable of union with a divine Person and influence.

CHAPTER FIVE

THE SENSITIVE KNOWLEDGE OF MAN

i

The Cognitive Conquest of Reality

The sensitive acts of man are functions of his animal nature. They are divided between his senses, his appetites, and his powers of locomotion. His senses generate animal knowledge; his appetites beget animal desire; and his powers of locomotion produce animal movements. Man's sensitive acts represent an improvement upon vegetative life by a gradual freeing of the soul from the cogencies and restrictions of matter. There is a permanent character to the nature of matter which defies all our efforts to convert it to our purposes. We may condense it, rarefy it, extenuate it by our processes of metabolism; yet it endures. Overcome and beaten down by the superior forces of vegetation, the inherent repugnance of matter to place itself at the disposal of the organism is never entirely vanquished. Generation is almost, but not quite, a creative modification. Metabolism brings matter under the subjection of the living body; yet it fails to accomplish the complete fusion which is the ideal of action, because the mere replacement of material parts, or juxtaposition of elements that are impenetrable, is opposed to such fusion.

It is in *knowledge* alone that a condition is realized wherein a subject, while remaining itself, becomes an object. We cannot speak of real possession except where there is interpenetration of two unifying principles, or where one becomes the other in some manner or other. "The noblest way of possessing a thing," says Aquinas, "is to possess it in an immaterial man-

111

ner, that is, by possessing its form without its matter. And this is the definition of knowledge." In knowledge, therefore, we see the beginning of the conquest of reality. Vegetative functions possess things, but in a manner that destroys or alters or negates what is possessed. Sensitive functions also possess things, but in a manner that perfects, rather than destroys, what is possessed.

ii

The Excellence of Knowledge

In the second book of his *Treatise on Truth*, Aquinas tells us that a thing may be excellent either in itself or in something else. Thus, a thing is said to be perfect in its own rightful being, first, when it is endowed with a specific nature which distinguishes it from the specific nature of other things; second, when it has all the attributes that are proper and essential to it as a particular kind of entity. But the very fact that it is particular indicates that its excellence is not absolute. It is one out of many; and, by contrast with other things in the universe, its being is imperfect. It is only a part of the total range of perfection represented by the world of cosmic reality. In order, then, that there may be some remedy for this imperfection of individual things, we find another mode of excellence in the universe, according to which the perfection which is proper to one thing is found in another. This perfection is what Aquinas means by knowledge, because, in the process of cognition, the thing that is known is somehow reproduced in the thing that knows. According to this mode of perfection, it is possible that the excellencies of particular things, which are imperfect in relation to the perfection of the whole, should be gathered together and given a communal perfection that they could not otherwise share in. It is a possibility that rests entirely upon the power of becoming something else, which every cognitive agent possesses.

iii

The Cognitive Union

We have just said that the object of knowledge is somehow reproduced in the subject of knowledge. Now, the being that knows can be looked at from two points of view. In one respect, it is itself, a particular entity with a specific nature. In another respect, it is the thing that it knows. The point to be remembered is that knowledge is not merely the possession of facts, but the identification of the subject of knowledge with the object of knowledge.

In man's vegetative acts, food is not simply possessed by the organism; it is converted into the organism, and the conversion involves a destruction of the nature of the food. In man's cognitive acts, on the other hand, food, as an object of knowledge, becomes identified with man, as a subject of knowledge, and with no conversion or destruction of its nature. In fact, it would be impossible to say that a subject of knowledge knows its object, if the process of cognition essentially changed the nature of the object which it knows. But, of course, it leaves the nature intact. Accordingly, subject and object must be identified in a manner different from the way in which the object actually exists. This means, in effect, that whatever is known is in the knower, not after the manner of the thing known, but after the manner of the knower. Because the soul possesses the power of becoming other things, it is said to be *quodammodo omnia:* everything, as it were. Herein lies the strange gift of beings that know. As John of St. Thomas says: "Things that know are nobler than things that have no knowledge, precisely in this: that they can receive into their being something else, exactly as it is something else; accomplishing their cognitive task in such a manner that, while remaining what they are in themselves, at the same time they are able to become things other than themselves." [a]

iv

Natural and Intentional Modes of Being

To know, then, connotes the entrance of one being into another. The life of the subject is enlarged and enriched by the addition of an object. Obviously, we are dealing with two different orders of being or existence when we speak of the object, as it exists in itself, and as it exists in the subject that knows it. The first, as Aquinas tells us, is *natural* existence; the second is *intentional* existence. The ability to give intentional existence to objects is precisely the thing that distinguishes cognitive being from nutritive being. For such is the flexibility of the knowing subject that it is capable of expanding and absorbing within itself the being of everything that falls in its power.

This is the gap that separates the sensitive from the vegetative acts of man. This, in a measure, is the dividing line between material and immaterial functions, because even sensitive knowledge, though common to body and soul, is yet immaterial in its way. In the hierarchy of man's acts, therefore, the operations of his senses are placed midway between the operations of his vegetative powers, which are purely material, though immanent and vital; and the operations of his rational powers, which are purely immaterial. Here, in a manner that is not true of his vegetative acts, he begins to manifest a certain freedom from the restricting influences of matter. It is not a perfect freedom, to be sure, nor comparable with the freedom achieved in the processes of pure intellection; yet it is a greater liberty than that found in his vegetative acts.

The basic principle along which all knowledge proceeds is remotion from matter. The higher the degree of immateriality, the higher the form of knowledge. To know is to become something other than oneself. This does not mean, in the teaching of Aquinas, that the subject becomes *like* the object, but that the subject *is* the object. Such a doctrine presupposes, on the one hand, the emergence of the knowing subject from the domination of matter—an emergence which is only faintly and imperfectly achieved in the subject of vegetation—and, on the other, the union of knowing subject with the object known, in a way that transcends the substantial union of matter and form in corporeal essences. To know, in short, is to exist. Knowledge, therefore, implies, not so much a doing something, as a being something or a becoming something. A soul with the power of knowing is limited only by its ability to become other things.

v

Knowledge a Separation of Form from Matter

What we have said up to this point chiefly concerns the subject of knowledge. It is manifest that certain requirements are also demanded of the object if it is to be known, that is, if it is to be united with the subject. Knowledge is possible only on the condition that subject and object have something in common. As we have already noted, a certain degree of immateriality is a primary requisite. A universe made up of matter alone would be simply unintelligible. What is it in the thing to be known that is capable of becoming the subject that knows? The answer is: its *form*. We shall recall, from our analysis of the hylomorphic doctrine, that a being is defined by its form. The part of an object, therefore, which can be assimilated by the knowing subject is its form.

To say, then, that a knowing subject becomes the object

which it knows is equivalent to saying that it becomes the form of the object which it knows. For Aquinas, this is the fundamental criterion in differentiating cognitive beings, such as animals and men, from noncognitive beings, such as plants and inanimate substances. "Things that are incapable of knowledge," he says, "have nothing except their own appropriate forms. Things that can know possess also the forms of the things that they know." In the same instant that the act of knowledge is completed, a new entity is brought into existence, made up of subject and object. The union of the two is unique, as Cajetan remarks, even more intimate than the composition of matter and form. "The knower is the thing known, either actually or potentially. But matter is never form. And from this difference as to being follows a difference as to unity: namely, that knower and known are more one than matter and form." For, matter and form in nature are united to produce a third something. The synthesis of subject and object in knowledge, on the other hand, involves the fusion of two beings that actually coincide at the moment of their union. And so, in the instant that the fusion takes place, the thing capable of being known and the thing that knows are made one and the same reality.

vi

The Meaning of Species or Intentional Form

We have arrived in our examination of the cognitive process at a point which demands the presence of the object known in the subject that knows. To show how this union is effected, that is, how subject becomes object, and yet remains essentially itself, Aquinas introduces us to the notion of cognitive species. The word *species* is very technical in meaning. Here it signifies, not a logical principle which determines predicational existence; nor an ontological principle which determines natural existence; but, if I may use the term, *an epistemological principle which determines intentional existence.* In its cognitive meaning, therefore, a species is an intentional form. As an intentional form it is an instrument of knowledge or an intermediary which enables the subject, without ceasing to be what it is by nature, to become the object, without destroying the nature of the object. In order to grasp the meaning of such an intermediary, which the fact of knowledge forces us to assume, we must abandon any attempt to picture it as a concrete image, such as the term "species" might conjure up. True, it is a medium through which the object is united with the knowing subject; but it is more than this. For, the species is really the object itself, under a new mode of existence. "Form," says Aquinas, "has one mode of being in the sense, and another mode of being in the sensible object. For, in the sensible object it has natural being; but in the sense, it has intentional and spiritual being." Only on condition that form has an intentional mode of existence is it allowable to say that the object acts effectually on the subject, since the species which unites them and makes them one in knowledge is the object itself existent after the manner of an intentional form. Only on this condition, moreover, can we maintain that *it is not the species which is primarily known, but the object by means of its species.*

vii

The Powers of Sensation

A. THE BEGINNING OF KNOWLEDGE

Man's sensitive knowledge proceeds from his senses, of which there are two general divisions: external and internal.

The external senses give rise to his sensations. The internal senses are responsible for his percepts, images, memories, and estimations. In the order of being and necessity, his external senses come first, since all his knowledge starts with sensation. In the order of excellence, however, his internal senses come first, since their knowledge is more perfect than the cognitions of the external senses. We are all familiar with the basic idea of a sensation. Perhaps the simplest way of describing it would be to say that it is *a vital operation, issuing in knowledge, resultant upon the stimulation of a sense organ by an appropriate object.* The knowledge, in this case, results from the impression of a stimulus on an external sense receptor. Further, the knowledge is accomplished in the sense organ, which means that the external sense is a true cognitive power since the form of its object is in it as in its proper subject.

B. THE OUTER SENSES

From the time of Aristotle, psychologists have been fairly well agreed upon the fivefold division of our external senses into vision, hearing, smell, taste, and body sense or somesthesis. Each of these sensoria embraces a large number of receptors that mediate the different sorts of sensations which we experience. For vision, we have cones and rods in the retina of the eye; for hearing, a mass of sensory cells in the organ of Corti which lies in the inner ear; for smell, olfactory bodies located inside the upper reaches of the nostrils; for taste, gustatory cells distributed over the surface of the tongue and in the mucosae of the epiglottis, larynx, and parts of the throat; and for body sense, a bewildering array of sensory cells and free nerve endings that mediate our sensations of pressure, pain, temperature, muscular movement, equilibrium, body needs, body satisfactions, body fatigues, body illnesses, and so forth.

C. OBJECTS OF THE OUTER SENSES

The world of corporeal being has many kinds of properties, and is so rich and abounding in action that the burden of recording it must be divided. Accordingly, nature has provided us with five outer senses, and assigned to each the task of registering some special aspect of cosmic being. This special aspect is what we mean by a *proper sensible*—an aspect so peculiar and reserved to one sense that it cannot be known by another sense. Thus, the lights and colors of the universe are the proper objects of vision; its sounds, the proper objects of hearing; its odors and flavors, the proper objects of smell and taste; its pulls and pushes, pressures and pains, warmth and coolness, roughness and smoothness, lightness and heaviness, and the rest, the proper objects of somesthesis. *Universals*

D. COMPARISON OF THE OUTER SENSES

From the foregoing we rightfully infer that man's outer senses do not all share the same ranking or importance in the list of his sensitive accomplishments. Aristotle, we remember, drew up some interesting comparisons which can be examined again with profit. Starting at the bottom, we note that somesthesis is the most wide-spread of all our external receptors. Every other outer power, in fact, is grounded somehow in somesthesis. Moreover, body sense is most closely allied to the nutritive and reproductive powers; so that to obliterate it means to stop life altogether. This truth is expressed in another way by saying that body sense has been given to us for our being, but the other senses for our well-being. By way of further comparison, it is observed that hearing is the most instructive of all our senses, sight the most ennobling, smell the most poorly developed, and taste the most closely allied to somesthetic power. I think that we may all agree with these insights of the Stagirite.

viii

The Act of Sensation

Sense, as we have already said, is a power of receiving forms without matter. When a stimulus impinges on an external receptor, it produces a modification in it. The process is likened by Aristotle to the impressing of a seal on wax. When the seal is applied to the wax, it leaves its outline behind, but not its matter. So, too, when the object is applied to the sense, it leaves its form behind, but not its matter. The analogy, however, is imperfect, because wax is a nonliving substance, indifferent to what goes on about it and wholly passive in its reception of an imprint. Sense, on the contrary, is alive and responsive. It is not only acted upon by the sensible object, but also acts in its own rightful way. And therefore Aquinas says very wisely: "From one point of view, sensation is a sufferance; from another, an operation. Thus, in respect to the receiving of sensible species, sensation is something passive. But, in relation to what follows upon the perfecting of the sense by species, sensation is something active." And so the sufferance or passion of sense is an effect of its natural tendency to receive the impressions of stimuli. The operation of sense, on the other hand, is born of its power to respond to such impressions.

The effect produced in the sense when an object impinges on it is neither wholly material nor wholly immaterial. It is not wholly material because, as we have said before, it is a removal or disengagement of form from matter; yet it is not wholly immaterial because the modification is wrought in a material organ. When, then, Aquinas refers to such modification as though it were a spiritual change, he is simply contrasting it with the changes of corporeal substance wherein matter and form are really, not intentionally, separated. For, certainly, the alteration of sense, in the act of sensing an object, is not an alteration of substance. Neither is the object substantially changed by the fact that it is sensed. Such is the mysterious nature of sensation that, when form is separated from matter, the sensible object is left whole and intact. It is clearer now, I trust, why Thomas speaks of the species or intentional form as a medium by which subject and object are united in the act of knowing, just as Aristotle speaks of it as a *mesotes* or ratio between stimulus and organ.

Because the sense is a material power, its operation is destroyed or nullified by excessive energizing of the sensible object. It has its threshold values, which involve the minimum amounts of material force necessary to set it into action; and its saturation point, beyond which its acuity in the sensing of objects is lost. This is not true of intellect, which has neither threshold values nor saturation points in its operations. As Aquinas points out, "Sense is rendered impotent by the action of a strong sensible object. We no longer hear well, for example, after excessive stimulation by loud sounds. And so with the visual and olfactory senses: it is quite impossible to see or smell properly when stimuli are too intense, because overmuch stimulation corrupts the organs of sense. But with intellect it is different. The very fact that we are thinking about something which is difficult to understand, makes it easier afterwards to think about something which is less difficult to understand. This would be the case with the senses too if they were not dependent upon material organs in their functioning."

ix

The Act of Perception

A. COMMON SENSE

Actually, sensations in their simple elemental form, as operations of the external senses, do not exist except as part of a more whole-making process which we term perception. This means that the external senses are functionless as isolated powers, or that they work only in conjunction with an internal power in which they are rooted and upon which they are dependent. This internal power is common sense, which is so named, as Aquinas points out, because it is the unit principle of all the acts of external sensation.

Common sense is the power from which all the proper senses are derived, to which all their impressions are relayed, and in which all their functions are unified. The external senses are affected by their own proper sensibles which are specific for each receptor. Common sense discriminates between these particular resultants at the same time that it unites them into perceptual wholes. It recognizes the difference between whiteness and sweetness, discerning, in the same moment, the fact that these two proper sensibles are linked together in a single object, sugar. For the perfection of animal knowledge, it is necessary that there be a central sense, which is able to apprehend *as one*, things that the external senses apprehend *as many*. Further, if, as experience tells us, the outer senses are conscious of their proper sensibles, it is because they are rooted in common sense. For this reason, the eye is said to perceive color, the ear to perceive sound, and so forth.

B. COMMON SENSIBLES

The act of common sense, however, does not consist merely in the conjoining of different sensations to form perceptual wholes. Its synthetic power has a much more significant rôle to play in the life of the animal and in man's sensitive cognitions. When we stop to reflect on the matter, every object that falls under the senses is quantified and localized by the laws of its cosmic being. It has definite spatial and temporal dimensions. It always exists and operates somewhere and sometime.

Now, these very facts immediately surround it with characteristics that are not entirely explicated in terms of colors, sounds, odors, flavors, and tangible properties.

A rose, for example, is not merely red and fragrant; it also has surface qualities, extension, shape, solidity, a measurable distance away from the eye, a definite size, perhaps even a local motion as it sways in the breeze. A song, for instance, is not merely a series of auditory stimuli. It also has a definite tempo, a meter, a distribution of accents, and a rhythm. Quite obviously, none of the spatial features of the rose, and none of the temporal characteristics of the song, are perceived by any one outer sense alone, in the same way that color is seen by the eye or sound is heard by the ear. Rather, they are aspects of the material object that simultaneously appeal to several external senses, representing an association of data that require the combined efforts of many senses if they are to be perceived. Aquinas, therefore, following the lead of Aristotle, calls them *common sensibles*.

Because these spatio-temporal aspects of an object are common sensibles, it might be supposed that they are the specifying factors of common sense. Such, however, is not the case, as Aquinas warns us. For, "common sense is a power wherein are terminated all the changes of the outer senses. . . . It is impossible, then, for common sense to have any proper object that is not the object of an external sense." The difference between the outer senses and common sense arises, accordingly, not from a difference of proper and common sensibles, but from a difference of the mode in which sensible objects affect the outer senses and common sense. Thus, in the case of the outer senses, the mode is one of proper sensibility alone. In the case of common sense, on the other hand, the mode is one either of proper sensibility or of common sensibility.[b]

C. INCIDENTAL SENSIBLES

Besides proper sensibles and common sensibles, both of which are capable of being perceived by common sense, there is another group of objects which Aristotle referred to as *incidental sensibles*, or sensibles by accident, since it is only by a contingency that they fall under the senses at all. Aquinas adopts the Aristotelian teaching on this point and comments on it as follows: "We say that Diares or Socrates is an object of incidental sensibility because it so happens that he is a white-colored thing. For, a thing is sensed *per accidens* when it happens to that thing in the course of its being sensed *per se*. Now, it so falls out that the white-colored object, which is a direct and immediate object of sense, is Diares. Accordingly, Diares is a sensible by accident." [c]

D. FUNCTIONS OF COMMON SENSE

The Thomistic doctrine on common sense gives a very satisfactory account of the wholeness of perceptual phenomena. Indeed, without common sense the external senses would have no significance whatever for the higher processes of knowledge. From it, they receive the supreme gift of consciousness and the power of sensing their own proper objects. Moreover, if we see that we see and are aware that we hear, it is by virtue of the intimate sovereignty of common sense over all the external senses. The eye, for example, knows only the luminous object by whose sensible form it is changed. Common sense not only perceives the luminous object, but also the visual act of the eye. Some of the discriminatory power of common sense is transmitted to the individual senses as when the eye perceives differences in the colors that it sees, and the ear perceives differences in the tones that it hears. But the higher function of selecting and combining data from the several external sensoria belongs to common sense alone. [d]

Each outer sense, as Aquinas tells us, "distinguishes between the stimuli that form its own proper objects. The visual power, for instance, knows the difference between white, black, and green. But neither vision alone nor taste alone can tell the difference between white and sweet, for the reason that the power which distinguishes between these two proper sensibles must know them both. Accordingly, the recognition of qualitative differences in our external sensations must be assigned to common sense, to which all the information supplied by the external senses is referred as to a common term." Ordinary observation tells us that even our simplest sense cognitions are organized. A patch of color on a background, a tone in its musical setting, is each observed by itself at the same time that it is brought into relation with its palpable surroundings. From the patch of colors common sense constructs a sunset; from tones, in combination, it fashions a song. Not sensations, then, but percepts patterned out of sensations, form the basic stuff of experience.

Finally, common sense is not only able to distinguish between the acts of the outer senses, but can also discern the difference between what is being actually sensed and what is merely imagined. Thus, "sometimes, while asleep, a man can judge that what he sees is a dream, differentiating, as it were, between things and their images. Nevertheless, common sense remains partly suspended; and therefore, although it discriminates some images from reality, it is always deceived in some particular." Manifestly, what it can accomplish in dream states, it is also able to accomplish in the waking state; and so the discernment of sensible appearances from sensible reality must be a further function of common sense. The possibility of its making such distinctions is due, of course, to the coign of vantage that it occupies, since it is situated midway between the exterior senses, on the one side, and imaginal power, on the other.

x

The Act of Imagining

A. IMAGINAL POWER

In order to function, both the external senses and common sense require the presence of an object actually impinging upon a receptor. But man possesses another power in his cognitive equipment which enables him to recall and live again the experiences of actual perception. It is called imagination, and its distinctive task, according to Aquinas, is to bring back on the screen of consciousness pictures of things that are no longer present to his outer senses. The only condition for the exercise of this remarkable power, which so lavishly broadens out the scope of our mental life, is that we shall have accumulated certain original impressions from the exercise of our external senses. For, obviously, it is impossible to imagine something we have never experienced before, in some fashion or other. Even the most riotous products of imaginal power represent elements of previous impressions, though the elements may never have been combined in the particular way that imagination now combines them. Winged horses and chimeras are pure vagaries of human fantasy, but wings and horses and all the individual parts of the chimera are matters of experience.

The term "image" is rather inadequate as a description of the product of imagination, because it is so immediately suggestive of something *seen*. The fact is, of course, that imaginal power is limited only by the limitations of sensitive experience. Accordingly, we have images arising from all the fields of sensation: visual, auditory, olfactory, gustatory, and somesthetic. Some people picture things seen more easily than things heard. They are better visualizers than auditors. Generally speaking, the visual, auditory, and somesthetic fields supply us with the greatest abundance of images.

B. FUNCTIONS OF IMAGINATION

The functions of imaginal power, as Aristotle pointed out, are of a double character: first, to picture things as more or less exact copies of original experiences—and this is simple *reproductive* imagination; second, to elaborate phantasms of things that have never been actually perceived by the senses—and this is *creative* imagination. In both cases, however, the contents of what is represented on the imaginal power must be drawn from previous experiences, even when chimeras and mountains of gold are fantastically created. For, in the teaching of Aquinas, imagination is aroused by the acts of the presentative senses, which, in turn, are thrown into operation by the impinging of sensible objects. Imaginal movements, in short, are caused by the senses in act; while movements of the senses are caused by the sensibles in act. The point about the matter is simply this: not that imagination does not require the presentations of sense in order to construct its own representations, nor that imagination is inoperative when the external senses and common sense are functioning, but that, even in the absence of the objects of sense, imagination is able to recall the images that are formed at the time of actual experience. This, in fact, is its special prerogative: to be capable of reinstating in consciousness the pictures of things that are no longer impinging on the senses. If, therefore, the proper object of common sense is always something present *qua* present, the proper object of imagination is always something absent *qua* absent. Herein lies the formal distinction of the two powers.

C. RÔLE OF IMAGINATION IN THE LIFE OF KNOWLEDGE

Like the percept, the image has a value for the mind which is both synthetic and whole-making. If remotion from matter is the true criterion of the immanence which a power possesses, then imagination is a more perfect cognitive instrument than common sense, to the extent that it does not require the presence of an object for the exercise of its functions. In this respect it is like the power of reason. Because of its freedom from the necessity of having its object actually present, it is described by Aquinas as a permanent principle of knowledge, a natural basis of intellectual operations. Its superiority over the presentative powers is further indicated by the fact that, while the judgments of physics terminate in the senses or with objects of the first degree of abstraction, the judgments of mathematics terminate in imagination, or with objects of the second degree of abstraction.

Because it does not require the presence of an object, imagination suffers from certain inexactitudes and failures of detail which that presence would relieve. The fact is, we are never sure that what is imagined corresponds exactly with what was originally experienced; and so we are obliged to recheck many of our images by reference to the percepts from which they derive. But, as with the products of common sense, so with the organized data of imagination, we are given a real starting point in the work of elaborating ideas. Further, the ease with which imaginal power supplies us with examples for illustration is of the highest importance for the development and exposition of our ideas. Even our most abstract problems are rendered less difficult if we can turn to the analogy of sensible objects for concrete cases and comparisons.

By imaginal power we are liberated from the restrictions set upon our powers of sensation and perception. By imaginal power we can live in other places and are able to project ourselves into situations that we have never actually experienced, working the old familiar patterns into designs that are fresh and new. Thus, imagination is a creative power; and all the world's great pioneers, inventors, dramatists, painters, poets, scientists, and philosophers of nature have been, unusually gifted with it. Because, in man, it is associated with intellect, imagination is subject to direction, control, and action toward a special goal; otherwise it could not serve the purposes of creative activity, as it does. "The passion of phantasy," says Aquinas, "is in us when we will; so that we are able to picture things as though they were happening before our very eyes." How truncated indeed our conscious lives would be if we were aware only of the things that are in our immediate environment!

xi

The Act of Remembering

A. MEMORIAL POWER

The proper object of imagination is something absent. But we are also able to identify things, not merely as absent, but also as *past*, and this function belongs to memory. It will be observed at once that there is a great deal of similarity between the operation of these two powers. Both presuppose original impressions of stimuli upon the sense receptors; both imply the unconscious retention of the effects of such impressions; and finally, both exhibit an ability to reproduce in consciousness the images of what has been previously experienced. It is easy to see, then, how imagination supplies a basis for memorial procedures. Yet the two powers cannot be identified, because of the difference in their formal objects. Memory always recognizes its revived products as images of past events, tracing them back to their origin in perceptual experience and placing them in a definite temporal context. Imagination does none of these things. The power to identify the past as past is an added excellence, and one which, like all excellences, is won only with difficulty. For, it is harder to remember things than simply to picture them on the imagination. I have no trouble at all in getting an image of a rose; but I am seriously perplexed in trying to remember the last rose I saw.

According to Aquinas, the principle of memory in animals is the experience of biological values, that is, of the usefulness or harmfulness of certain things. Just as imagination is complementary to common sense, whose objects it is able to conserve when they are absent, so memory is complementary to estimative sense, whose objects it is able to recall when they are past. The point about the matter is this: that although memorial power can exercise itself with any sensible event that has previously occurred, it is particularly designed, in its pragmatic aspect, to enable the animal, and ourselves as animals, to remember the objects that have special biological implications.

B. SENSITIVE AND RECOLLECTIVE MEMORY

As in the case of imagination, memory gains definite advantages from its adjacency to reason. It is not only capable of recalling past events, but, as Aquinas points out, is also able to inject insight and control into its memorial procedures, so that it can proceed syllogistically, as it were, in its efforts to recapture the past. But even in its pure form, that is, apart from the influence of intellect and will, memory functions in virtue of certain connections that exist among its images and govern their reinstatement. For it is obvious that these images are associated in the same way that the *parts* of the original experience are linked together to form the *whole* of the original experience. Accordingly, when a part of the previous experience is recalled, it tends to bring back all the remaining parts of the whole with it. This is the basic principle along which all spontaneous association of images advances.

C. LAWS OF ASSOCIATION

The well-known laws of association were first formulated by Aristotle. They are founded on the principle that the things we experience are naturally *similar* to each other, *opposed* to each other, or *close* to each other; and that the images of these things are therefore related by the same kinds of bonds: likeness, contrast, and propinquity. Note, however, that the laws of association are really laws of reminiscent or syllogistic memory, rather than of simply reproductive memory. This is patent from the examples which Aquinas employs. Thus, Plato reminds one of Socrates because both were very learned men; Hector immediately suggests Achilles by virtue of their mutual oppositions; and father and son are naturally placed together because of their close lineal connections. In the first case, like produces like; in the second, like produces unlike; and in the third, like produces near-like, the nearness being one of time, place, generation, and so forth. The influence of reason on these three types of association is detected especially in the second, where insight is obviously required to appreciate the opponencies of relationship.

xii

The Act of Estimating

A. ESTIMATIVE POWER

Over and above his powers of perceiving, imagining, and remembering things, man also possesses an ability to discern the *useful* or *obnoxious* character of certain objects. In its purely sensitive state, it is known as estimative power. Aristotle, we recall, refers to it simply as nature or natural faculty. Animals must depend entirely on the informations of their estimative sense in adjusting themselves to the critical situations

of their lives, such as those involving their individual and racial survival.   The numerous ways in which the estimative
power manifests itself are nothing short of marvellous. Aquinas
was quite familiar with many of these exhibitions of animal
prudence. "Some things," he says, "act without judgment of
any sort. A stone, for example, moves in a downward direction
solely because of gravitational pull; and so with regard to all
things that lack knowledge. Again, some things act by judgment, but the judgment is not free, as in the case of the brutes.
For instance, when a lamb sees a wolf, it concludes that here is
something to be avoided. But its decision results from a natural and not a free judgment, since it is formed entirely on a
basis of instinctive knowledge and not by rational comparisons. This, in fact, is the case with all the judgments of animals." The point about such sensitive judgments is that they
represent an awareness of concrete relations only.   Rational
judgments, on the contrary, always imply a knowledge of abstract relations. The former are founded on a collation of particular images; the latter on a comparison of universal ideas.

B. INSTANCES OF ANIMAL PRUDENCE

A dog, for example, is trained to fetch a certain sponge which
its master uses when cleaning his boat. But when the sponge is
not in its accustomed place, the dog does not bring back a cloth
instead.   To do so would indicate a power of abstraction.
Again, an ape learns to pile one box on top of another, in order
to get the fruit that is out of its reach. But it never solves its
problem ideationally, though the tools for such a solution are
placed conveniently at hand. What the animal does, in cases
like these, is remarkable, of course; yet its behavior demands
no rational insight, but only an apprehension of the way that
objects are concretely related.

Aquinas cites an example from the hunt which illustrates

well the whole question of animal prudence. "A hound in following a stag, comes to a crossroad, and tries by scent whether the stag has gone by the first or second road. Finding that it has not passed there, and being so assured, the hound takes to the third road without trying the scent; as though it were employing the principle of exclusion and reasoning thus: the stag did not go by the first two roads; therefore, it must have gone by the third since there is no other road." What are we to say to this case of apparent rational procedure? Here is the answer of Aquinas, framed in such general terms that it can be applied to all instances of animal prudence: "The power of a mover appears in the movement of the thing which it moves. Accordingly, in all things moved by reason, the order of reason is made manifest even though the things themselves are without reason. Thus, an arrow shot by an archer goes straight to the target, as though it were directing its own course by reason. The same phenomenon is witnessed in the movement of clocks and other instruments devised by the art of man. Now, as artificial things are compared to human art, so natural things are compared to Divine art. Wherefore it is said, in the [Stagirite's] second book of *Physics*, that order is just as apparent in the things moved by nature as in the things moved by reason. And so it comes about that in the accomplishments of irrational animals, we detect certain signs of sagacity, in so far as they are moved by nature to set about their actions in a most orderly way—being prompted in their skills by the wisdom of Divine art. For this reason, then, and not because they think or choose, animals are said to be prudent or sagacious."

C. PARTICULAR REASON

Estimative power in man is linked up immediately with his intellect and takes on something of its rational nature; and so Aquinas calls it cogitative power or particular reason. For, whereas animals perceive the useful or harmful intentions of things by an illumination which they receive from nature or natural instinct, "man perceives these same intentions by means of a collation of ideas. . . . Therefore, his cogitative power is also called particular reason . . . because it compares individual intentions, just as intellectual reason compares universal intentions." By intentions, here, are meant the insensate qualities of objects, so called because they cannot be apprehended, as such, by common sense or imaginal power.[e]

Intentions of this sort obviously refer to matters of special biological significance to the animal. There is nothing, for example, in the lamb's simple perceptual or imaginal apprehension of a wolf, to tell it that the wolf is its mortal enemy; yet the lamb possesses such information. The harmfulness of the wolf, in this case, is an insensate quality which can be recognized only by the lamb's estimative power. The faculty of estimation, which is shared by man and brute alike, represents the cognitive part of what the modern psychologist calls *instinct*, the other parts being supplied by the sensitive appetites and the faculty of locomotion.[f] But, to repeat, in man the estimative power works like a particular reason: so that the insensate aspects of objects are appreciated by him either ideationally, or by particular reason operating in conjunction with universal reason. The special discursive activity of particular reason terminates in what Aquinas calls an *experimentum*—the highest type of sensitive experience possible to man.[g]

D. RÔLE OF PARTICULAR REASON IN CONCEPTUAL PROCESSES

Further, because it is the special office of the cogitative power to compare and relate individual intentions, it at once assumes a rôle of capital importance in the formation of our concepts by giving the final synthetic touches to the phantasms or sensory data from which intellect derives its ideas. Being a kind of reason, it enjoys a superiority over all the other senses—working over, comparing, and organizing their products in much the same way that common sense unifies the data of external sensation. And thus, while it is true that imagination, memory, and cogitative power all have the task of forming phantasms upon which intellect operates in the genesis of its ideas, yet the phantasmal products of cogitative power would appear to be most perfect and therefore the fittest material for intellectual abstraction. Finally, in the Thomistic economy of knowledge, cogitative power has special offices to perform with reference to our intellectual knowledge of singulars, as we shall see in a later chapter.

xiii

The Formation of Impressed and Expressed Species

A. THE PRESENTATIVE SENSES: IMPRESSION

We have already observed how the mystery of sense knowledge implies a kind of immateriality at the same time that it is the act of a material organ. It is the mystery of the action of the cosmic universe on our sensitive apparatus, an action wherein the form which constitutes and specifies an object in its natural existence, is detached and impressed upon the sense organ, so that the object is now united intentionally with the cognitive subject. The object of the external senses is attained, not by the formation of expressed species, but by the action or impression of itself on the sense organ. Thus, sensation terminates with things as they are or exist in themselves. This means that sensation is an operation which is accomplished in the senses, as in its proper subject, and terminates with the object precisely as the object acts on the senses. The individual sense receptor spontaneously responds to the impression of a stimulus, receiving its object by the special material qualities which the object brings to bear on the organ. In this self-oblation of the object, which Aquinas calls the sensible in act, a species is impressed on the sense organ. Note that it is an impressed species, and its function is to specify the organ which it modifies. The action of the object may be compared to the sowing of a seed within the fertile depths of the sense which thus becomes intentionally the sensible object itself. And so Aquinas declares that sense and sensible object, in the actual performance of their individual tasks, are a single principle of operation for the acquiring of knowledge.

In the Thomistic teaching, therefore, no expressed species is formed either by the outer senses or by common sense. Such a species would be useless, since the sensible object is immediately present to the senses and is itself sufficient to terminate the act by which the subject knows. Moreover, as Aquinas clearly holds, the species is not *that which* is known primarily, but *that by which* the object is known. To abandon this distinction is to fall into a purely idealistic view of knowledge. Further, the cognitive process is not essentially aimed at the production of a term; because even when such a term is actually produced, as in the formation of images by the re-presentative senses and of ideas by intellect, knowledge continues after its production and is, in fact, perfected by contemplation of the term produced. This means that the expressed species is generated for the sake of knowledge, and not the other way about.

B. THE RE-PRESENTATIVE SENSES: EXPRESSION

Stimuli, proceeding from the external senses through common sense, act upon the imaginal power and produce an impressed species. Imagination reacts to such impression by forming an expressed species or image. This image, in turn, acts as a stimulus for memory and cogitative sense. In the same manner as imagination, the memorial and cogitative powers react to stimulation by forming their own expressed species or images. As we have already pointed out, the images of imagination, memory, and cogitative sense are called phantasms; and their significance for intellectual abstraction has been hinted at. Just how they contribute to the process of ideogenesis will be apparent later, when we discuss the rational acts of man. What I should like to emphasize once more, however, is the fact that the cognitive species is simply the instrument or medium of knowledge. When we say, then, that the species determines or specifies a power, we really mean that the object accomplishes this important function by virtue of its species. For, the species is the form of the object, with an intentional mode of existence. Its purpose, therefore, may be described as twofold: first, to make possible the union of subject and object, without which knowledge could not be perfected; second, to enable the subject to know the object by actually becoming the object in an intentional way.

xiv

Psychosomatic Nature of Man's Senses

Man's senses are composite in nature. Belonging to body and soul together, they have immediate dependencies upon material structures, and especially upon the nervous system, for their operation. The external senses react to direct stimulation, as does common sense too. The remaining internal senses function through stimulations that are furnished by the acts of the perceptual senses. Cortically speaking, our external senses operate through direct connections with what are called primary projection centers in the brain. Our internal senses, on the other hand, are not restricted to these primary areas but apparently involve the whole cortex or at least very large areas of it.

Though the cortex is basic to sensational experience, it does not follow that our sensations are not localized in the organs of sense. On the contrary, the testimony of common observation is consistent in placing them there. Such testimony cannot be discarded until scientific reason is advanced for eliminating it. A reason of this sort was thought to have been found in the fact that visual and auditory impressions could be aroused by direct cortical stimulation of the centers involved. But it should be noted that such results have not been demonstrated in the case of individuals who have never seen or heard. Moreover, the impressions so produced are not of any definite object, but of vague and indefinite lights and sounds, in which imagination may have some part to play. There is nothing extraordinary in the view that sensations actually take place in the sense organs when we remember that the complete functional unit of each sense receptor embraces not only sensory cells and sensory fibers, but also sensory centers in the cortex. In addition to these physiological considerations, there is the still more important psychological fact that our external senses are rooted in common sense and thus participate in its life of consciousness.

xv

Noetic Character of Man's Senses

In conclusion, it may be well to reiterate the fact that the sense powers of man are instruments of a rational soul and are, by that very fact, elevated above the limited operational dimensions of pure sensitivity. Accordingly, it is quite impossible to make accurate comparisons between man and animal on a basis of their commonly shared faculties. The animal has perceptual powers, but their discriminations have no intelligence to aid them, as man's perceptual powers most surely possess. The animal has imagination that simply reproduces; but man's imagination also creates. The animal has memory to recall the past; but man's memory can also reminisce on the past. The animal has instinct which tells it all that is necessary to its individual and specific survival; but man has cogitative power which acts like a particular reason to discover his instinctive needs. In short, man does a sort of thinking with his senses which is quite impossible to the animal. His senses furnish him with the proximate data of ideation, and this fact alone is sufficient to indicate the wide gap which separates his sensory equipment from that of the brute. In the animal, the life of sense is limited to pragmatic self-interests. Its goods are appreciated, not for their own sake, but because they subserve the welfare of the individual or the species. Everything is estimated by norms of pleasure or utility. In man, on the other hand, the life of sense is extended by his rational regard for absolute values; so that even the operations of his nonrational powers are intellectually conditioned to the extent that he employs them in a human way—by proper consideration for these absolute values.[h]

READINGS FROM AQUINAS

Summa Theologica, part I, question 78, articles 3 and 4.

CLARIFICATIONS

(a)

Difference between cognitive and noncognitive corporeal substances

Cajetan explains the difference between cognitive and noncognitive corporeal substances by saying that the latter receive their forms through the action of some extrinsic agent which operates on them efficiently, while the former receive their forms and are constituted actually knowing entities by their own operation. Accordingly, the efficient principle which makes the cognitive agent know is the cognitive agent itself and not something extrinsic to it. The form of the sensible object, impressed on the sensitive power, or the form of the intelligible object, impressed on the intellectual power, does not combine with the power to produce a third thing, as in the case of the hylomorphic union, where matter and form are combined to generate a new substance. Rather, the intentional form simply actuates the power to know. In this manner, the form of the knowable object becomes the form of the knowing power which, thus actuated, becomes the object in an intentional manner.

(b)

Common sensibles are aspects of quantity

Aquinas says: "Size, shape, and the like, which are called common sensibles, are midway between accidental sensibles and proper sensibles, which are the objects of the senses. For, the proper sensibles first and of their very nature, affect the outer senses, since they are qualities that cause alteration. But, the common sensibles are all reducible to quantity. As to size and number, it is clear that they are species of quantity. Shape also is a quality about quantity, since the notion of shape consists in fixing the bounds of magnitude. Movement and rest, too, are sensed according as the subject is affected in one or more ways by the magnitude of its mass or of its local distance, as in the movement of growth or of locomotion; or again, according as it is affected in some sensible qualities, as in the movement of alteration. And so, to sense movement and rest is, in a way, to sense one thing and many. Now, quantity is the proximate subject of the qualities that cause alteration, as surface is of color. Therefore, the common sensibles do not move the senses first and of their own nature, but by reason of some sensible quality; just as a surface [affects the senses] by reason of its color. Yet, they are not accidental sensibles, for they produce a certain variety in the immutation of the senses.

Thus, sense is immuted differently by a large surface and a small one, since whiteness itself is said to be large or small and is therefore divided according to its proper subject."

(c)

The incidental objects of sense

Professor Adler makes the point that Aristotle and Aquinas both failed to give an adequate account of the primary object of perception, namely, corporeal substance as opposed to corporeal accident. They were right in saying that corporeal substance, for example, this patch of white which is the son of Diares, is only incidentally an object of the outer senses; but they were wrong in not saying that the same corporeal substance is the primary object of the senses *in toto*, mainly, of course, of the internal senses, and especially of the internal senses as dianoetically operative. I should also like to add the point that the determinate qualities of corporeal substance are not the primary objects of all the senses but only of the presentative senses.

(d)

Common sense and reflection

Aquinas says that by common sense "I see that I see." As Professor Adler points out, this seems to suggest that sense has a certain reflexivity which the Angelic Doctor elsewhere reserves to intellect alone. The difficulty is resolved by the consideration that no single sense is able to reflect on itself. Thus, common sense is really perceiving, not its own act, but the act of another power, when we see that we see. It is as though one were to say, "By my common sense I perceive that I am seeing by my visual sense." In other words, common sense merely perceives the act of sight or that visual sense is acting; and the same is true when it perceives the acts of the other external senses. Intellect, on the other hand, reflects on its own act. It understands that it understands; and, in the act of understanding, it is able to know both its act and itself.

This is the Thomistic meaning of reflection, which Aquinas, of course, inherited from Aristotle. By such a criterion, no sensitive power can reflect on itself. The basic reason why sense is unable to make a complete return upon itself is the material texture of its being. A faculty that is able to reflect upon itself is necessarily devoid of *all* matter; and so its object is not limited like that of the senses. If it be said that I have strained the meaning of *video me videre*, and that common sense is aware of its act, I should still hold that "to see that I see" is not an act of reflection because, in its performance, common sense knows neither the nature of its act nor the nature of itself.

(e)

The insensate objects of animal prudence

When the Thomist refers to the object of estimative power as something insensate, he does not mean that it is something nonsensible, but simply that it is not capable of being sensed, in the first instance, by any of the other sensitive powers. I say *in the first instance*, because it is obvious that, once there has been experiential knowledge of biological situations, the animal can repicture such situations either imaginatively or memorially. The point about the insensate object is that it is sensible, properly, only for estimative power; otherwise, there would be no grounds for postulating such a power in the animal's makeup.

As Aquinas says, "If an animal were moved by pleasing and disagreeable things only, as affecting the senses, there would be no need of attributing to it any power beyond that of apprehending those forms which the senses perceive, and in which the animal takes pleasure, or from which it shrinks in distaste. But the animal needs to seek or to avoid certain things, not only because they are pleasing or otherwise to the senses, but also on account of other advantages and uses, or disadvantages: just as a sheep runs away from a wolf, not because of its color or shape, but because it is a natural enemy: and again a bird gathers together straws, not because they are pleasant to the sense, but because they are useful for building its nest. Animals, therefore, need to perceive such intentions, which the exterior sense does not perceive. And some distinct principle is necessary for this; since the perception of sensible [or sensate] forms comes from an immutation caused by the sensible object, which is not the case in the perception of these [insensate] intentions."

(f)

Estimative power and instinct

The modern notion of instinct includes three distinct factors: first, recognition of the utility or harmfulness of certain objects; second, experience of emotion as a result of such knowledge; third, motor behavior. Obviously, such a notion calls for a manifold of powers in the animal's makeup: cognitive, appetitive, and locomotive. From the Thomistic point of view, therefore, it is improper to speak of instinct as a single faculty, since it is really a combination of several faculties. Estimative power, as pictured by Aquinas, corresponds only to the cognitive factor in instinct, as pictured by the modern psychologist. Perhaps the closest approach which Aquinas makes to our present-day concept of instinct—at least as far as human instincts are concerned—is in his description of man's sensitive inclinations, as distinguished from his natural inclinations, on the one hand, and his rational inclinations, on the other. The following passage brings out the point:

"In man there is, first of all, an inclination to good in accordance with the nature which he possesses in common with all substances: inasmuch as every substance tends to preserve its own being, according to its nature. . . .

"Secondly, there is in man an inclination to things which appertain to him more specially according to the nature that he shares with the animals: and in virtue of this inclination, those things are said to belong to the natural law 'which nature has taught to all animals' (as we read in the *Pandect of Justinian*, I, tit. 1), such as sexual intercourse, education of offspring, and so forth.

"Thirdly, there is in man an inclination to good, according to the nature of his reason, which nature is proper to him. Thus, man has a natural inclination to know the truth about God, and to live in society."

(g)

The meaning of experimentum in the Thomistic psychology

Sensible cognition, though not the total and perfect cause of our intellectual knowledge, is nevertheless the *materia causae* or "matter of the cause" of intellection, in the words of the Angelic Doctor. Let us briefly recount the moments involved in our sensible apprehension of reality, the terminal point and ultimate consummation of which is reached in an *experimentum* or *experience*, as Aristotle and Aquinas teach.

First of all, observe that sense is a passive power, fashioned and molded by its very nature to receive the stimulations of external objects. From the impression of such objects on the organs of sense, the vital act of sensation is produced. It is manifest, however, that the outer senses are not affected by absent objects; so that, were we in possession of our presentative senses alone, there could be no sensitive cognition except in the presence of sensibles actually impinging on the sense receptors. Yet, we are able to hold on to the objects of sensation even when they are absent, and to reproduce them in consciousness under the form of an image or phantasm. Moreover, if such objects have biological values, we are also able to remember their usefulness, harmfulness, and so on.

We infer, then, that the concrete and individual objects of sense are known separately by the external senses, and collectively by common sense: whence they are passed on to imagination and memory where they are retained as phantasmal products and recalled as occasion demands. Estimative power, which is also a representative or image-forming sense, is concerned with the insensate aspects of sensible objects. In man it is called particular reason, since he apprehends the utility or obnoxiousness of sensible objects by a kind of discursive activity, that is to say, by an estimative power which is immediately subject to his intellect.

Although the imaginal, estimative, and memorial faculties of man are more excellent than these same powers in the animal, yet they do not attain to more than what is particular and individual. They cannot, therefore, report one object or aspect of sensible reality which would be common to all objects or aspects. Their knowledge, in short, is never universal in character. Nevertheless, they are able to prepare the way for such knowledge, by the total patterning of their activities; and this brings us, once more, to the *experimentum* which, as we stated at the beginning, represents the perfect form of sensitive cognition and the highest achievement of our sensitive powers—a result that is accomplished in the *collatio* or synthesized product of particular reason. It is in such a product that intellect finds its proper object which is the common or universal nature of corporeal being.

Aristotle refers to the *experimentum* as arising "from much memory." Yet, as Aquinas points out, it is not a simple collection of things remembered, but a whole-making experience wherein the things of actual perception are linked together with what has been perceived in the past. Thus, the *experimentum* may be said to have its origin in a kind of discourse, exercised by particular reason working under the guidance and control of intellect. It cannot be called rational discourse, in the strict sense, because it is concerned with particulars. We may, however, dignify it by the name of sensitive discourse, since its function is to draw together and compare all the concrete informations of both the external and internal senses. The principle is illustrated in the example cited by Aquinas: "When some one recalls that this particular herb has cured many people of fever, the apprehended fact that this particular herb is a specific against fever is said to be an *experimentum*. Intellect, of course, does not rest with this experience of particulars, but goes on, from the many particulars experienced, to draw out the one element which is common to them all. This *unum commune* is laid up firmly in the soul, and intellect considers it without considering anything of the singulars [from which it was abstracted]. This one common element it accepts as the principle of its artistic knowledge [when it is a question of making things] and of its theoretic knowledge [when it appertains to matters of speculation]."

(h)

Adjacency of the senses to reason in man

Although all of man's senses are influenced by his intellect, as I think, yet the degree of this influence varies with the remoteness of the sensitive power from the intellectual power. Thus, the presentative senses, which comprise the outer senses and common sense, are situated between the external world and the re-presentative senses. The latter powers, in turn, which include imagination, memory, and estimative faculty, are placed between the presentative senses and intellect. It is easy to understand, then, how the re-presentative senses should receive more abundantly of the influence of both reason and will. Aristotle speaks of the dianoetic as well as the aesthetic or purely sensitive functions of the re-presentative senses. But nowhere, to my knowledge, does he make such a distinction in the acts of the presentative senses.

Despite the overflow of reason into man's sensitive channels of activity, there are no grounds for making human senses distinct in kind from the corresponding cognitive powers of the animal. The differences here, according to Aquinas, are not differences of **nature** or **species**, but of excellence or nobility.

CHAPTER SIX

THE PASSIONS AND ACTIONS OF MAN

i

Knowledge and Desire

Man, like the animal, is a creature of emotion. Sense knowledge, of itself, does not suffice to guarantee the performance of necessary tasks within the sphere of material action. Indeed, this is true of any kind of knowledge. Our cognitive acts, as Aquinas tells us, require a complement of some sort. As isolated entities, they are sterile and unable to produce fruitful results within the practical dimension. They need to be fecundated, therefore, if the measure of our lives is to be full. For knowledge brings only the forms of things to us— forms separated from matter and deprived of their rightful existence. Intentional being is a truncated kind of being, at best; yet it is the only kind of existence that the object can enjoy in the cognitive subject. Thus, while it is true that the soul is intentionally everything that it knows, it does not follow that the soul physically possesses the objects of its knowledge.

The cognitive organism is really not satisfied with the mere fact of knowing. It needs more than this. We may say the same thing about the object that is known. Its nature is not complete in the intentional mode of existence which it shares with the subject of knowledge, but cries aloud to be absorbed whole and entire and in its proper objective mode of being. And so there is engendered in the cognitive subject a desire to possess the object and hold it as it is in itself. The aspiration, thus created, tends to project the soul toward a union which

147

will be *real*, and not merely *intentional*. The life of man and beast alike would end in indigence and fatuity unless it could pour itself out in desire.   Nature, however, has provided against this need, by supplying us with appetites. Now, the law of appetite is the law of love; and love, in turn, begets action.   In this wise, then, by knowledge, love, and action, the cycle of conscious life is complete, and the powers of man and the animal are brought to perfect fruition.

ii
The Notion of Appetite

The act of a sense is sensation. Similarly, the act of an appetite is appetition. Aristotle referred to the acts of appetency as *orexis;* and the term is coming into general use once more in modern psychology. Appetency or orexis, therefore, is a function of our appetitive powers. Aquinas makes a distinction between several kinds of orexis, according to the sort of appetite that engenders it. First, there is the *natural orexis* of creatures that lack knowledge, which proceeds from properties or powers that are lodged in their very essence. A chemical, for example, displays a natural affinity for other chemicals with which it can enter into combination. In like manner, a plant exhibits a natural desire to feed and propagate itself. Note, that in all such cases we are dealing simply with the basic tendencies of powers to be thrown into action by their appropriate objects; and the range of operation is limited solely by the number of properties, living or nonliving, that the appetitive subject reveals. Secondly, there is *sensitive orexis* which is determined by knowledge that proceeds from the senses. This is the type of appetency which man shares with the animal. It is concerned with goods of a material and transitory nature, and is always limited to particulars, just as the cognitions of sense are always limited to particulars. Finally, there is *intellectual orexis* which is proper to man alone since it is based upon rational insight. This sort of appetency proceeds from will, and is limited only by the finite character of our concepts.[a]

iii

The Appetitive Union

We are interested here only in those forms of orexis that are determined by knowledge. Further, since our analysis is concerned with the animal functions of human nature, we shall treat only of the phenomena of sensitive orexis. Such phenomena are generally grouped under the headings of feeling and emotion. They are acts of our sensitive appetites. There is a clear distinction between the senses and the sensitive appetites. The first are cognitive powers. The second are appetitive powers. The fruit of the first is knowledge. The fruit of the second is desire. The difference between knowledge and desire, or between cognition and appetition, is briefly expressed by Aquinas when he says, "The function of a cognitive power is completed by the very fact that the object which is known is in the subject that knows. But the function of an appetitive power is completed only when the subject which desires is carried towards the object that is desirable."

Thus, the term of the process is different in each case: for cognition, it is the object in the subject; for appetition, it is the object in itself. Or, to put it in another way: the term for cognition is the object with intentional existence; for appetition, it is the object with real existence. In both cases, it is a question of uniting subject with object. But the appetitive union is closer than the cognitive union. Again Aquinas expresses the idea very lucidly when he says, "Knowledge is perfected when the object known is united, by its intentional form, to the subject knowing. Love is perfected when the object itself is united with the lover. Hence the union of lover with the thing loved is more intimate than the union of knower with the thing known." This means that the union of appetite with its proper object is closer than the union of sense with its proper object, since the latter terminates with intentional possession, while the former ends with real possession.

iv

The Concupiscible and Irascible Appetites

Even in beings that are completely devoid of knowledge one discerns, with Aquinas, two basic kinds of desire: the first, an impulsion to conserve what is proper to their existence; the second, an urging to combat what would endanger or destroy this existence. So, in creatures whose desires are conditioned by knowledge, one discovers the same fundamental tendencies—to obtain the things that are suitable to nature, and to impugn the things that are opposed to nature. Now, man and the animal are equipped with sensitive appetites whose objects are the goods of sense. Some of these goods are simply good, and as such are objects of *concupiscible appetite*. Others are arduously good, and as such are objects of *irascible appetite*. In the former there is pleasure for pleasure's sake. In the latter there is struggle for pleasure's sake. "Wherefore," says Aquinas, "it is necessary that the animal secure the victories of irascible appetite, so that concupiscible appetite may enjoy its sensual delights without let or hindrance. Joys of this sort are chiefly concerned with sex and food; and it is a significant fact that the major battles of the animal kingdom are fought over such matters." In some cases, however, the animal may occupy itself with unpleasant things, apparently for the sole purpose of exercising its irascible appetite; and this is additional proof, for Aquinas, that the two appetites cannot be reduced to the same principle of operation.[b]

Because concupiscible appetite is only concerned with the goods and pleasures of sense, it is moved to act through knowledge of the perceptual and imaginal sort. Because irascible appetite is occupied with the hardships and dangers that surround these sensible goods, it is moved to act through knowledge of the estimative and memorial sort. Since the nature of appetence follows the nature of knowledge, it is likely that something analogous to the cognitive species is produced in the act of orexis. If the cognitive species is an intentional form, the orectic species is a tendential form. Further, just as intentional form is the determinant of knowledge, so tendential form is the determinant of orexis. On the presumption that such tendential forms or species exist, they proceed as impressions from common sense and imagination, in the case of concupiscible appetite; from estimative sense and memory, in the case of irascible appetite.[c]

v

The Meaning of Passion

The act of a sensitive appetite is called a passion. The term "passion" is almost lost to modern psychology, and this is a great misfortune. It is a strong term, vibrant with meaning, just as the passionate phenomenon itself is vibrant with action and biological significance. Nowadays, if passion is referred to at all, its meaning is limited either to erotic movements of the sort that we associate with carnal love, or to impulses of an angry nature. Perhaps the moderns are impatient at the idea of designating the acts of our animal appetites by a name that would seem to connote passivity, especially in view of the fact that these appetites are so obviously connected with outer behavior. But this is a total misunderstanding of Aquinas's teaching. For him, passivity indicates an active-reactive condition of the organism, or a power of being acted upon in a manner that determines the organism to act. In a more profound sense, passivity means a capacity for suffering; and so the passions are sufferances, wherein the living organism allows itself to be affected by the presence of certain objects in its environment, making its own responses according to the demands of sensitive life.[d]

All this is difficult for the investigator to grasp; and, as a result, the word "passion" has been practically eliminated from his psychological nomenclature. Instead, he employs the terms "feeling" and "emotion" to indicate the acts of our sensitive appetites. There is no quarrel with him on this score. Indeed, I should say that there is something of an advantage if by feeling and emotion we mean to indicate varying intensities of sensitive orexis. There can be no doubt about such quantitative differences, even though the qualitative aspects of feelings and emotions are identical, since both are functions of sensitive appetites. Thus, we might think of our emotions as having high intensities, and of our feelings as having low intensities. Because intensities are quantitative in character, they must proceed from the body in some manner. They are, in fact, the physiological changes that Aquinas regards as an essential part of every passion. So true is this that only creatures possessed of bodies can rightfully be said to elicit passions. The differences between feeling and emotion, therefore, are simply differences in the amounts of organic disturbance that each act of the appetite provokes.

vi

Feeling

A. BASIC ACT OF APPETENCY

Feelings are difficult to describe—except to say that they are acts of our sensitive appetites. In their broadest characteristics, they are referred to as pleasant or unpleasant. Feelings are associated with the operations of all our cognitive powers, demanding knowledge as their basis and point of departure. The presence of feelings in every phase of conscious life is indubitable. Their ubiquity is clearly recognized by Aristotle, as when he says that "pleasure supervenes on all our acts . . . just as the beauty of youth supervenes on those in the flower of their age." Aquinas, too, proclaims the wide incidence of feeling states. Thus, any cognitive act, in so far as it is perfect and well rounded, tends to produce feelings of a pleasant nature. On the other hand, any cognitive act that is shortened and truncated or impeded by some kind of obstacle results in feelings of an unpleasant character. "There is pleasure not only in touch and taste, but also in the exercise of every sense; and not only in the exercise of the senses, but also in the functioning of intellect, as when our rational speculations bring us certitude about various matters. Among the operations of sense and intellect, those yield us most pleasure that are most perfect in their results . . . and so we may conclude that every cognitive act is pleasurable, to the extent that it is perfect."

B. FEELING AND SENSATION

The close relationship between feeling and sensation has led some of the modern investigators into the mistake either of identifying the two or of making one simply an aspect of the

other. This is particularly the case in dealing with organic
sensations, such as hunger, thirst, and erotic experience,
where, unquestionably, the orectic background of the sensation is very pronounced. But, because the cognitive and
appetitive phenomena are conjoined, it does not follow that
they are one and the same in nature. Actually they belong to
different categories of experience since one proceeds from a
power of knowledge and the other from a power of appetency.
Some philosophers, not satisfied with merely identifying
sensations and feelings, would even blot out the differences of
sensations among themselves, by spreading an orectic film
over all the modalities of sense. Visual phenomena, for example, are continuous with auditory phenomena, because both
are affectively pleasant. Such a theory, however, fails to take
account of the fact that the conscious qualities of each of
these two types of experience are different—as they obviously
are and must be, if the testimony of introspection can be
relied upon.

C. BIOLOGICAL VALUE OF FEELING

The story of our feelings is a story of deep biological significance. When they are pleasant, they point to conditions
that are favorable to the organism. When they are unpleasant, they are symbols of distress, indicating that organs are
overtaxed and energies depleted. Our powers were meant to
be exercised in moderation; and our feelings are the surest
signs of excess or defect. As Aquinas puts it, "Action is delightful only when it is proportionate and connatural to the
agent. Now, since our human powers are finite, there is a
proper rule and measure for the expenditure of their energies.
And thus if one exceeds or falls short of this measure, his acts
will be neither balanced nor pleasurable, but full of labor and
tedium."

vii

Emotion

A. ACT OF SENSITIVE APPETITE

A passion of low intensity is identified as a feeling. A passion of high intensity is known as an emotion. Both are acts of our sensitive appetites. Both are determined by knowledge of some sort. Both are a complex of psychic and somatic elements. But whereas the body changes of feeling are scarcely discernible, those of emotion are marked and strong. Aquinas frequently speaks of the physiology of orectic experience. In emotion it takes numerous forms. Sometimes there is acceleration of the activities of the body, causing increase in glandular secretions, speeding up of heartbeat, quickened respiration, and so forth. Sometimes there is a retarding of organic functions, inducing a state of temporary paralysis in the muscular system, delayed peristalsis in the alimentary tract, and so on. The point about these body changes is the fact that, for Aquinas, they are an essential part of the emotional procedure. They may be present without emotion; but with emotion, they are never absent. The modern investigator states this somewhat differently when he says that we never have emotional experience without exhibiting emotional behavior, though we may exhibit emotional behavior without having emotional experience. The interesting thing about these body disturbances is that they do not provide any sure clue to the kind of emotion which we are experiencing, since they are frequently the same for several emotions. How, then, are we to distinguish between our different emotions? ᵉ

B. MILD AND EMERGENCY EMOTIONS

If we follow the lead already given by Aquinas the answer is simple: powers are differentiated by their formal objects.

Now, the object of any appetite is an apprehended good. Accordingly, the powers of animal appetency are distinguished in conformity with the diverse ways by which the senses apprehend sensible goods. First, as we have noted, there is the object which is apprehended simply as good. To it is opposed the object which is apprehended simply as evil. The good attracts the appetite. The evil repulses it. Modern psychologists make the same distinction when they speak of the favorable and unfavorable stimulus, or the pleasant and unpleasant situation. The passions aroused by such stimuli and situations are classified today as mild emotions. Aquinas refers to them as movements of the concupiscible appetite. In all such cases, to repeat, it is a question of goods that are cognized simply as good; and of evils that are cognized simply as evil.

Second, there is the difficulty factor which is apprehended to be present with certain goods and evils. What appetite wants, it finds hard to get; and what it does not want, it finds hard to avoid. As a result, we observe a real difference in the emotional reaction. For the stimulus or situation is not merely good, but arduously so; not merely evil, but strenuously so. Orectic phenomena, appearing under stresses and strains of this sort, are known today as emergency emotions. Aquinas refers to them as movements of the irascible appetite.

viii
A Map of Man's Passions

A. MOVEMENTS OF THE CONCUPISCIBLE APPETITE

In regard to the object that arouses our sensitive appetites, "the good exhibits a power of attraction, while the evil manifests a power of repulsion. Thus, good things generate in the concupiscible appetite a certain inclination, aptitude, or con-naturalness in respect of the good. Such an inclination pertains to the passion of *love*, to which *hatred* is opposed in respect of the evil. Again, if the good which is loved is not yet possessed, it arouses in the appetite an impulse to acquire it. This pertains to the passion of *desire*, to which *aversion* is opposed in respect of the evil. Finally, when the good is possessed, it causes the appetite to rest, as it were, in the satisfaction of attainment. This pertains to the passion of *joy*, to which *sorrow* is opposed in respect of the evil."

B. MOVEMENTS OF THE IRASCIBLE APPETITE

"With the irascible passions, on the other hand, the inclination is to pursue after difficult goods and to flee from difficult evils. All movements of this sort, it should be observed, are founded on impulsions of the concupiscible appetite, which tends towards its object simply as good or evil. Thus, in respect of the good not yet possessed, we have the passions of *hope* and *despair;* and in respect of the evil not yet avoided, we have the passions of *courage* and *fear*. As for the difficult good already possessed, there is no passion in the irascible appetite, because such a good no longer has the aspect of difficulty. But with regard to the difficult evil which actually inflicts itself on the appetite, there is another kind of movement in the soul, which is the passion of *anger*. . . . Altogether, then, there are eleven different species of passion: six in the concupiscible appetite and five in the irascible appetite. Under these, all the other passions of the soul may be included." The accompanying diagram shows how the basic impulsions of man's sensitive appetites are speciated by the Thomist.

DIAGRAM 3. THE PASSIONS OF MAN

Concupiscible	good	love	affective complacency
		desire	affective approach
		joy	affective possession
	evil	hatred	affective repugnance
		aversion	affective retreat
		sorrow	affective possession
Irascible	arduous good	hope	affective approach to the attainable
		despair	affective approach to the unattainable
	arduous evil	courage	affective retreat from the vincible
		fear	affective retreat from the invincible
		anger	affective possession

ix

The Primacy of Love

When we sift the matter down, it will be found that love is at the root of every passion. It is, in a sense, the beginning and end, the alpha and omega, of all the movements of our appetites. "Love," writes Aquinas, "is the cause of everything the lover does." We can broaden out this statement, I believe, and say that love is the cause of everything that anyone does. What a profound thought for our meditations! All our hatreds and repulsions, all our sorrows, hopes, despairs, all our enterprises, fears, and angers, ultimately point, like fingerposts, to the place where our treasure of love lies. If there were no love, there could be no hatred; for, we hate the things that endanger our loves. If there were no love, there could be no hope; for, our ambitions always center about the things that we love. By love we are judged; for, the things that we love no longer exist on their own account, but solely for the sake of the pleasure that they give us. It is in this way that the hedonist loves the food that he eats, the clothes that he wears, the money that he hoards, the woman that he embraces, the children that he begets. His life is spent on the sights and sounds, the tastes and odors that enthrall his senses, and the tangible seductions of matter that fill his appetites to repletion. We estimate the character of men by the price that they set upon their material loves.

Thus, love drags us down or lifts us up, according to the value of the thing that we love. And so, love becomes the principle of all our actions, since it is the principle of all our passions. There is, of course, a higher form of love which proceeds from the will; but we are concerned here only with the loves of our animal nature; and we cannot disguise the fact that such loves play an enormous rôle in our ordinary lives, impelling us to link ourselves with the physical goods of the universe. It is of this type of passion that Augustine speaks when he says that all the emotions of the soul spring from concupiscence. And the reason? Because, as Aquinas explains, every passion implies movement toward something or repose in something. But movement and repose are due to the fact that there is some basic kinship between the appetite and the object which it desires. Now, love is precisely this kinship. And so Aquinas concludes that there is no passion in the soul of man which is not founded on love of some kind.

x

The Psychosomatic Nature of the Sensitive Appetites

Like the senses, our animal appetites are psychosomatic powers. They are rooted in the synolon or composite, which means that they belong partly to the soul and partly to the body. This is quite obvious from the character of our passions. It will be recalled that Aquinas refers to emotional experience in establishing the substantial union of soul and body. He could do this, of course, because of the psychic and somatic elements that every passion reveals. The psychic factor is the inclination of the appetite toward its proper object. The somatic factor involves not only the nervous system, but also the glands, tissues, and organs that are concerned in the physiology of an emotion. The important point, for Aquinas, is the fact that both the somatic and psychic features of a passion constitute one affective phenomenon, a unit of orectic or appetitive experience. Body and soul, in such a case, are acting as a single principle of operation. This means that the physiological changes, so readily discerned in every emotion, are part of its very essence. It would be just as impossible to separate matter and form, in a corporeal substance, as to separate the psychic and somatic factors in an emotional event.

For Aquinas, therefore, there is no question whether the experience of emotion precedes or follows the changes that disturb the body. This is a problem which troubles the modern investigator. The answer of Aquinas rests upon his hylo-morphic analysis of the nature of man as a being made up of soul and body, with certain powers that belong to the soul alone and others that are shared by soul and body together. Our animal appetites are powers of the latter nature; and so are the acts of these powers. To repeat, then: the passions of man are composed of two factors, revealing the parts out of which they are made: first, a psychic or affective element which is traced to the soul; second, a somatic or physiological element which is traced to the body—both parts being united to produce the whole of emotional experience, just as the soul and body are united to form the whole of human nature.

xi

Passion and Reason

A. RATIONAL SOUL THE ULTIMATE PRINCIPLE BY WHICH MAN ACTS

It would be well to recall, at this juncture, a point of capital importance bearing on what we have called the anthropological approach to the study of psychology. All along reference has been made to man's psychosomatic functions as acts of his vegetative and sensitive powers. This is perfectly true from a proximate standpoint, since acts proceed immediately from powers. But in the final analysis it is man himself who lives, senses, and feels, since he is the ultimate subject of his powers and acts. Moreover, the principle by which he performs all his vegetative and sensitive operations is his rational soul; so that his lower appetites, like his senses, may gain something from their close association with his powers of thinking and willing.

B. COMPARISON OF APPETITES IN MAN AND THE ANIMAL

There is a distinction in the relative excellence of the animal's cognitive faculties which may be observed in its appetites too. Thus, if its estimative sense is superior to its power of perception because it is more like man's intellect, then its irascible appetite is superior to its concupiscible appetite because it is more like man's will. "Concupiscible appetite is moved by the simple pleasures of sense. But irascible appetite, leaving these pleasures behind, goes forth to do battle and seek victory, which it wins only at the price of sorrow. . . . And so irascible appetite is nearer to reason and will than concupiscible appetite." Therefore, incontinence of anger is less base in a man than incontinence of lust because, in the first instance, he is more deprived of the power of reasoning. The example is significant of the difference between the passions of men and of animals. For, the passions of men may be determined by thought or volition; but the passions of animals are motivated entirely by the principle of sense knowledge. The brute has no higher force to control its exercise of appetite. It cannot, therefore, be held responsible for what it does. Its animal cognitions must be the sole criteria of what it shall seek and what it shall avoid.*

C. CONFLICT OF PASSION AND REASON

Man has instruments of a rational order, to help him moderate the acts of his sensitive appetites. But alas! he does not always take advantage of these superior abilities in his nature. The conflict between passion and reason makes up a major portion of the drama of his existence on earth; and when the struggle is over, passion very often emerges the victor. This is the sad epic of humanity from the beginning. "For I do not that good which I will; but the evil which I hate, that I do. . . . I see another law in my members, fighting against the law of my mind and captivating me." The law of the mind is the rule of reason; but the law of the body is the rule of passion. Now the rule of reason, as Aquinas tells us, is like the rule of a king—sweet, gentle, and enlightened. But the rule of passion is like the rule of a despot—harsh, crude, and blind. Man acts as man when he follows the rule of reason; but he acts as an animal when he follows the rule of passion.

Passion, however, has not been given to man without a purpose. It is nature's best guarantee of action. If passion is, at times, unruly in the face of reason's counsels and will's commands, it is also a stout cooperator when great effort is demanded of our higher powers. As Aquinas profoundly observes, "It is not possible for the human will to be moved intensively towards an object, without a passion being aroused in the sensitive appetite."

xii

Passion and Action

A. THE LOCOMOTIVE POWER

Out of the ample bosom of passion, action is begotten. By action, we mean *external behavior*. The fact that we possess matter in our nature and live in a world of material dimensions calls for some sort of outward expression of the internal phenomena of consciousness. Man, like the animal, tends to project his knowledge and desires into matter, to clothe his thoughts and volitions in cosmic behavior. It will be noted that there are motions of a local character involved in our vegetative acts. But such movements do not depend upon consciousness. They are simply reflex acts of the involuntary musculature, and are under the control of the autonomic nervous system. In their sum total they constitute what we may call the schema of plant behavior. There are also movements of a local nature involved in our sensitive acts. They result from cognition and orexis and are executed by the voluntary musculature. On their physiological side, they are integrated and controlled by the cerebro-spinal nervous system. In their totality they constitute what we may call the schema of animal behavior.

B. THE ANIMAL'S OUTER BEHAVIOR

Aquinas has given us numerous examples of typical animal behavior. The knowledge of danger, for instance, generates a passion of fear; and fear, in turn, naturally leads to flight. In the behavior pattern we discern three elements: cognition, which is at the bottom of the procedure; orexis, which determines the particular direction—approach or retreat—that the action shall take; and muscular movement, which carries out the action. In explaining outer behavior, Aquinas refers to the cognitive factor as informative; to the orectic factor as imperative; and to the muscular factor as executive. The senses make known the situation; the appetites issue the orders; and the locomotive power carries out the orders. At once we see the position of autocracy that the sensitive appetites occupy in the generation of outer movements. In the animal there is no choice but a blind obedience to their commands. Everything the brute does—apart from the training that it sometimes receives from humans—is done as a result of its orectic impulsions. It acts as it is driven to act by the weight and force of its passions.

C. MAN'S OUTER MOVEMENTS

Man's life, too, is guided very largely by the current of his feelings and emotions. Even the drift of his thoughts and judgments, his outlook on affairs, his interpretation of people and events, are influenced, in great measure, by the depth and intensity of his emotions, and by the patterns of his appetitive behavior. But man is not limited to the knowledge of his senses or to the desires of his animal appetites. And so he can employ his voluntary muscles with greater freedom and for more ultimate purposes than the brute. The information on which he acts may come from his intellect; the orders on which he acts may come from his will. The behavior of muscle and bone is given rational patterning and made to serve as a basis for skills and craftsmanship that are quite beyond the capacities of the brute.

READINGS FROM AQUINAS

Summa Theologica, part I, question 81.
———   part I–II, questions 22–48; question 77.
Contra Gentiles, book I, chapter 89.
———   book III, chapter 27.

CLARIFICATIONS

(a)

The Meaning of Conation

For Aquinas and those who follow his teaching, man's orectic life is divided between sensitive appetency and rational appetency. Modern psychologists (and this is true of the philosophers as well as the scientists) speak of conation, conative impulses, conative urges, conative tendencies, and so forth, as conscious data distinguishable from cognitive states, on the one hand, and from feeling states, on the other. The word "conation" is found in the writings of Ralph Cudworth, the Cambridge Platonist (1617–88); but it was first given prominence by Sir William Hamilton in his well-known trichotomy of cognition, feeling, and conation. The division is repeated in almost every non-Aristotelian textbook of psychology that has appeared since Hamilton's time. It is wrong on two scores: first, because it is redundant; second, because it is unbalanced. The redundancy arises from a violation of the principle of the minimum, since feelings and conations are both appetitive phenomena. The lack of balance arises from the fact that, even on the assumption that feeling here means sensitive appetition and conation means rational appetition, there should be a corresponding dichotomy of cognition into sensitive cognition and rational cognition.

(b)

Distinction of concupiscible and irascible appetites

That the concupiscible and irascible appetites cannot be reduced to a single principle of operation is inferred by Aquinas from two experiential facts: first, "because the soul sometimes occupies itself with unpleasant things against the inclinations of the concupiscible appetite, in order that, following the impulsions of the irascible appetite, it may fight against obstacles"; and second, "because the passions of the irascible appetite counteract the passions of the concupiscible appetite: since lustful desires, on being aroused, diminish anger; and anger, being aroused, diminishes lustful desires." And he adds: "All the passions of the irascible appetite arise from the passions of the concupiscible appetite and terminate in them. Anger, for instance, is caused by sadness, and having wrought its vengeance, comes to an end in joy."

(c)

Motives of sensitive appetency

Aquinas says: "Sensitive appetite is naturally moved, not only by estimative power in the animal and by cogitative power in man, but also by imagination and sense."

According to Professor Mailloux, the apprehensions which move the sensitive appetites in all cases arise from estimative or cogitative power: either directly and immediately, when it is a question of purely estimative forms of knowledge; or indirectly and mediately, when it is a question of perceptual, imaginal, and memorial forms of knowledge. In favor of this view, we have the following texts from the Angelic Doctor:

"In brutes, the sensitive appetites are naturally moved by estimative power."

"Just as the imagining of a form, without some estimation of its usefulness or harmfulness, does not move the sensitive appetites; so neither does the apprehension of the true move [the rational appetite] without the aspect of goodness and desirability."

"Appetite is not acted upon or moved by such simple knowledge of a thing as imagination proposes. On the contrary, it is necessary that the thing be apprehended under the aspect of good or evil, of usefulness or harmfulness, and so on. . . . Accordingly, the appetites of the animal are motivated by natural estimation."

(d)

Passivity of human powers

When Aquinas refers to the powers of man as passive, he does not simply mean that they can be acted upon by some outside agent. Obviously, in this sense, every created power is passive. Even purely mechanical forces are governed by the laws of action and reaction. For, when such forces are directed upon an object, the object, in turn, reacts upon them, compelling them to undergo its action which is the result of theirs. But a living power is termed passive or receptive in the sense that, in order to be able to exercise its proper function, it requires an *intrinsic complement*, a sort of informing coprinciple, to complete its aptitude for such exercise and to determine the direction of its activity. Without some such determination, a cognitive power, which is capable of knowing certain objects, would never be aware of such objects unless they had been actually submitted to the exercise of its energy. In the same manner, the power of appetition could never be exercised *in the concrete* unless knowledge or motive were supplied to the appetite by the apprehension of the value thus intended to be a motive.

(e)

Order of events in an emotional experience

The scientific psychologists are divided today between two accounts of emotion: the *James-Lange theory*, named after the American William James and the Danish Carl Lange, both of whom discovered it at the same time but separately; and the *thalamic theory*, founded by Walter B. Cannon and so called because the thalamic area of the brain is regarded as the coordinating center of the physiological changes involved in sensitive orexis. According to the James-Lange theory, the order of events in an emotion is as follows: first, knowledge; second, physiological changes; third, affective experience. According to the thalamic theory, the arrangement is thus: first, knowledge; second, affective experience; third, physiological changes. The sequence, here referred to, is not one of time but of causality. The researches of Cannon, it may be added, have given us two important insights regarding the nature of emotional life: first, affective behavior may be present in an individual without true affective experience; second, emotions cannot be classified on a basis of the kinds of physiological change that accompany an affective experience, since, as pointed out in the text, the same kinds of physiological change may be present in different kinds of emotion.

(f)

Obedience of the passions to reason and will

"In man," says Aquinas, "the sensitive appetites are naturally moved by particular reason. But this same particular reason is naturally guided and moved according to universal reason, since in syllogistic matters particular conclusions are drawn from universal propositions. Accordingly, it is clear that universal reason directs the sensitive appetites, which are divided into concupiscible and irascible; and these appetites obey it. But, because to draw particular conclusions from universal principles is not the work of intellect, as such, but of reason, therefore the irascible and concupiscible appetites are said to obey reason rather than to obey intellect. Anyone can experience this in himself: for by applying certain universal considerations, anger or fear or the like may be modified or excited.

"To will also is the sensitive appetite subject in execution, which is accomplished by the motive power. Thus, in other animals movement follows at once the concupiscible and irascible appetites. For instance, the sheep, fearing the wolf, flies at once, because it has no superior counteracting appetite. Man, on the contrary, is not moved at once, according to the irascible and concupiscible appetites, but awaits the command of will, which is the superior appetite. For, wherever there is order among a number of motive powers, the second only moves by virtue of the first. Accordingly, the lower appetite is not sufficient to cause movement, unless the higher appetite consents."

CHAPTER SEVEN

THE INTELLECTUAL KNOWLEDGE OF MAN

i

The Life of Intelligence

The intellectual acts of man are the most immanent and therefore the most perfect operations of life on earth. Up to this point in our analysis we have been moving within the realm of matter. Both the vegetative and sensitive functions of man are bounded by the limitations of time and space, of material organs and material objects, though we discern varying degrees of immanence and remotion from matter in the activities of our psychosomatic powers. But now, with the advent of thinking processes, a completely new world is opened up to us: a universe of ideas and volitions, an immaterial expanse of creativeness, a region liberated from the palpabilities of sense. The human mind uses no organ in its actual elaboration of thought, however much it may be extrinsically limited by cortical substance, nerve centers, nerve pathways, sensations, images, and all the material paraphernalia that form the necessary preliminary to its intellectual achievements. Because it can overreach the restrictions of matter and rid itself of all time-space dimensions, it is truly *quodammodo omnia*, infinite in its potentialities of understanding, a microcosmos which, by its ability to know and become the universe, *is* actually the universe.

This, says Aquinas, is the earthly goal of man: to evolve his intellectual powers to their fullest, to arrive at a maximum of consciousness, to open the eyes of his understanding upon all things, "so that on the tablet of his soul the order of the whole universe and its parts may be enrolled." His senses receive the species of all things understandable; with the result that his soul is everything, after a fashion, through its possession of sensible and intelligible forms. "For this reason we may say that beings which have intellectual knowledge approach in a special manner to the likeness of the Creator, in Whom all things pre-exist." The highest type of living activity consists in the intellectual grasping of reality. This penetrative power of mind presupposes, as Aquinas points out, that what is real is by that very fact intelligible—otherwise it has no title to reality. Absolutely speaking, mind comes first, and all being is for mind—as an object of, or a preparation for, intellectual operation.

ii

The Cognitive Conquest of Reality

A. SENSE AND INTELLECT

The conquest of reality by the knower varies with the degree of immanent activity which is enjoyed by the knowing subject. It is quite obvious that the senses do not capture the inner meaning of things. They are in surface contact, so to speak, with their objects; and the best they can do is to register the accidental or phenomenal qualities of matter. Intellect, on the other hand, reaches within. It penetrates to the core. It deals with substances or essences. The life of sense is a dispersed type of knowledge, at best. The life of intellect is concentrated, because it is truly comprehensive. It plunges beneath the surface and grasps the very thing which holds all phenomenal qualities together. The senses exist in a sort of perpetual twilight. Their cognitions and discernments are exhausted by what is good or bad for the animal organism. Intellect, by contrast, moves in the clear atmosphere of immaterial knowledge.

Man alone, of all earthly creatures, exhibits a complete emergence from the conditions of subjectivism that make the animal's knowledge concrete and particular and restricted to the tangible realities of sense. "Intellect," says Aquinas, "reaches out to a large number of objects. Sense, on the other hand, is confined to a few. This greater latitude of intellectual power, however, does not mean that its knowledge is dissipated. On the contrary, it is actually more unified, in its apprehensions of many things, than is sense in its apprehensions of few. The reason for this fact lies in the cognitive medium which is of a more comprehensive nature in intellectual operations than in the acts of sense."

Of all souls, man's possesses the most perfect power of otherness, because his intellect can grasp things in their universal character and also because it can reflect upon itself. Now, it is quite manifest that a power which is capable of grasping the universal nature of its objects and of reflecting upon itself must be rooted in a substance that is completely devoid of matter; and further, that its proper stimulus, to be able to set it in motion, must be immaterial also. At once we see the possibilities of a most intimate union between subject and object—an intimacy which is entirely denied to the senses. Aquinas puts it plainly when he says: "Sense, by its apprehensions, is linked to things in a very superficial manner. Intellect, on the contrary, reaches in to grasp the very essence of things. . . . By our union with immaterial forms, we penetrate more deeply to the heart of reality than by the palpable conjunction of sense and object which is manifest in animal cognition."

B. THE INTIMACY OF INTELLECTUAL KNOWLEDGE

Thus, the only activity that is perfectly acquisitive of objects is the intellectual operation. Far from widening the gap that separates mind and reality, this immanence is the very condition of the passage of object to subject. For, to repeat what we have already said so frequently, it is only by becoming a thing that we know it. Further, such perfect intimacy, proper to intellectual acts alone, serves to deepen the subject's knowledge of himself. The possession of objective knowledge means the possession of subjective knowledge. "The better a thing is understood," says Aquinas, "the closer is the knowledge of it to the knowing subject and the nearer it is to being one with the knowing subject."

This prominent feature of unity, which is so constantly proclaimed by Aquinas, throws a flood of light on the profound immanence of intellectual knowledge, which has no counterpart in the life of sense; and on the extensiveness of our rational insights, which make our souls so truly universal in their interests. It is precisely because man desires to know all things, and cannot do so except by a succession of intellectual acts, that he finds pleasure in the movements of thought. Unity of intentional being is an essential condition of ideation. In fact, since an idea is a second self, inasmuch as it is self as thought, it should possess the same oneness that characterizes the self with which, for the moment, it is identical. "Intellect, in its act of understanding, is perfectly identified with the thing that it understands. . . . This does not mean, however, that the essence of the intellect becomes the thing understood or the image of the thing understood; but simply that, in the moment that it actually understands, it is completely informed by the species of the thing understood."

C. THE EXCELLENCE OF INTELLECTUAL KNOWLEDGE

Thus, becoming something else, by a process of remotion from matter, represents the whole Thomistic economy of knowledge. Those who are familiar with the writings of Aquinas will agree, I think, that this is the pith of his doctrine on the cognitive procedure. There is scarcely a page in all his vast tomes that does not contain some reference to his views on knowledge and its processes. The degree of remotion from matter furnishes the clue to the perfection of the knowing subject. This is what sets man head and shoulders above the animals and all other earthly creatures. "The most excellent beings are intellectual, since intellect is potentially everything, having within itself, as it were, the excellence of everything." And again: "By the fact that a being is endowed with intelligence, it is capable of possessing within itself all other being." Further: "Intellectual apprehension is not limited to particular things but extends itself to everything."

From these sample texts, which could be multiplied over and over again, it is easy to determine the attitude of Aquinas on the supreme importance and intrinsic perfection of intellectual life. Here is immanence in its highest earthly reaches. Here is cognition at its greatest remove from matter. Here is an act which, by its complete intus-susception of the object which it grasps, most perfectly fulfills the conditions of a vital function—that is, of a process which is at once receptive and creative, spontaneous and self-perfecting.

iii

The Body an Instrument of Intellectual Knowledge

A. MATTER THE COPRINCIPLE OF RATIONAL FORM

Man is by nature a composite creature. His soul requires a body for the perfection of its being. Indeed, any explanation of human knowledge in which the body does not share, or shares only in an incidental manner, would be straightway disqualified in the mind of Aquinas. Further, if the union of soul and body is a design of nature, then it must be natural for man's intellect to be conditioned by the administrations of his senses. Human knowledge, then, must show forth the original condition of human nature—a nature which, as Aquinas loves to repeat, operates at the crossroads of two worlds, the one of matter, the other of spirit. The body of man places him in contact with the universe of physical dimensions, with matter and all its tangible properties. The mind of man enables him both to create and to live in a realm of metaphysical realities. Because all our knowledge begins with the cognitions of sense, the body must therefore be regarded as a necessary instrument of knowledge.

Now, the closer our grasp on reality, the better it is. If, then, in the pursuit of knowledge, recourse must be had to certain auxiliary factors which are not of a purely intellectual nature, the reason must be that such information as is possible to the human mind is too vague to delineate reality in all its fullness. Foreshortened as our perspective on the universe of being is, it would be still farther removed from the concrete truth that things actually possess were it not for the fact that intellect is conjoined to sense, that mind is assisted by material agents in the elaboration of its ideas. Let us suppose, says Aquinas, that we got our concepts without resorting to sense imagery. "Such knowledge would be imperfect, of a general nature, and confused. The very constitution of things requires a union of body and soul on the part of man, if he is to have a proper idea of the world." The impressions of sense objects are designed to produce a correct knowledge of themselves. With regard to such objects, the soul of man is like an uneducated person who needs concrete examples to help him understand. The greater good of the soul, therefore, demands its union with the body; in order that, from its immediate contact—through the body senses—with the world of corporeal reality, it may develop a proper and adequate knowledge of sensible things.

Accordingly, nature has ordained that the human soul should receive its rational perfection from the body to which it is conjoined. Otherwise, there would be no reason for its having a body. More to the point: nature has ordained that the light of man's intellect, which is without actual specification, should be kindled from without, by the action of the body on the soul. For, man's senses have their roots in matter as well as in spirit. They function in a material medium and upon material objects. The phantasms that they produce are the pictures of material phenomena.

Now, all these pyschosomatic powers are, in fact must be, at the disposal of intellect. In the first stages of knowledge man is utterly dependent upon them. His senses are continuous, so to speak, with the world of time and space in which he lives; and the ideas which he wrests from the impressions of sense have the seal of their material origin upon them. What, then, is the sort of thing with which the mind of man naturally deals? The answer is easy. Man himself is a creature composed of body and soul. He is a corporeal substance. Quite naturally, therefore, the proper object of his intellect is the essence of corporeal being. More simply, man's mind is born to understand material things. Such knowledge is acquired only by degrees. Its first information is to the effect *that* there is a universe of sensible reality. From this point on, its quest is to know *what* this universe is. The way is long and tortuous, and the journey is really never ended. We do not mean to say, however, that the human mind knows only material objects, but merely that these objects form its proper diet. They are connatural to it, the soil from which it gathers its first information. With such knowledge securely laid away, it can go on to know immaterial realities by means of the material things that it understands. But to repeat: the object of human intelligence must be proportionate to it, since object and subject become one in the act of knowledge. Now the subject, in this case, is man; and man is composed of matter and form. The proper object of his intellect, then, must be the universe of sensible being which, like man, is also composed of matter and form.

iv

The Problem of Human Knowledge

A. APPROACH TO THE PROBLEM

Philosophers who have tried their hand at a solution of the problem of ideogenesis have been committed to one of three great traditions, all of which have come down from the Greeks. The first is the tradition of *sensism*. It may be said to begin with Democritus. It is materialistic in character. In its description of the birth of the idea it represents an overemphasis of the object of knowledge, which is material, at the expense of the subject of knowledge, which is immaterial. The second tradition is that of *intellectualism*. It may be said to begin with Plato, in whose writings we find its first complete exposition. It is idealistic in character. In its account of the birth of the idea it represents an overemphasis of the subject of knowledge, which is immaterial, at the expense of the object of knowledge, which is material. Finally, there is the tradition of *moderate realism*. It begins with Aristotle. It is partly materialistic and partly intellectualistic in character, since it requires both sense and intellect for the generation of the idea. To sum up, therefore, the tradition of Democritus interprets ideogenesis as a purely sensory event; the tradition of Plato explains it as a purely intellectual event; and the tradition of Aristotle represents it as a manifold of both. All theories of knowledge may be included within the limits of these three main traditions.

B. THE TRADITION OF MATERIALISM

Democritus taught that we know objects because of minute images that stream off their surfaces and eventually reach mind through the avenues of sense. The essential features of this interpretation, which reduces all our higher forms of knowledge to the dimensions of sense experience, have been resurrected again and again in the history of psychology. In modern times, the associationalists, represented by Hume, Bain, James Mill, Reid, Spencer, and their followers, have been sensists; and many of our contemporary schools, either openly or by implication, hold to such views. Titchener, for example, and the structuralists describe our ideas as images or sensations of a faint, elusive, and obscure character. Watson and the behaviorists make the birth of an idea a purely physiological phenomenon, construing it as a vocal reflex. Köhler and the gestaltists trace back all cognitive events, even our rational insights, to cortical activities which regulate themselves. It is difficult to see how theories of this sort can possibly escape the naïve materialism of Democritus.

C. THE TRADITION OF IDEALISM

Plato taught that our ideas are not derived from the data of sense experience. They are, in fact, totally independent of any antecedent sensitive process. Accordingly, the only way of explaining their presence in intellect is to say that they are inborn. Plato's position was founded on the presumed impossibility of deriving ideas, which are abstract and immaterial, from the data of sense, which are concrete and material. There have been several historical repetitions of the Platonic theory. All of them may be resolved ultimately into the view that what is universal in nature cannot arise from what is singular in nature. Augustine, who was a keen lover of the philosophy of Plato, said that no intellectual knowledge can originate from sensations. If we have ideas, it is because the soul draws them out of itself, even when it appears to discover them. Descartes, as we have seen, revived the exaggerated Platonic dualism of mind and matter. Geulincx fell in with this position and taught that the process of forming ideas is parallelled by certain sensitive functions but is not in any way connected with the latter. Malebranche and Gioberti also were disciples of Descartes and developed an ontologistic theory of ideation, arguing that, because extended matter cannot make an impression on unextended mind, our ideas must be replicas of ideas in the Divine Intellect.

As we approach modern psychology, we note an attenuation of the idealistic motif. The emphasis today is on matter rather than form, on the principles of sensism rather than the tenets of intellectualism. Still, it may be pointed out that the act psychology of Brentano, stressing the object of thought as intended rather than existent, savors somewhat of Plato's attitude toward the products of intellect. So, too, the mental creation of form qualities, as expounded by the school of Graz, is at least reminiscent of the Platonic doctrine that intellect is independent of sense for its abstract contents.

D. THE TRADITION OF MODERATE REALISM

Solidly reared against the extreme views of Democritus and Plato is the ideogenetic theory of Aristotle. With the former, it holds for the need of sense in the beginning of human knowledge. With the latter, it defends the primacy of intellect in the perfection of human knowledge. Ideas are neither the actual products of sense nor the innate contents of intellect. Yet, they are derived from sensory data, through the instrumentality of intellect. The object of sense is a sensible, and the object of intellect is an intelligible. The medium of knowledge, in both cases, is a species. An image is a species of a sensible order of being. An idea is a species of an intelligible order of being. An idea is not an image of a superior sort. To identify them is to be guilty of sensism. This is the position of the materialists in psychology. On the other hand, the idea is derived in some manner from the image. To say that they are not related is to be guilty of intellectualism. This is the position of the idealists in psychology. The task of Aristotle was to show how, by a process of abstraction, our ideas are wrested from images; how a sensible datum is transformed into an intelligible datum; how an object capable of being apprehended by sense is elevated to the status of an object capable of being grasped by intellect.

v

The Process of Ideogenesis

A. ABSTRACTING AND UNDERSTANDING

In accounting for such a transformation, Aristotle recognizes in human intelligence a dual power: first, the ability to abstract; second, the ability to understand. Aquinas takes over the Stagirite's distinction and makes it the basis of his own ideogenetic theory. The ability to abstract he calls *agent intellect*. The ability to understand he names *possible intellect*. The functions of agent intellect are active or creative. The functions of possible intellect are passive or receptive. The proper object of sense is a sensible. But a sensible is only potentially intelligible. As a datum of sense, it is material. In order to be understood, it must be made immaterial. The datum of sense is presented to agent intellect in the form of an image or phantasm. It has all the concrete characters of a material object. It is the product of a material power, enveloped in material conditions. It belongs to the category of the here and now. It is, in short, individualized. The act of illumination, which is proper to agent intellect, is brought to bear on the phantasm. The concrete characters of the datum of sense are left aside. This is the movement of abstraction. Only the nude nature of the object represented in the phantasm remains. But a nude nature, or a nature stripped of its individuating notes, is something capable of being understood. The content of the phantasm is no longer material and determinate but has been raised to the level of intelligibility.

Thus, the work of agent intellect is to illumine and abstract, and, in the very act of illuminating and abstracting, to change the object of sense into an object of intellect. The effect of its creative functioning is to produce a species which, by virtue of its immaterial action, can fecundate possible intellect with the germ of knowledge. The task of possible intellect, however, is not only to receive and be fecundated, but also to produce in its own right; and so it gives expression to its representational power by forming a species of its own. This species is the idea or concept.[a]

B. FUNCTION OF THE INTELLIGIBLE SPECIES

To distinguish between the two sorts of species involved in the operation of our intellectual abilities, the followers of Aquinas refer to the product of agent intellect as an *impressed intelligible species*, and to the product of possible intellect as an *expressed intelligible species*. By the fertile seed which is sown in possible intellect, the faculty of understanding is determined to a new mode of existence wherein it becomes, intentionally, the object which it understands. Thus spurred on to act, it generates within itself a living fruit which is a mental word or concept, an image of an intelligible order, bringing the object which it represents to a sovereign degree of immanent union with the understanding subject. For, in the consummation of this union, possible intellect becomes the very object which it understands, according to the Aristotelian dictum: the intelligible in act is identical with the intellect in act. The whole process which we have just described consists in a progressive elaboration of an object which is first made intelligible in act by the formation of an impressed species; then is actually understood through the production of an expressed species. It is to be noted that, in the explication of Aquinas, the expressed species is not that which we understand, but that by means of which we understand. "What is known in the first instance," says Aquinas, "is the object itself."

C. SPECIES THE MEDIUM OF KNOWLEDGE

In the Thomistic analysis, therefore, the idea is simply an instrument of knowledge, representing both its medium and its content, but not, let it be noted again, its object. Of course, it is true that ideas may become objects of knowledge in a secondary sense, to the degree that we reflect upon them. This is to know that we know what we know. As instruments of knowledge, our ideas refer intentionally to what intellect understands, that is, to the order of reality or of extramental existences. The root of all subjective idealism may be traced to the confusion of what we know with the medium whereby we know. Locke is the responsible agent of this sort of error in modern times. In his *Essay Concerning Human Understanding* he defines idea as an "object of the understanding when a man thinks." Berkeley and others carried the Lockian theory to its logical conclusion and became enmeshed in the extremes of idealism.

If the Thomistic interpretation of the idea as a medium of knowledge is ignored, no grounds are left for distinguishing between the thing as it is in itself, and the thing as it is known to us. But without such a basis it would be impossible to separate truth from falsity, since we could have no wrong ideas of things. This, however, is manifestly contrary to experience. On the other hand, to neglect the intentional factor in our knowledge, that is, its essential relation to objects, is to obliterate the distinction between things as they are in themselves and things as they are known to us—in which case we should be prisoners of our own thoughts, with a purely idealistic vision of the world. Subject and object must in some manner be related if we are not to lose our grip on reality. Related they certainly are, by the relation of intentionality. But separated, too, they must be, if existence in the intentional order is different from existence in the real order.

D. THE MOMENTS OF IDEOGENESIS

In the initial stage of its life, the human intellect shows a striking resemblance to first matter. Thus, before it is conjoined to first form, first matter actually is nothing. So, before it has images from which to abstract, man's intellect actually knows nothing. But, first matter, by its nature, is capable of becoming everything. So, man's intellect, by its nature, is capable of knowing everything. At the start, it is void of all notions, like a tablet on which nothing is written. The primitive stimulus to knowledge comes from experience. The cosmic world impinges on the outer senses, impressing its qualities on organs that are specially designed to receive such stimulation. The products of the external senses are differentiated, compared, and synthesized by common sense, and made over into perceptual wholes. Percepts, in turn, provide stimuli for the operations of the other internal senses—imagination, memory, and cogitative power—each of which is capable of forming an image or phantasm of the object presented to sense. Agent

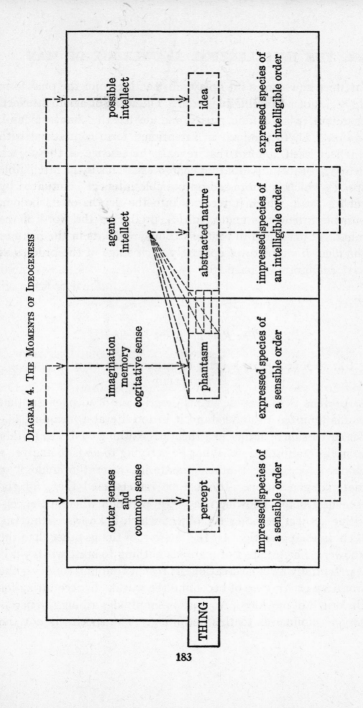

DIAGRAM 4. THE MOMENTS OF IDEOGENESIS

THING

outer senses
and
common sense

percept

impressed species of
a sensible order

imagination
memory
cogitative sense

phantasm

expressed species of
a sensible order

agent
intellect

abstracted nature

impressed species of an intelligible order

possible intellect

idea

expressed species of
an intelligible order

183

intellect now comes into play, abstracting from the phantasm a species of an intelligible order. The work of agent intellect, therefore, is to illumine, purify, and idealize the phantasm, and, in doing so, to produce an intentional form connatural with intellect itself, a form that reveals the essence of the object, denuded of its individuating characters. This is the intelligible species which is impressed on possible intellect. Actuated by such a form, which it receives into the depths of its bosom, possible intellect is made fruitful, producing the word of the mind. It may help to fix the various moments in the birth of the idea, if we picture separately each stage of the process as in our diagram on page 183.

vi

The Rôle of Agent Intellect

A. PRODUCTION OF SPECIES COMMENSURATE WITH POSSIBLE
INTELLECT

Aquinas is so graphic in his description of ideogenesis that one is tempted to understand it in too literal a meaning, like the succession of scenes in a theater. Nothing would be farther from his real intention. What he is trying to do is to analyze a mode of becoming that is immaterial, after the analogy of material generation. It must be remembered that, for the Angelic Doctor, knowing is a vital operation wherein the cognitive subject becomes the object which it knows. Its term, then, is the possession, by the knower, of things other than the knower. The intellect of man has nothing to start with, yet it is potentially a whole creation. It reaches out and conquers the world by the process of becoming the world. In accounting for the origin of our ideas, Aquinas is simply describing the necessary preliminaries to this becoming. The species is not the thing which is known, but only the cognitive instrument whereby a knowledge of the thing is made possible. Our power of intelligence is passive as well as active, receptive as well as creative. This implies that knowledge is an apprehension of objects as they are, as well as a development of self by the assimilation of things to mind. The task of understanding requires a certain connaturality of subject and object. Intellect must be made like the object that it understands, sharing with it a common nature. But a union of this sort could not be achieved if the object were not transformed by the act of abstraction. Only on the condition, then, that an impressed intelligible species is formed can the mind of man be determined to know.

B. PERPETUAL ILLUMINATION

It would be a mistake, however, to think that the rôle of agent intellect stops short at the formation of impressed species. Aquinas had a much higher view of its function and importance. The radiance of agent intellect is a sign, set upon man, of a divine light. At first he knows nothing. His mind is completely empty of concepts. But within its limitless depths, it possesses the seeds of that perfect kind of immanence which is characteristic of mental life. Possible intellect is capable of becoming other things. Because it is a capacity, it must be actualized; and it is reduced to act only by the movement of an illuminative power which is always in act. The very nature of agent intellect is such that it is "always in act according to its very substance; in which respect it differs from possible intellect which is in potency according to its substance and in act only when it is informed by its proper species." If possible intellect is able to function at all, it is solely because of the perpetual light that is diffused by agent intellect, transmuting the object of sense into an object of understanding.[b]

C. INTERMEDIARY BETWEEN SENSATION AND THOUGHT

Agent intellect is already, by its nature, at the supreme degree of actualization without any object in its presence. It is possessed by man in order to illuminate, and not in order to become. To become is the rightful function of possible intellect. But agent intellect is the necessary complement of possible intellect, the root of all its energy, "the active principle," as Aquinas remarks, "by which we are made actually to understand." And thus it is under the urge of agent intellect that possible intellect, made fruitful by the germ of an impressed species which has been abstracted from the object of sense, now produces within itself an expressed species or concept which is a mental symbol of the thing that it understands. In the Thomistic analysis of knowledge, therefore, understanding requires a preliminary act of abstraction, just as abstraction requires a preliminary act of sensation. This brings us back to the point from which we started in explaining the origin of our ideas: that the soul of man requires a body if it is to reach the level of excellence that nature meant it to have.[c]

vii

The Mind's Knowledge of Singulars

A. THE COGNITIONS OF SENSE

Our intellects do not create the world which they know. Rather it is the other way about: the world of reality is the cause of our knowledge of it. But the cosmic universe is a world of singular entities, bathed in a flux of contingency. How, then, are we to explain our cognition of singular and constantly changing things, when our ideas are of universal and necessary natures? First of all let us observe with Aquinas that "the singular does not resist understanding because it is singular, but because it is material, since nothing is understood except immaterially." Further, the senses attain to singulars by a direct and immediate movement. That is the very goal of their operations. It must be by a return to the administrations of sense, therefore, that the universal is concretely realized. Ideas are abstracts from phantasms, and phantasms are potential ideas. Our knowledge of singulars, accordingly, is indirect, achieved "by a kind of reflective procedure wherein, from an apprehension of its intelligible object, the human mind reverts to consider: first, its own act of understanding; next, the intelligible species which is the principle of its operation; and, finally, the origin of its species. And thus it comes to analyze the phantasm [from which it derived its universal idea] and the singular, with which the phantasm is concerned." [d]

B. FUNCTIONS OF THE PHANTASM

For Aquinas, then, the phantasm is a necessary factor, both in the acquisition of our ideas of singulars and in every subsequent intellectual reinspection of these ideas.[e] A cognitive power is always proportioned to its object; and because the soul of man is naturally conjoined to a passible body, the cognitions of intellect are naturally directed to corporeal substances. Now, it belongs to the very essence of corporeal being to exist in an individual and singular entity. Thus, it is proper to the nature of a rose that it have its being in this particular rose; just as it is proper to the nature of humanity that it exist in this particular man. Hence, the nature of any corporeal substance cannot be known completely, and as it is, unless it be known as existing in this singular and concrete thing. But, we apprehend singulars directly and immediately, by the senses. And so, in order that intellect may understand what properly belongs to the dimension of sensitive cognition, it is necessary that it return to the phantasms of sense, to discern therein the universal nature concretized in the singular.

C. NEED OF RETURNING TO THE SENSIBLE OBJECT

By our reflex ideas, then, we have indirect knowledge of singulars. The importance of this knowledge in the Thomistic theory may be gathered from the fact that for Aquinas any science or philosophy of nature which does not return to the singular is neither science nor philosophy, but a dream. "The goal at which our knowledge of nature is terminated is the thing attained by the senses, above all by the sense of vision. As the cutler does not seek for any deeper knowledge of the knife than is required by the work in hand, which is to fashion this particular knife, so the philosopher seeks to know the nature of a stone or a horse simply in order to discover the essential properties of the things that fall under his senses. And just as the judgment of the cutler would be deficient if he ignored the functions of the knife, so the judgment of the philosopher would be lacking in something if he ignored the evidence of his senses. Even the immaterial things that are known by our intelligences, in the present state of the soul's union with the body, are known by means of some comparison with material things." *f*

D. DEFECTIVENESS OF HUMAN KNOWLEDGE

Though the essences of corporeal things are the proper objects of human intellection, yet these essences are really very obscure in our vision because of the matter in which they are enshrouded. "The vast majority of the properties of sensible objects escapes our knowledge, just as the meaning of the properties that fall under the cognitions of sense is unknown to us in most cases. At times we are constrained to employ accidental instead of essential differences—a procedure which is legitimate to the extent that these accidental differences are signs of essential differences which are concealed from us."

It is possible to reach certain specific conclusions regarding the nature of man, his person, operations, habits, and powers; but below man, for the most part, it is seemingly impossible to penetrate to the core of matter, or to beat down the resistance which matter presents to human understanding. This means that the essences of corporeal things are opaque rather than translucent, so far as our ability to understand them is concerned. Certainly the little knowledge that we possess of them is not the kind of cognition that plunges at once into the heart of reality. It is not the intuitive sort of knowledge that is natural to pure spirits. It is least of all the perfect and unclouded type of knowledge which is proper to the Godhead. It is not central but radial knowledge. It proceeds inward from without, and reaches the center only by starting from the periphery. It apprehends the essences of sensible things, not in themselves, but in the symbols which these essences manifest to the senses.[9]

viii

Sensible Form and Intelligible Form

In the explication of our human modes of knowledge we see the full implications of the hylomorphic doctrine, as Aquinas developed and applied it. Thus, everything in the cosmic universe is composed of matter and form. Everything is concrete and individual. Hence the forms of cosmic entities must also be concrete and individual. Now, the process of knowledge is immediately concerned with the separation of form from matter, since a thing is known precisely because its form is received in the knower. But, whatever is received is in the recipient according to the mode of being that the recipient possesses. If, then, the senses are material powers, they receive the forms of objects in a material manner; and if intellect is an immaterial power, it receives the forms of objects in an immaterial manner. This means that in the case of sense knowledge, the

form is still encompassed with the concrete characters which
make it particular; and that, in the case of intellectual knowledge, the form is disengaged from all such characters. To understand is to free form completely from matter. Moreover, if
the proper knowledge of the senses is of accidents, through
forms that are individualized, the proper knowledge of intellect
is of essences, through forms that are universalized. Intellectual knowledge is analogous to sense knowledge inasmuch as it
demands the reception of the form of the thing which is known.
But it differs from sense knowledge so far forth as it consists in

DIAGRAM 5. SENSIBLE AND INTELLIGIBLE FORMS

(in the senses)

FORM
INDIVIDUALIZED

THING

received without matter, but not without the concrete conditions of matter; informing a material
power; restricted to here and now

agent
intellect

FORM
UNIVERSALIZED

received without matter, and without the concrete
conditions of matter; informing an immaterial
power; not restricted to here and now

(in the understanding)

the apprehension of things, not in their individuality, but in their universality.

The separation of form from matter requires two stages if the idea is to be elaborated: first, the sensitive stage, wherein the external and internal senses operate upon the material object, accepting its form without matter, but not without the appendages of matter; second, the intellectual stage, wherein agent intellect operates upon the phantasmal datum, divesting the form of every character that marks and identifies it as a particular something. Abstraction, which is the proper task of active intellect, is essentially a liberating function in which the essence of the sensible object, potentially understandable as it lies beneath its accidents, is liberated from the elements that individualize it and is thus made actually understandable. The product of abstraction is a species of an intelligible order. Now possible intellect is supplied with an adequate stimulus to which it responds by producing a concept. The two stages involved in the ideogenetic separation of form from matter are shown in the diagram on page 190.

ix

The Dependency of Intellect on Sense

A. PHANTASM A POTENTIAL IDEA

The senses can grasp things only by sensible forms. Intellect, on the other hand, can understand things only by intelligible forms. This is simply another way of saying that the proper object of the senses is a singular, whereas the proper object of intellect is a universal. The restriction of the sensitive power to the apprehension of singulars is due, of course, to its psychosomatic nature. It is inherently dependent on matter for all its operations. By contrast, the extension of the intellectual power to the apprehension of universals is due to its purely psychic nature. It is inherently independent of matter in all its operations. This does not signify that intellect is free of the administrations of sense. Quite the opposite! As Aquinas so repeatedly insists, sense products represent the potential matter of intellection. "Phantasms are images of particular things. Ideas, on the contrary, are universals, abstracted from particularized conditions. Accordingly, phantasms are universals in potency."

Again: "Understanding, viewed from one aspect, is proper to the soul alone; but seen from another point of view, it is an operation of body and soul combined. We observe, therefore, that there are attributes and operations of the rational soul which are dependent upon material things, both instrumentally and for their object. Vision, for example, has a material stimulus . . . since color, which is the proper object of vision, is found only in corporeal substances. Hence, though vision is an operation of the soul, it can take place only through the organ of vision . . . which serves it as an instrument. This shows that vision is an operation not only of soul, but also of a bodily organ. There is another function, however, which depends on the body merely for its object, since it does not act through a material instrument. The act of intellectual knowledge does not take place through a material instrument, though it requires a corporeal substance for its object. As Aristotle points out . . . sense imagery is related to intellect in the same way that colors are related to vision. This means that images are the objects of intellect. And since one cannot have imagery without a material organ, it seems clear that there can be no intellectual operation without the cooperation of matter."

To understand the true nature of its dependency on sense, therefore, it is necessary to distinguish intellect's proper operations, which are immaterial, from the conditions of its exercise, which are material. Senses and intellect must work together in the production of the idea; but the dependency of the latter on the former is merely of an objective or extrinsic sort, inasmuch as the senses furnish the data from which intellect abstracts its intelligible species. As Aquinas puts it, the phantasm is "matter for the cause" of ideation, the total cause being found in the joint operations of intellect, acting as principal agent, and of sense, functioning as secondary and instrumental agent.

B. FACTS OF COMMON OBSERVATION

The dependency of intellect on sense is indicated by Aquinas in several ways. In the first place, people congenitally deprived of any outer sense are deficient in ideas corresponding to this special field of experience. Those born blind, for example, have no ideas of color. In the second place, if cortical tissue is injured, imaginal and memorial powers may be definitely impeded in their functions. In such cases, a person is prevented from understanding things of which he had previous knowledge. This would indicate that the presentations of sense are necessary, not only in the acquisition of our ideas, but also in their subsequent recall. In the third place, all of us have the common habit of drawing on the contents of both imagination and memory in order to get concrete examples of what we are trying to understand. The same device is used when we attempt to explain anything abstruse or difficult to another person. Finally, there are the usual phenomena of dream life in which the perceptual powers are more or less in a state of quiescence, with the result that it is extremely hard to distinguish appearances from reality. Judgments are formulated upon bizarre premises, and fact and fancy seem to merge into a single logical system. Here, obviously, the weakness of the reasoning power is due to the condition of the senses.[h]

C. FACTS OF SPECIAL OBSERVATION

Observations of this kind are matters of public experience; yet the results of experiment and clinical research are also in substantial agreement with the conclusions of the Angelic Doctor. We know, from inductive study, that the cerebral cortex possesses certain primary reception and projection areas for the different types of sensation and body movements. More than this, we can point out, in some detail, the actual cortical topography of our sensitive functions. Injuries to particular sections of the brain may exterminate the activities of the outer senses or destroy special fields of imaginal or memorial experience. But there is no neurological evidence for the localization of intellectual functions in any part of the cortex. On the contrary, the scientific records would tend to show that, despite the loss of sense organs or parts of the cortex, intellectual life can still be pursued. It may be impaired, of course, by such material losses; but it cannot be obliterated without the total annihilation of all our sensitive acts. The power of understanding continues to operate so long as the cerebral cortex and the organs of sense are sufficiently intact to provide materials upon which intellect can work.

Another type of evidence refers to threshold values and saturation points, which may be definitely established in the case of the senses, but which are unknown to intellectual power. The fatigues that are sometimes associated with heavy mental effort are now experimentally known to be muscular in character and origin. To be sure, such fatigues may have their effect on intellect. Reaction times are lengthened and errors of judgment appear, as the physical strain on the senses is prolonged or increased. But intellect is affected by such factors only in a roundabout way, to the extent that the acuity of the external receptors is reduced, or the powers that produce phantasms are obstructed in their work.

D. DEPENDENCY OF SOUL ON BODY

Thus the fact of the human mind's dependency on sense is easily discerned and readily admitted. It is not the fact, indeed, that should interest us, but the reason of the fact, which, ultimately, goes back to what we have said many times before —that the soul of man is designed by nature to be united with matter which it needs in order to accomplish its perfection. Such being the case, we should not be surprised to find that all the soul's powers, without exception, are somehow conditioned by material structures. As Aquinas profoundly observes: "Because the soul of man is the form and actuality of matter, there proceed from its essence certain powers affixed to material organs from which it accepts the object of its immaterial knowledge." And so it is that the rational soul, which can neither acquire knowledge, nor use the knowledge which it has acquired, *without converting to phantasms*, verifies completely its definition as a form which is naturally meant to be immersed in matter.

x

The Essential Superiority of Man over the Animal

To sum up: although man's intellect exhibits an objective need of the ministrations of sense, there is no proof of any subjective dependency upon such ministrations. On the contrary, all the evidence points to an essential distinction between the products of sense and intellect. The point is critical, because if it could be shown that sense knowledge does not differ from intellectual knowledge, it would mean that man is no different from the rest of the animal kingdom. That this is not the case may be shown in two ways.

In the first place, our analysis has revealed that the instrument of sense knowledge is a sensible species and that the medium of intellectual knowledge is an intelligible species. Now, a sensible species is an individualized form, that is, a form which has not been freed from the concrete characters that limit it both temporally and spatially. An intelligible form, on the other hand, is a universalized form, that is, a form which has been denuded of all its concrete characters and thereby removed from the dimensions of space and time. A sensible form, then, is something material. An intelligible form is something immaterial. But, knowledge by sensible species is proper to the animal, just as knowledge by intelligible species is proper to man. Unless, therefore, material and immaterial mean one and the same thing, it is impossible to identify the cognitions proper to man with those proper to the animal.

In the second place, the external fruits of man's knowledge are so superior to the animal's accomplishments that one is forced to conclude to a difference of cognitive principles. Witness the products of human craftsmanship, the works of human art, the achievements of human language! Witness, too, the outward expression of man's moral and religious sentiments, the drama, humor, and pathos of life which are appreciated, obviously, only by man. Now, all of these things are based on rational insight; and none of them are found in the animal kingdom. It is lawful, then, to infer that the animal has no reason.

xi

The Degrees of Intelligence

A. DISCURSIVE NATURE OF THE HUMAN INTELLECT

A final problem concerns itself with the position which the human mind occupies on the scale of intelligences. Let us recall, first of all, that for Aquinas the act of understanding is the perfect and supreme function of life. Man enjoys such an excellence to the extent that his intellect can reflect upon itself. At one and the same time it can know reality and itself. But this is only the beginning of intellectual perfection. Phantasms are necessary for the acquisition of our ideas, and for the reinspection of ideas once acquired. Further, our minds must seek knowledge by a kind of circular movement wherein they advance, through the successive stages of time, from one truth to another.[i] As Aquinas says: "Men are called rational because they come to know truth by the methods of discourse, being constrained to follow such a device because of their feebleness in comprehending things." Because our souls are conjoined to bodies, they are operative within the boundaries of space and time. Indeed, body must act first, through the senses, before soul can act through the intellect. Our minds are completely without knowledge until matter has supplied them with an object. Moreover, the initial ideas that we get from the cosmic universe are imperfect and confused; and so we are obliged to fill them out with information of a more determinate nature, always approaching closer and closer to the reality which nourishes and sustains our thinking processes at the same time that it is never exhausted by them.

B. INTUITIVE NATURE OF THE ANGELIC INTELLECT

Thus, man is constrained by nature to seek his knowledge from below. His mind is a potency that always needs to be activated, with the result that he must wrest his knowledge, piecemeal, from the world of sensible phenomena.

In the angel, on the other hand, there is no darkness of unrealized knowledge, no weakness of unrealized power. For, the angelic mind is always in act, with regard to what it can understand. Yet, even the angel has its natural limitations. Its mind does not exhaust reality: neither is its thought identical with its substance. "No created intellect is related as act to the realm of universal being, for in such a case it would have to be infinite. It follows, then, that every created intellect, by the fact that it is created, is not the act of all that is understandable, but is related to the understandable as potency is related to act. Now, potency is connected with act in two ways: first, when it is always in act; second, when it is not always in act but must be reduced to act. The intellect of the angel is always in act with respect to what it can know. The intellect of man, on the other hand, is in potency with respect to what it can know."

C. SUBSTANTIAL NATURE OF THE DIVINE INTELLECT

Over and above every created intellect is the mind of the First Cause, which stands to universal being as the act of everything that is. Such a mind, of course, is the very essence of the Godhead. In it, every creature pre-exists—formally, as in its exemplary cause, and virtually, as in its efficient cause. This is the mind that measures all creation, but is itself unmeasured and unmeasurable, a mind wherein no interior resistance, no shadow of material darkness, no potentiality of any sort, is possible. For, everything in the depths of the divine mind is infinitely conscious, infinitely in act; everything subsists there as an idea of divine reality. Consciousness in this supreme plenitude does not entail any opponency of subject to object, since the perfection of the act of knowing all things can have no internal or external limitations to surmount.

READINGS FROM AQUINAS

Summa Theologica, part I, question 79, and questions 85–88.
Contra Gentiles, book I, chapters 44–50.
———— book II, chapters 73–78.

CLARIFICATIONS

(a)

Kinds of abstraction

"Abstraction may occur in two ways," as Aquinas shows: "First, by way of composition and division; and in this way we understand that one thing does not exist in some other, or that it is separate therefrom. Second, by way of simple and absolute consideration; as when we understand one thing without considering another. . . . This is what we mean by abstracting the universal from the particular or the intelligible species from the phantasm; that is, by considering the nature of the species apart from its individual qualities represented by the phantasms."

(b)

The Augustinian doctrine of illumination

In the teaching of Augustine, intellect always needs the light of God, its Sun, in order to understand. This divine illumination, without which the soul cannot attain to truth, is not an objective revelation, but a production within the mind of a cognitional species which determines us to know. It is a *lumen sui generis*, a light which is not God, yet is emitted by God. As the senses perceive by the light of the cosmic sun, so intellect understands by the light of the divine countenance. The illumination theory of Augustine exercised a profound influence on the philosophers of the Middle Ages. Aquinas would readily admit that the radiant activity of agent intellect is a sign, set upon man, of the perpetual splendor of the mind of God, according to the words of the psalmist: "The light of Thy countenance is signed upon us, O Lord." But he would deny that a supernatural illumination is necessary before man's intellect can understand. All that is required in the human soul is a power of lighting up the phantasms and of abstracting universal forms from their particular conditions.

(c)

Memory and intellect

Aquinas raises the question: is there an intellectual memory distinct from intellect itself? His reply is as follows:

"The condition of past may be referred to two things, namely, to the *object which is known*, and to the *act of knowing*. These two are found together in the sensitive part, which apprehends something from the fact of its being immuted by a present sensible: wherefore, at the same time, an animal remembers to have sensed before in the past, and to have sensed some past sensible thing. But, as concerns the intellectual part, the past is accidental, and is not in itself a part of the object of the intellect. For, intellect understands man, as man: and to man, as man, it is accidental that he exist in the present, past, or future. On the part of the act, however, the condition of past, even as such, may be understood to be in intellect as well as in sense, since our soul's act of understanding is an individual act, existing at this or that time, inasmuch as a man is said to understand now, or yesterday, or tomorrow. And this is not incompatible with the intellectual nature: for, such an act of understanding, though something individual, is yet an immaterial act . . . and therefore, as the intellect understands itself, though it be itself an individual intellect, so also it understands its act of understanding which is an individual act, in the past, present, or future. In this way, then, the notion of remembrance, in so far as it regards past events, is preserved in intellect, forasmuch as it understands that it previously understood; but not in the meaning that it understands the past as something [restricted by the conditions of] here and now."

It is the same power, namely, possible intellect, which receives intelligible species and retains them. For this reason, it is called by Aristotle a *topos eidon*, or storehouse of species. "Wherefore" as Aquinas concludes, "it is clear that memory is not a distinct power from intellect, since it belongs to the nature of a passive power to preserve as well as to receive." The retention, it should be noted, is after the manner of a habit. Now, habit acts as a power when it becomes fully entrenched in the power. Memory in intellect, accordingly, is simply a developed skill in the use of one's ideas. From the point of view of recall, it involves active as well as possible intellect, since ideas are never brought back to consciousness for reconsideration except by a conversion to phantasms, and the presence of phantasms implies an exercise of the abstractive functions of agent intellect.

(d)

The intellectual apprehension of singulars

According to the Thomistic interpretation, man's intellect does not grasp singulars directly, but by an indirect movement wherein it returns to consider the phantasm from which it abstracted its universal idea and thereby comes to analyze the singular thing represented by the phantasm. It is obvious that, for the achievement of such indirect knowledge, some kind of continuity must be effected between intellect, on the one side, and sense, on the other. In the teaching of Aquinas, this mutual extension of material activities into the sphere of the immaterial, and of immaterial activities into the sphere of the material, is accomplished through the cogitative faculty or particular reason. From the point of view of the knowable object, the movement of continuity implies that singulars are somehow present to intellect, even though they are material in nature. From the point of view of the knowing subject, the movement of continuity further implies that intellect has thrown itself against the barrier which matter presents, even though it cannot overcome it completely and is compelled to take a roundabout route in order to reach its cognitive goal. As Aquinas tells us, it is not the singularity of a corporeal substance, but its materiality, which prevents us from grasping it directly. The act which accomplishes the necessary contact of intellect with sense is not only collisional, but also cognitional, since by it intellect gains at least indirect information about the singular. Such information is evidenced in our judgments about particular things, in our use of proper names and possessive pronouns, and so forth.

This brings us to a final important consideration, namely, that the present problem concerns not only singular things to be known, but also singular actions to be performed. And since knowledge is translated into action through the intermediation of the appetites, it is manifest that we must have the same continuity between will and singular actions to be performed as we have between intellect and singular objects to be known. Thus when prudence dictates some concrete line of conduct, and will undertakes to carry through the prudential judgment and make it an actional reality, it is cogitative power which functions in the rôle of intermediary, making it possible for intellect to conclude, by a final practical decision in which will has a hand, that *this* ought to be done.

(e)

The theory of imageless thought

Aquinas says: "It is impossible for man's intellect, in the present state of life in which the soul is united to a body that is capable of sufferance, to understand anything actually, excepting by a conversion to phantasms." This is the case "not only when it acquires fresh knowledge, but also when it applies knowledge already acquired." To illustrate: "Anyone can experience for himself, that when he tries to think about something, he forms certain phantasms to serve as examples wherein, as it were, he examines what he is desirous of understanding. For the same reason, when we want to help someone else grasp a truth, we lay examples before him from which he forms phantasms, in order to help him understand." Even incorporeal substances, "of which there are no phantasms, are known to us by comparing them with corporeal things of which there are phantasms." The position of Aquinas here is quite clear and emphatic.

The modern psychologist has formulated what is known as "the theory of imageless thought." The theory is the result of a great deal of experimental work performed by Alfred Binet in France, Oswald Külpe and the Würzburgers in Germany, Robert Woodworth and Thomas Verner Moore in America, and others. To understand the significance of the theory, it is necessary to distinguish between the single-concept aspect of thought, and its judicial or inferential connotations. This is the familiar Thomistic distinction between simple apprehension and the compositional and divisional achievements of intellection which result in judgment and reasoning. In the modern psychologist's nomenclature, simple apprehension is referred to as *meaning*, while judgment and reasoning are broadly classified under the heading of *proposition*. For practical purposes of discussion, therefore, we may say that there are two ways in which thinking can be differentiated in the theory of imageless thought: first, as meaningful or conceptual; second, as propositional or judicial. It may be added at once that, in proposing his theory, the modern psychologist has in mind chiefly the second type of thinking; and he points to concrete evidence which, in its cumulative force, certainly seems to indicate that there can be a mode of intellection that is unaccompanied by any corresponding imagery. On the other hand, when it is a question of the first type of thinking, he does not say that simple concepts are or can be derived from experience without a conversion of intellect to phantasmal data, but merely that, in the reinspection of any one of these concepts, the image to which intellect converts need not be the one from which the concept was originally abstracted.

At no point, so far as I can see, is there any conflict between the experimental evidence and the teaching of Aquinas, when each is properly interpreted. There would be a serious difficulty, of course, if it could be shown that meanings appear in consciousness without some image appearing at the same time. The Angelic Doctor is very positive in his assertion that every single concept is derived from some sort of phantasm. Indeed, there is no other way of getting at a meaning except through the data elaborated by the senses. Here ancient teaching and modern experimentation are in basic agreement, since philosopher and scientist alike admit the impossibility of excluding the cooperation of intellect and sense in the genesis of our ideas. At the same time, Aquinas does seem to allow that, in going over ideas that have already been wrested from sensible data, intellect is not bound to convert to the phantasm from which it made its original abstraction. He was familiar, moreover, with what are called today "constructed concepts," that is, concepts which have been refined by additional knowledge and which are made up of the contributions of several kinds of sensible data. Such concepts, e.g. our notion of potency and act, square root, physical hypothesis, and so forth, are really not abstracted directly from any one sensible datum, but are built up by the creative power of intelligence. Although all concepts of this nature involve several elementary factors in their construction, they are not usually reinspected by converting to the particular phantasms from which their elements were abstracted in the beginning. It may be that, in the recall of constructed concepts, particular images are irrelevant, and that the important thing is simply the arousal of some kind of imaginal activity.

With regard to the compositional and divisional types of thinking, where the essence of the procedure consists, not in simple apprehension, but in the discernment of a relationship between things, the Angelic Doctor is again in agreement with the experimental findings, if I understand these findings aright. Thus, there is no phantasm that can possibly picture the essence of a proposition *as such*, that is, the affirmation or negation of an abstract relationship. Speaking of our rational acts, Aquinas says: "Intellect, in forming quiddities [or simple apprehensions] has nothing except an intelligible species of the thing which exists outside of intellect; just as sense has nothing except a sensible species of the thing [which exists outside of sense]. When, however, intellect begins to judge about the thing which it has simply apprehended, its judgment is something that is strictly proper to itself, since there is nothing outside intellect and in the thing, [which corresponds with the apprehended relation of the judgment]." This being the case, it would also follow that there is no phantasm which corresponds with the apprehended relation of the judgment. On this basis, I should say that Aquinas would have accepted the experimental observations which point to the existence of imageless thought, so long as such observations are certified and refer only to the propositional types of thinking. I should like to repeat, however, that there is no fact or finding in the experimentalist's record which eliminates the necessity of some sort of image in conceptual thinking. And even in the case of the propositional modes of thought, the drift of the evidence must not be interpreted to mean that no imagery is present. Thus, propositions are made up of terms, and terms represent simple apprehensions to which some kind of imagery is always attached. It is the apprehended relational element of the proposition to which, as Aquinas says, there is nothing really correspondent outside the mind, since it is a pure achievement of intellect.

(f)

Knowledge of material and immaterial things

Aquinas says: "The object of knowledge is proportionate to the power of knowledge. Now, there are three grades of cognitive powers. For, one grade of cognitive power, namely, sense, is the act of a corporeal organ. And therefore the object of every sensitive power is a form as existing in corporeal matter. And since such matter is the principle of individuality, consequently every power of the sensitive part can have knowledge only of the individual. There is another grade of cognitive power which is neither the act of a corporeal organ, nor in any way connected with corporeal matter. Such is the angelic intellect, the object of which is a form existing apart from matter; for, though angels know material things, yet they do not know them save in something immaterial, namely, either in themselves or in God. But, the human intellect holds a middle place: for it is not the act of an organ; yet it is the power of a soul which is the form of matter. . . . And therefore it is proper to it to know a form existing individually in corporeal matter, but not as existing in this individual matter. But, to know what is in individual matter, yet not as existing in this individual matter, is to abstract the form from the matter which is represented by the phantasms. Accordingly, we must needs say that our intellect understands material things by abstracting from phantasms; and through material things, thus considered, we acquire some knowledge of immaterial things; just as, by contrast, the angels know material things through the immaterial."

(g)

Order of human knowledge

"In our knowledge," as Aquinas points out, "there are two things to be considered. First, intellectual knowledge in some degree arises from sensible knowledge: and, because sense has singular and individual things for its object, and intellect has the universal for its object, it follows that our knowledge of the former comes before our knowledge of the latter. Secondly, we must consider that our intellect proceeds from a state of potentiality to a state of actuality; and every power thus proceeding from potentiality to actuality comes first to an incomplete act, which is the medium between potentiality and actuality, before accomplishing the perfect act. The perfect act of intellect is complete knowledge, when the object is distinctly and determinately known; whereas the incomplete act is imperfect knowledge, when the object is known indistinctly and confusedly, as it were. A thing thus imperfectly known, is known partly in act and partly in potentiality; and hence the Philosopher says (in the first book of his *Physics*) that 'what is manifest and certain is known to us at first confusedly; afterwards we know it by distinguishing its principles and elements.'

"Now, it is evident that to know an object that comprises many things, without proper knowledge of each thing contained in it, is to know that thing confusedly. In this way we can have knowledge not only of the universal whole, which contains parts potentially, but also of the integral whole; for, each whole can be known confusedly, without its parts being known. But, to know distinctly what is contained in the universal whole is to know the less common, as to know *animal* indistinctly is to know it as *animal;* whereas to know *animal* distinctly is to know it as *rational* or *irrational*, that is, to know a man or a lion. Therefore, our intellect knows animal before it knows man; and the same reason holds in comparing a more universal idea with a less universal.

"Moreover, as sense, like intellect, proceeds from potentiality to act, the same order of knowledge appears in the senses. For, by sense we judge of the more common before the less common, in reference both to place and time. Thus, as regards place, when a thing is seen afar off it is seen to be a body before it is seen to be an animal; and to be an animal before it is seen to be a man, and to be a man before it is seen to be Socrates or Plato. And the same is true as regards time, for a child can distinguish a human being from a non-human before he distinguishes this man from that man. . . . The reason of this is clear: because he who knows a thing indistinctly is in a state of potentiality as regards its principle of distinction; just as he who knows gender is in a state of potentiality as regards difference. And so it is evident that indistinct knowledge is midway between potentiality and act.

"We must therefore conclude that knowledge of the singular and individual is prior, as regards us, to knowledge of the universal; just as sensible knowledge is prior to intellectual knowledge. But, in both sense and intellect, knowledge of the more common precedes knowledge of the less common."

(h)

Sensible origin of our ideas

The sensible origin of our ideas is exemplified by many of the words which we employ in designating the act of intellection. The following list can be completed by consulting any standard dictionary.

DIAGRAM 6. WORD SYMBOLS AND THE SENSIBLE ORIGIN OF OUR IDEAS

Consider	*sidera*	(to gaze at) the stars
Contemplate	*templum*	(to enter) the soothsayers' place of observation
Reflect	*reflectere*	to bend back
Ponder	*pondus*	(to use) a weight
Comprehend	*prehendere*	to take hold of
Deliberate	*librum*	(to balance on) a scales
Conceive	*capere*	to seize on
Discern	*circus*	(to mark off with) a circle or ringed area
Envisage	*visus*	(to use one's) power of vision
Cogitate	*agitare*	to shake up or turn over

(i)

Simple apprehension, judgment, inference

"The human intellect," as Aquinas tells us, "must of necessity understand by composition and division. For, since intellect passes from potentiality to act, it has a likeness to things that are generated, which do not attain to perfection all at once but acquire it by degrees. So, likewise, the human intellect does not acquire perfect knowledge by the first act of apprehension; but it first apprehends something about its object, such as its quiddity, and this is its first and proper object; and then it understands the properties, accidents, and the various relations of the essence. Thus, it necessarily compares one thing with another by composition or division; and from one composition and division it proceeds to another, which is the process of reasoning."

(j)

Truth and falsehood in sense and intellect

"Sense," says Aquinas, "is not deceived in its proper object—as sight in regard to color—save accidentally, through some hindrance occurring to the sense organ. For example, the taste of a fever-stricken person judges a sweet thing to be bitter, through his tongue being vitiated by ill humors. Sense, however, may be deceived in regard to common sensible objects, such as size or figure—when, for example, it judges the sun to be only a foot in diameter, whereas in reality it exceeds the earth in size. Much more is sense deceived concerning accidental sensible objects, as when it judges that vinegar is honey because the color of both is the same. The reason of this is evident. For, every faculty, as such, is *per se* directed to its proper object; and things of this kind are always the same. Hence, so long as the faculty exists, its judgment concerning its own proper object does not fail.

Now, the proper object of intellect is the quiddity of a material thing; and hence, properly speaking, intellect is not at fault concerning this quiddity. It may, however, go astray as regards the surroundings of the thing in its essence or quiddity; or in referring one thing to another in respect to composition and division; or in the process of reasoning. But, in regard to those propositions which are understood as soon as the terms thereof are understood, intellect cannot err, as in the case of first principles from which arises infallible truth through the certitude of demonstrated conclusions.

"Intellect, nevertheless, may be accidentally deceived about the quiddity of composite things, not by a defect of its organ—since it is a power that is independent of any material instrument—but on the part of the composition affecting the definition. Thus, the definition of a thing may be false in relation to something else, as when the definition of a circle is applied to a triangle; or the definition may be false in itself because it involves the composition of things that are incompatible, as when an object is described as a rational winged animal. Hence, as regards simple things not subject to composite definitions, we cannot be deceived, unless, indeed, we understand nothing whatever about them."

CHAPTER EIGHT

THE VOLITIONAL LIFE OF MAN

i

The Perfection of Will

A. THE POWER OF INTELLECTUAL OREXIS

The life of intellectual knowledge does not suffice for man. It demands a complement, as Aquinas tells us. Just as nature has endowed us with sense appetites which spend themselves and are spent upon the material goods of the universe, so she has enriched our being with a rational appetite which can pour itself out in longing for the things of the spirit. This does not mean, of course, that man's will finds its sole happiness in values of an immaterial character; but simply that our intellectual desires are grounded on intellectual apprehensions. We have already seen how, in the teaching of Aquinas, the proper object of the human intellect is found in material essences. Should not these same material essences, then, form the connatural objects of his will? *ª* But reason does not rest content with its knowledge of material things. Through the visible things of the universe it is able to lift itself up to a universe of invisible realities. So, too, will can focus its desires upon goods that are completely devoid of matter. The quest after truth which begins in the human mind with the dawn of understanding is a pilgrimage that can end only in eternity. Similarly, the thirst for happiness which engulfs the human heart upon the first stirrings of love will never be slaked till it is swallowed up by a goodness that is infinite. "Thou hast made us for Thyself" cries Augustine to his Creator; "and our hearts will be restless till they rest in Thee."

B. THE TENDENTIAL NATURE OF WILL

All our appetites are cognitively determined. In the case of the animal passions, the determination has to do with the singular and concrete, since the object of sense is a sensible. In the case of the will-act, the determination has to do with the universal and abstract, since the object of intellect is an intelligible. As Aquinas clearly explains, sense is unable to apprehend its object without material conditions, being immersed in the contingencies of time and space; and so sense appetite is directed to its object in the same manner, that is, to a good which is particularized. Intellect, on the other hand, can apprehend its object without material conditions; and so intellectual appetite is directed to its object in the same manner, that is, to a good which is universalized.

If the sensitive appetites require an image to provide a motive for the passions, the intellectual appetite requires an idea in order to be similarly stimulated to volition. Things are said to enjoy an intentional mode of being in our knowledge of them. So, they may be said to enjoy an analogous tendential mode of being in our desire of them. By the fact that they are known, they tend to exert a pull on the appetites. The difference between cognition and appetition, says Aquinas, is like the difference between rest and movement. "The function of a cognitive power is completed when the object is in the knowing subject. The function of an appetitive power is completed when the desiring subject is borne towards the desirable object. Therefore, the action of a cognitive power may be likened to a state of rest; while the action of an appetitive power may be compared to a state of motion." Because of this difference in respect to goals, the operation of an apprehensive faculty is not so properly called a *movement* as the operation of an orectic power.

ii

The Appetitive Union

A. THE IMPULSION OF LOVE

It is important to remember, from the outset, that the act of will is no less immaterial and pure in itself than the act of intellect.   Two kinds of generation may be discerned in our higher powers, as Aquinas points out: first, the generation of knowledge, wherein subject becomes object through the medium of an idea; second, the generation of desire, wherein object becomes subject through the medium of an act of love. If we speak of the *birth of a concept* in the processes of knowledge, we may also speak of the *birth of an impulsion* in the processes of love. Moreover, the knowable object is in the knowing subject by the instrumentality of this concept; so the object of love is in the lover by the weight of this impulsion. The mystery of the cognitive union obliges us to postulate an intentional mode of being for the objects that we know.   In the same manner, the mystery of the appetitive union obliges us to postulate a tendential mode of being for the objects that we love. Further, just as the intentional mode of being is material in the case of the senses and immaterial in the case of intellect, so the tendential mode of being is material in the case of the animal appetites and immaterial in the case of will.

B. THE INTIMACY OF LOVE

We said a moment ago that the immateriality of the acts of will is not less pure than the immateriality of the acts of intellect. Yet there is this major difference between the two powers: that the acts of will are less separated from things in themselves than the acts of intellect.   Our volitions are always turned toward objects in their concrete state; but our thoughts are the products of abstraction and may rest content to deal with generalities. Perhaps we can make the comparison clearer by saying that intellect is essentially the basis of theory and speculation; will is essentially the basis of practice and production. The fundamental distinction between the two powers is found in the difference between the true and the good, the former being an object of knowledge and the latter an object of love. In knowledge, the union of object with subject is wrought through the agency of a similitude or intentional form. In love, the union of subject with object is accomplished as a result of a tendential weight or impulsion. Further, the appetitive union is more intimate than the cognitive union. As Aquinas puts it: "Knowledge is perfected by the thing known being united, through its likeness, to the knower. But the effect of love is that the thing itself which is loved, is, in a way, united to the lover. Consequently, the union caused by love is closer than the union caused by knowledge."

C. BENEVOLENT AND CONCUPISCENT LOVE

Two kinds of love proceed from the will of man: first, the love of friendship or benevolence, which is a love of being; second, the love of concupiscence, which is a love of well-being. Each of these loves, as Aquinas tells us, is generated by an apprehension of the oneness of the thing loved with the lover. "When we love a thing with the love of concupiscence, we apprehend it as belonging to our well-being. In like manner, when one man loves another with the love of friendship, he wills good to him, just as he wills good to himself. And so he apprehends his friend as his other self, so far forth, namely, as he wills good to him as to himself. Therefore, a friend is called a man's other self."

D. THREE KINDS OF UNION POSSIBLE TO LOVE

Union, as Aquinas teaches, has a threefold relation to the act of love: first, when it is the *cause* of love; second, when it is the

very *essence* of love; and third, when it is the *effect* of love.
The first type of union is substantial. It is exemplified in
the love that the soul bears to the body. The second type of
union is according to a bond of affection. Here the lover is related to the object of his love as to himself, if it be a love of
friendship; or as to something belonging to himself, if it be a
love of concupiscence. The third type of union is accomplished
by a physical conjoining of lover and loved one. Now, each is
actually present to the other. This sort of union is the natural
fruit of love. In referring to it, Aquinas mentions a passage
from the writings of Aristophanes who says that lovers desire
to be fused into one. But, since this would entail the destruction of both, they seek a more practical outlet for their love,
by living together, speaking together, and being united in
other things of a similar nature.

iii

Natural and Deliberate Volition

In a previous chapter, we distinguished three kinds of appetitive tendency in creatures: the natural desires of inanimate
matter and plant life; the sensitive desires of animal life; and
the intellectual desires of human life. The first have no basis
whatever in knowledge. The second are grounded on the cognitions of sense. The third proceed from rational insight. It
would be a mistake, however, to confine the meaning of natural desire to the impulsions of chemicals or plants. The fact
is that *every* created power has a basic tendency to be attracted
by its appropriate object. The eye, for example, is naturally
designed to see, which means that it has a natural desire for
light. So, too, the highest of our cognitive powers, intellect,
has a natural desire for truth. What we have said of the senses
and intellect is also verified in the case of will which manifests

a natural desire of good. But, does not truth compel the assent of intellect? And if this is the case, does not good compel the love of will?

In reply to both these questions, Aquinas makes an important distinction. There is a good which has the same meaning for will that first principles have for intellect. There are other goods which have the same meaning for will that deductions from first principles have for intellect. Now, in the presence of first principles intellect is powerless to refuse its assent; otherwise it would be acting contrary to its nature, which is to apprehend truth. In the presence of inferences from first principles, however, intellect may agree or disagree, dependent upon the logical appeal of such inferences. The situation is the same for will. There is the good which is necessarily linked up with the happiness of man. In its presence, will is powerless to refuse its love; otherwise it would be acting contrary to its nature. To this object, therefore, will must adhere as to its last end. Such an object, of course, can be nothing short of *universal good*. It is, in fine, the supreme and final goodness of the Creator. There are other goods, however, that are not necessarily connected with man's happiness. He can be happy without them; and even when he possesses them, they do not make him completely happy. These are *particular goods*, that is, goods which do not exhaust his concept of good. Accordingly, will is not obliged to love them or desire them, even when intellect shows them to be valuable.

The impulsion of will toward universal good may be called *natural volition*. It is the act of will as nature. Similarly, the movement of will toward particular goods may be called *deliberate volition*. It is the act of will as will. Particular goods, as Aquinas tells us, are really the means to happiness rather than the end of happiness, since they cannot be man's final goal. It is important to note this point, because human freedom is

properly exercised with particular goods, to which there are
alternatives, and not with supreme good, to which there can
be no alternative.[b]

iv

The Elicited and Commanded Act of Will

Moreover, just as the liberty of man is not constricted by
the natural impulsions of his will toward good in general or supreme good, so it cannot be touched by physical forces that
may be brought to bear upon his outer behavior. Here, again,
Aquinas clarifies the matter with a distinction between the acts
of will that proceed directly from will, and the acts of the other
powers that are under the control of will. The first are *elicited*
by will; the second are *commanded* by will. Obviously, a man
may be coerced into doing something that he does not want to
do. But coercion can be employed only on the body and its
members. It cannot reach in to shackle the movements of will;
neither can it propel will toward an object that it does not
want. And so, again, the area of human freedom is further
limited by the boundaries of its elicited acts. To sum up: the
problem of man's liberty has certain definite dimensions.
First: it is not concerned with the basic impulsions of will toward good in general or supreme good, but with volitions that
are focused upon particular goods. Second: it is not concerned
with the commanded acts of will, but with its elicited movements.[c]

v

The Act and the Object of Free Will

A. WILL AND FREE WILL

Will differs from free will, says Aquinas, in the same way
that understanding differs from reason. Thus, understanding

deals with first principles, whereas reason is concerned with conclusions. So, will is directed toward the end of man, whereas free will regards the means to this end. In matters of knowledge, we assent to the conclusion on account of the principles. Similarly, in matters of love, we desire the means on account of the end. "Wherefore, as intellect is to reason, so is will to free will, which is the power of choice. But it belongs to the same power to understand and to reason. . . . Accordingly, it belongs to the same power to will and to choose. And so will and free will are not two powers, but one." [d]

B. EXERCISE AND SPECIFICATION OF FREE WILL

Freedom of choice refers either to the act of will, or to the object of will. In the first instance, there is freedom of exercise; in the second, freedom of specification. *Freedom of exercise* means that will is at liberty to choose or not to choose, to operate or not to operate. The point to be emphasized here is not the mere absence of action on the part of will, but the fact that it is not compelled to act. *Freedom of specification* means that will, having established a particular goal, is at liberty to choose among the several courses of action that can lead it to its goal. A man, for example, is free to walk or not to walk; and after he has made up his mind to walk, he is still free to walk wherever he pleases.

vi

The Problem of Human Freedom

A. HISTORICAL APPROACH TO THE PROBLEM

The first great scholar on record who attempted to solve the problem of human freedom was Socrates. According to this philosopher, man desires only good. If he wills what is evil, it must be on grounds of ignorance, since malicious impulses can never be the true offspring of free will. This means, of course, that man is determined in his actions by the amount of knowledge that he possesses. Plato modified the Socratic theory to some extent by saying that only true knowledge is invincible in its effects upon will. Opinion, on the other hand, being a kind of ignorance, may be followed or not followed as one wishes. Of course, a settlement of this sort does not really come to grips with the problem, but only makes it less difficult for us to continue to believe in freedom.

Although Aristotle did not give a complete exposition of the matter of human liberty, he is, nevertheless, decidedly against the views of both Socrates and Plato. He points out, very soundly, that a man must be held morally responsible for his opinions, that is, for what appears to him to be good. For, if he is not thus accountable, it would be impossible to say that virtue is any more voluntary and meritorious than vice. The Stagirite, accordingly, rejects the Socratic formula that no man is willingly bad—even if his badness arises from opinion rather than from science. Aquinas, as we shall presently see, followed the Aristotelian position. His teaching was particularly opposed to the Averrhoists of his day, who held that receptive intellect is the same for all men, thereby destroying the basis of human freedom—since individual choice is founded upon individual understanding.

B. POSITION OF THE EXTREME DETERMINISTS

The views of modern psychologists, outside the tradition of Aristotle, are divided between the extremes of determinism and indeterminism. It is scarcely necessary to add that a scientific psychologist is a determinist or an indeterminist by implication, rather than by explication, since the problem of human liberty is a philosophic one, and it is not the business of the investigator to deal with such problems. Keeping this fact in mind, then, we can proceed to divide all modern deterministic theories into three major groups.

First, any psychologist who holds to the idea of a completely rigid causality in natural events, identifying the psychic with the physical, is a *physical determinist*. The strict application of such an unbroken law must inevitably destroy freedom of action on the part of will. The fact is, of course, that the operations of the cosmic universe exhibit only a relative sort of determinism. Such operations suppose that only material agents are at work. To draw an argument in favor of absolute determinism from the status of physical determinism in nature is simply a piece of trickery. The behavior of free agents is, by the very notion of freedom, outside the domain of the material. The point is that the action of free will, properly understood, causes no changes in the laws of matter. Neither is will itself affected by such laws. As we have already explained, no material force can coerce the elicited acts of will, though it may influence its imperated acts.

Second, any psychologist who puts forward the relentless reign of animal impulses in all human conduct is a *biological determinist*. Such is the modern Freudian; and to his company may be added the behaviorist, who makes all human activity boil down to the inflexible consistency of a reflex arc. But neither animal instincts nor vegetable reflexes represent the total, or even the essential, range of man's operations; and the laws that govern his lower powers, with their dependencies on matter, are not the same as the laws that govern his higher powers, with their independencies of matter.

Third, any student of mind who says that will must accept the strongest motive or choose the object of greatest value when it acts is a *psychological determinist*. On this basis, will is forced to follow a recognized order of goods. Leibniz, for example, was committed to such a view by his principle of sufficient reason; and the present-day school of Alfred Adler falls into the same category by its accentuation of the sheer power of intellectual processes in the forming of human character. The importance of will is admitted by the Adlerians; but there is a definite implying, at the same time, that mere acquaintance with the demands of reality, or mere recognition of positive values that are best fitted to answer these demands, *alone* suffices to change the course of one's life. The facts of ordinary experience, however, make us question the position of Adler. Thus, we actually select things which intellect tells us are lesser values; or, the other way about, we do not always choose the best things among the goods that are presented by intellect to will. Choice is consequent upon the last practical judgment which suggests a preference of one value over another, as we shall see presently.

To sum up: no power outside of will—either material force, or physiological reflex, or instinctive urge, or even intellect itself—can so determine the human will as to leave it trapped and helpless in the face of superior agencies.

C. POSITION OF THE EXTREME INDETERMINISTS

Sinning by defect in the other direction is the school of extreme indeterminism. Here the position is such that will is left without a single reason for acting—not even the motive of intellect. Exaggerated notions about the indeterminate character of will and its acts may be traced to the teaching of Descartes. Now the power of choice is pictured as entirely free of necessity, even the necessity of having a proper motive upon which to operate. This point of view is not very common today, it is true; yet the implications of it are found in such unwarranted phrases as wish without reason, preference without knowlege, unconscious motivation, and so forth, met with in some of the current psychologies.

Will, in a theory of this kind, must be entirely autonomous. Its acts must arise, not from insight or rational judgment, but from the incalculable depths of its own bosom. But, obviously, to speak of volition without a recognized motive, or of intellectual desire without intellectual knowledge, is to lose sight of the whole meaning of the will-act. Orectic experience that is not founded on cognitive experience is impossible; and this statement is true not only of the sensitive appetites and their movements of passion, but also of will and its acts of volition. Appetite of any sort is a blind power. It cannot know what it wants. If it moves at all, therefore, it must be on a basis of information supplied to it by a cognitive power.

vii

Solution of the Problem of Human Freedom

A. INTELLECT NOT DETERMINED TO ONE

The position of Aquinas is clear-cut. It is midway between the extremes of determinism and indeterminism. First of all, will is a rational appetite. This means that it is moved by the knowledge of intellect. In the nature of intellect, therefore, Aquinas discovers the roots of human freedom. Choice is out of the question if the judgment on which it depends is, itself, a matter of determination. What are the facts of the case? To begin with, man has some notion of good in general, or of what perfects him completely. Such a notion is abstract and universal. It cannot be restricted to here and now, or determined to any one thing. Its very essence is to be free of contingency. Accordingly, man is always able to compare the particular good which is presented for his consideration with his universal concept of goodness.

The result, of course, is an indifference in his judgment, since only goodness as such, which is complete and absolute good, can necessitate approval. Aquinas puts it clearly when he says: "Particular goods, insofar as they are lacking in some good, can be regarded as nongoods." Manifestly, then, the judgment of intellect must be indifferent in regard to such goods. It is as though a man were in converse with himself, just before he makes his choice: "What I want, ultimately, is good without limit or supreme good. What I see before me is a particular good. It does not exhaust my idea of good. I can even regard it as a nongood. So I am not bound to desire it. From one point of view it is attractive; from another, it has no appeal whatever. Compared with supreme good, it is nothing. My will can approve it or set it aside." Such a mode of reasoning is rarely, if ever, explicit; nevertheless, it does really represent a man's state of mind immediately before he chooses. Further, it shows that *the roots of human liberty are lodged in man's rational nature*, since his intellect knows the universal meaning of value, and cannot be determined in its judgments to limited and imperfect goods. But, if the judgment of reason is indetermined, then so is the choice that follows it. Will, therefore, is a free agent, with mastery over its acts.

An argument of this kind can have no weight with sensistic psychologists, like the structuralists, who confound ideas with images; or the behaviorists, who identify thinking with tacit vocalization; or the gestaltists, who explain even the highest achievements of intellect in terms of physical or cortical patterns of energizing; or the Freudians, who make all human activities emergences from instinct. Ultimately, these are the materialists in psychology. As materialists, they are bound to a denial of freedom since matter and reason, or particulars and universals, are mutually exclusive. For such theorists, there can be no human liberty, because there is no intellectual apprehension of good on which to found it.

But man, as Aquinas points out, is limited neither by matter nor by instinct in his thinking procedures. Unlike the stone which is forced toward the center of gravity, or the animal which is driven by instinct to seek the goods of sense, man is guided by reason in the conduct of his affairs. Now, the function of reason is to compare and, in the very act of comparison, to be inclined to several alternatives. Its judgment, therefore, in such contingent matters, "may follow opposite courses and is not determined to one. Forasmuch, then, as a man is rational, it is necessary that he have a free will."

B. THE PERSUASION OF PUBLIC EXPERIENCE

The fact of human freedom is also evident from other sources. Thus, to deny it is to run counter to public experience. Even those who in their private speculations make much of its nonexistence would appear to conduct themselves as though they were free. This is especially the case in the critical situations of life when the responsibilities of our human actions are more deeply felt.

The idea of human liberty is just as widespread as the idea of being answerable for our behavior. The two notions are correlative, since no one can be held worthy of praise or blame if he is compelled to follow a certain course of action. "Take away freedom from the will of man," says Aquinas, "and you take away the meaning of counsels, exhortations, commands, prohibitions, rewards and punishments." What purpose, for example, could advice serve, if we were unable to amend our judgments and so act in a manner different from what we first intended? Moreover, even after a map of conduct has been decided upon, it is still possible, as experience shows, to work in opposition to the original plan, to change it upon better information, or to abandon it altogether if we are so inclined. It is even possible to degenerate from our good intentions, by refusing to allow for those motives that would improve the course of our actions. Such is the perversity of our human nature that we do not always elect to follow the procedure that is best. Rather, knowing what is better, we often choose what is worse. This, of course, is the problem of moral evil, to which we shall return in a moment.

viii

The Scope of Human Freedom

The fact that there are certain boundaries within which will must exercise its freedom is really no argument against that freedom. What the very nature of will bids us do we cannot but do; so that, if it belongs to nature to desire the perfect good when in its presence, will must necessarily seek such a good. But, the impulsions of will, *as nature*, really have nothing to do with free acts. What is essential to the liberty of man is that he have some management over particular goods, since these alone are the objects of choice. Does this mean that we are entirely free in reference to particular goods? Obviously not, because it sometimes happens that only one particular good is offered as a motive. In such a case, there is no objective freedom since will cannot select between this or that alternative. It can, however, refuse to act at all. The point is that liberty of exercise is sufficient to ensure human freedom, when liberty of specification is absent.

ix

Function of the Last Practical Judgment in Choice

Choice of particular goods, according to the Thomistic teaching, is always consequent upon the last practical judgment of intellect. This means that will fixes on the object which rational insight says is the thing that ought here and now to be chosen. Does intellect, then, compel will to make its decision? Or how do the two powers operate together, without infringing on the rights of freedom? Briefly, the followers of Aquinas reply that intellect moves will by specifying the objects of its choice, while will moves intellect to form its last practical judgment.[e]

The relation that obtains between the two powers is like the relation of a blind man who can walk, to a paralytic who can see. The combination of a good pair of eyes in the one with a good pair of legs in the other makes for a joint action on the part of both which would be otherwise quite impossible. Will needs intellect to show it the desirability of its object, and to furnish it with a motive for choosing as it does. Intellect, on the other hand, needs will in order to formulate the last practical judgment upon which choice is immediately consequent. Intellect, apart from will, can determine what is desirable in the abstract. But choice is essentially concerned with what is desirable in the concrete, that is, with what is here and now good for the individual. Without will, then, intellect could not make its judgment practical, since it could come to no decision relative to the concrete situation in hand. Unlike a speculative proposition, the practical judgment derives its truth, not from formal adequation of intellect with thing, but from the fact that it is orchestrated with a sane and healthy will. Now, the nature of man's will is such that no particular good can compel its choice. The structure of human freedom requires, therefore: first, that intellect should determine will, by showing the desirability of the object of will; second, that will should determine intellect, by applying the judgment of intellect to what it here and now desires.

It may be objected that if intellect must determine the act of will, and if will must determine the judgment of intellect, we are caught in a vicious circle. The difficulty is resolved, however, when we reflect that it is one and the same act of will which determines the practical judgment of intellect and is determined by the selfsame judgment. The fact is that both intellect and will act simultaneously, so that it is not a question of a priority of time in their effects. We have many instances of the principle of simultaneity in other quarters. Thus, matter determines form and makes it something individual; at the same time, form determines matter and makes it something specific.

When, then, the last practical judgment is about to be made, will applies intellect to the task of judging determinately what is to be done, and receives in return the guidance and determination of intellect in deciding that this or that particular course of action is to be settled upon. There is an analogy in the behavior of the motorist who switches on his lights in order to see, and then fixes the direction of his movements by the light which he produces. Thus, the last practical judgment is not purely a phenomenon of intellect, since it contains an admixture of volition. Intellect deliberates about the value of several particular objects. Will puts an end to this deliberation and makes its choice when one of these particular objects sufficiently appeals to it to give it satisfaction. The goodness of the object is here judged in relation to the appetite which it arouses. In all its operations, whether from choice or necessity, man's will follows the lead of his intellect. Nevertheless, the determination of intellect is effective in moving will only because will, of its own initiative, enters into this relation of dependence. In fine: intellect enjoys a primacy of knowledge in which will cannot share; will enjoys a primacy of election in which intellect cannot share. Yet, both powers are required for the *liberum arbitrium* or deliberated reason which is the basis of human liberty—a liberty that is terminated, *cognitively*, by the last practical judgment of intellect; and, *appetitively*, by the free and spontaneous choice of will. [f]

x

The Mystery of Sin

We have said that will, of its nature, desires supreme happiness. When face to face with goodness itself, it is drawn by an ineluctable movement of love. Still, is it not possible to discover some sort of freedom with reference to absolute goodness? In answering the question, we note, once more, the dual liberty which the human will enjoys: first, in respect to the act which it exercises; second, in regard to the object which it specifies. Now, freedom of specification signifies that there is an alternative to the good which we choose. But, absolute goodness excludes an alternative, so that freedom of specification is impossible in its regard. With liberty of exercise, however, the case is somewhat different. As long as he remains on earth, it is within the power of man to will or not will his final end, in the sense that he is not obliged to consider his ultimate destiny. He may even refuse to let his intellect think about the matter. The mystery of sin is the mystery of the human mind's failing to reflect on the goodness of God, and of the human will's falling short in its love of that goodness.

The roots of sin, says Aquinas, are three: ignorance, malice, and passion. Ignorance puts a shroud over the eyes of intelligence; malice twists and distorts its vision; and passion interferes with the clarity of its judgments. Now, where the knowledge of intelligence is defective, the love of will must also be defective. As a result, men frequently set the particular goods of this life above the goodness which is eternal. But liberty such as this is not true liberty; and the best that Aquinas can say for it is that it is the appearance rather than the reality of freedom. Passion, ignorance, and malice are so many obstacles to knowledge, and therefore to the love which is conditioned by such knowledge. Just as physical health is a surer token of life than physical pain and weakness, though both are witnesses to the principle of vitality, so, virtue is a surer token of freedom than vice, though both give evidence of the power of election. Indeed, to be incapable of sin is to be free in the highest degree. As Aquinas tells us, it belongs to the perfection of liberty to be able to select the things that will bring us to our goal; but to its imperfection to be able to choose the things that turn us away from our end. Far better, says Augustine, not to be able to do wrong, than to be able not to do wrong.

xi

A Comparison of Intellect and Will

For the Angelic Doctor, intellect occupies a position of definite superiority over will. "Something is required for the perfection of knowledge that is not required for the perfection of love. For, knowledge belongs to reason, whose task is to distinguish things that are in reality united, and to unite things that are in some manner distinct. . . . Therefore, the perfection of knowledge demands that a person should know distinctly all that is in a thing, such as its powers, properties, perfections, parts, and so forth. Love, on the other hand, springs from appetite which regards a thing as it is in itself. Wherefore, it suffices for the perfection of love that a thing be loved according as it is known in itself." Again, intellect possesses its object as form is possessed by matter, whereas will is directed to its object as to a goal. But form is something within, while a goal is something without. Now, "all things considered, it is better to be in possession of the nobility of another being, than to have a relation to a noble being which remains beyond it." Intellect, then, is a more excellent power than will.

It is also significant of the attitude of Aquinas that he refuses to base his hierarchy of living things on the different kinds of appetition, but establishes it on a cognitive foundation.

"Orexis," he says, "does not constitute any special grade of life." This means that appetite is always in function of something else, to be explained in terms of what is not really itself. Thus, sensitive appetite is in function of sense; and intellectual appetite is in function of intellect. The mind of man is a power of otherness, since it is able to become reality through its grasp of the form of reality. Its acquisitive function, by which it transforms the universe of being into its very self, represents the highest kind of act that man can perform. And so intellect is described, in the theory of Aquinas, as the reason and measure of appetite, wherever found.

With all these concessions to intellect, however, there is a meaning in which will is more closely attached than intellect to the physical reality of being. In cognition, the known is in the knower after the manner of the knower. In volition, the thing is in the lover after the manner of the thing loved. Our knowledge of supreme goodness is imperfect and restricted; yet our love of supreme goodness may be perfect and without bounds. "A thing can be loved more than it is known, since it can be loved completely even though it cannot be known completely." Furthermore, although it is true that love demands knowledge as its basis, it is also true, as Aquinas points out, that love may work reflexly on our knowledge, impelling us to greater study and making us more ambitious for deeper insights into the things that we love. "The lover is said to be in the beloved according to apprehension, inasmuch as the lover is not satisfied with a superficial knowledge of the beloved, but strives to gain more intimate information about the object of his love—if possible, to penetrate into the very soul of the beloved." Thus, it is the nature of love to urge us on to greater knowledge; and it is the nature of knowledge to lead us, in the end, to a fuller love by making us more deeply acquainted with the reasons for love.[g]

xii

Human Freedom and Divine Causality

Human intelligence bears only the faintest resemblance to the intelligence of God. So, too, human liberty is but a dim replica of the freedom of God. The point about the divine will to be noted here is the fact: first, that it is supreme and universal in the order of causality, and nothing can escape its motion; second, that when it moves creatures, it moves them infallibly. Does this mean that the freedom of man is merely a figment in the eyes of the Creator? Of course not! The divine motion can do no violence to our wills. On the contrary, its influence is in deepest conformity with all the stirrings of our rational appetites. Indeed, if we are free at all, it is precisely because we have been created in freedom. Only the movement of the First Cause can reach into the sanctuary of the human will; only a divine agent can rouse its deepest love, carrying it confusedly through all the degrees of good before inclining it to stretch out toward some particular good. No finite being can exist apart from the infinite being of its Creator.

No secondary liberty, such as man enjoys, can be separated from the primary liberty of the Godhead. It can exist only on condition that it be caused and moved by the latter. And why should not God have the power of producing infallibly, in us and with us, the freedom of our acts? Of course, He must move us in accordance with the nature of our wills; so that He cannot generate in us a free act unless it be determined freely on our part. As Aquinas says: "If will were moved by another in such a manner as not to be moved by itself from within, the act of will could not be imputed for reward or blame. But since its being moved by another does not prevent its being moved by itself from within, it does not thereby forfeit the motive for merit or demerit." And again: "We must remember that properly speaking the necessary and contingent aspects of a thing are consequent upon the being of the thing, as such. Hence, the mode both of necessity and of contingency falls under the foresight of God, Who provides universally for all being." Necessary and contingent, as Aquinas explains, are the primary modes into which being is divided. Now, the divine will exists outside the order of created being, as the cause which produces the whole of being; so that, if the will of man displays a contingent manner of being, it is precisely because the Creator has endowed it with this sort of existence.

The whole teaching of the Angelic Doctor on the relation of man's freedom to the infallible action of God is summed up in a well-known passage from his *Summa Theologica:* "Free will is the cause of its own movement, because by his free will man moves himself to act. But, it is not a necessary part of freedom that what is free should be the cause of itself; just as, for one thing to be the cause of another, it is not necessary that it be the first cause. Now, God is the first cause. As such, He is the cause of movement in both natural and voluntary causes. And just as, by moving natural causes, He does not prevent their acts from being natural, so, by moving voluntary causes, He does not deprive their acts of being voluntary. Rather, He is the cause of this very freedom in them. For He operates in each thing according to its proper nature."

READINGS FROM AQUINAS

Summa Theologica, part I, questions 82 and 83.
————   part I–II, questions 8–10; question 13, articles 1, 3, 6.
————   part I–II, question 27, article 2.
————   part I–II, questions 75–78.
Contra Gentiles,   book I, chapter 85.
De Potentia Dei,   question 6, article 1.

CLARIFICATIONS

(a)

Motives of volitional movements

As Aquinas tells us, "will is moved not only by universal good apprehended by reason, but also by good apprehended by sense. Wherefore, we can be moved to some particular good independently of a passion of the sensitive appetite. For, we will and do many things without passion and through choice alone; as is most evident in those cases wherein reason resists passion."

(b)

Natural and deliberate volition

Will is moved in two ways, as Aquinas tells us: "first, as to the exercise of its act; secondly, as to the specification of its act, derived from the object. In regard to the first way, no object moves the will necessarily, for no matter what the object be, it is in man's power not to think of it, and consequently not to will it actually. But, in respect to the second manner of motion, will is moved by one object necessarily, by another not. For in the movement of a power by its object, we must consider under what aspect the object moves the power. . . . Now, good is the object of will. Wherefore, if will be offered an object which is good universally and from every point of view, it tends to such an object of necessity—if it wills anything at all—since it cannot will the opposite. If, on the other hand, will is offered an object that is not good from every point of view, it does not tend to it of necessity. And since any lack of good is really a nongood, therefore that good alone which is perfect and lacking in nothing is such a good that will cannot not will it: and this is Happiness. Particular goods, on the contrary, so far forth as they are lacking in some good, can be regarded as nongoods; and from this point of view, they can be either set aside or approved by will, which can tend to one and the same thing from various standpoints."

Natural volition does not differ *in kind* from deliberate volition, since the latter is merely an application to a particular good of the original movement of will toward good in general. Aquinas says: "Since the species of an act is derived from its object, considered under its formal aspect, it follows of necessity that it is specifically the same act which tends to an aspect of the object and which tends to the object under that aspect. For instance, it is specifically the same visual act whereby we see the light and whereby we see the color under the aspect of the light." Now, it is under the aspect of good in general that the rational appetite moves toward any particular good. This is simply another way of saying that it is specifically the same impulsion of will which tends to good in general and which tends to a particular good under the aspect of good in general.

What is true in the order of nature is also verified in the order of grace. Thus, "the aspect or ratio under which our neighbor [a particular good] should be loved is God [Who is good in general], since what we ought to love in our neighbor is that he may be in God. Hence it is clear that it is specifically the same act whereby we love God and our neighbor."

Aquinas is at great pains, however, to point out that the natural desire which man has for supreme good is not to be confounded with the desire for the Beatific Vision. The first can be achieved by a purely human effort. The second requires a supernatural help. Here are two texts bearing on the matter:

"The end towards which created things are directed by God is twofold: one which exceeds the proportion and power of created nature; and this end is the life eternal which consists in seeing God. . . . The other end, however, is proportionate to created nature, to which end a created being can attain according to the power of its nature."

And more explicitly: "To see God in His essence, wherein the ultimate happiness of the rational creature consists, is beyond the nature of every created intellect. Consequently, no rational creature can have a movement of will directed towards such happiness, except it be moved thereto by a supernatural agent; and this is what we call the help of grace."

So uncertain, subjectively considered, is the object of natural volition that Aquinas is content to describe it as a *bonum in communi* or good in general. "There exists in man an appetite for his final goal in general, that is to say, an impulsion by which he desires to be entirely perfected in goodness. But in what this perfection consists, whether in the practise of virtue, or in knowledge, or in pleasure, is not determined for him by nature."

(c)

Denominations of the will-act

The act of will is designated by Aquinas in several ways. Thus, with reference to the end, there is *volition*, whereby will regards the end absolutely; *fruition*, in which will considers the end as its place of rest and enjoyment; and *intention*, wherein will considers the end as the term toward which something is ordained. Again, with reference to means, there is *use*, whereby will employs different ways in achieving its end; *consent*, in which will approves of several means; and *choice*, wherein will selects one means in preference to another. Should there be only one means, then, as Aquinas points out, "consent and choice do not differ in reality but only in our way of looking at them; so that we call it consent according as we approve of acting in a particular way; and choice according as we prefer this particular way to other means that do not meet with our approval."

(d)

Intellectual appetite a single species of power

"Why," asks Aquinas, "are there two sensitive appetites, namely, concupiscible and irascible, and only one intellectual appetite, namely, will? The answer is: because powers are distinguished according to their formal objects. Thus, the object of an appetitive power is an apprehended good. But, intellect and sense do not apprehend good in the same manner, since intellect apprehends good according to the universal notion of good, while sense apprehends it under some determinate aspect of good. Wherefore, the appetite which follows the apprehension of intellect is a single power. The appetites which follow the apprehensions of sense, on the other hand, are diversified according to the different ways in which sense apprehends good."

(e)

Interaction of will and intellect

"Will moves intellect as to the exercise of its act," Aquinas explains, "since even the true itself, which is the perfection of intellect, is included in the universal good, as a particular good. But, as to the determination of the act, which the act derives from the object, intellect moves will; since the good itself is apprehended under a special aspect, as contained in the universal true. It is therefore evident that the same is not mover and moved in the same respect."

(f)

Liberum arbitrium

As Aquinas explains: "The proper act of free will is choice: for we say that we have a free will because we can take one thing while refusing another; and this is to choose. Therefore, we must consider the nature of free will, by considering the nature of choice. Now, two things concur in choice: one on the part of the cognitive power, the other on the part of the appetitive power. On the part of the cognitive power, counsel is required, by which we judge one thing to be preferred to another; and on the part of the appetitive power, it is required that the appetite should accept the judgment of counsel. Therefore, Aristotle (in the sixth book of his *Nichomachean Ethics*) leaves it in doubt whether choice belongs principally to the appetitive or the cognitive power: since he says that choice is either 'an appetitive intellect or an intellectual appetite.' But, (in the third book of the same work) he inclines to its being an intellectual appetite when he describes choice as 'a desire

proceeding from counsel.' And the reason of this is that the proper
object of choice is the means to the end: and such an object is
in the nature of that good which is called useful. Wherefore,
since good, as such, is the object of appetite, it follows that choice
is principally the act of an appetitive power. And thus free will is
an appetitive power."

Free action, since it is rational, must have a motive. Freedom
consists precisely in the control of motive, since we choose the
motive to which we shall respond. *Liberum arbitrium* or free choice,
then, is really a combination of two elements: the motive of intellect
and the selective act of will. We judge the situation, set the stage
for our performance, and then choose the reasons for acting in the
way that we do. We are masters in our own theater of life, and
nothing within or without can deprive us of the rôle that is rightfully ours to play. Only the vision of supreme good has the power
of moving will irresistibly. With any other kind of good, will
remains essentially indifferent and detached.

What I have pictured here is, of course, the ideal state of affairs.
In practice, we are not always so completely free as not to be
influenced by our egotisms, passions, and prejudices, arising from
physical constitution, upbringing, environment, and so forth.
Weakness of will is often no more than an inability to fix the
intellect on those motives that would move will effectively to
command what should be done.

(g)

Comparison of intellect and will

As Aquinas says: "The superiority of one thing over another
can be considered in two ways: absolutely and relatively. Now, a
thing is considered to be such absolutely which is considered such
in itself: but relatively as it is such with regard to something else.
If, therefore, intellect and will be considered with regard to themselves, then intellect is the higher power. And this is clear if we
compare their respective objects to one another. For, the object
of intellect is more simple and more absolute than the object of

will, since the object of intellect is the very idea of appetible good; and appetible good, the idea of which is in intellect, is the object of will. Now, the more simple and the more abstract a thing is, the nobler and higher it is in itself; and therefore the object of intellect is higher than the object of will. Accordingly, since the proper nature of a power is in its order to its object, it follows that intellect, in itself and absolutely, is higher and nobler than will.

"But, relatively and by comparison with something else, we find that will is sometimes higher than intellect, from the fact that the object of will occurs in something higher than that in which the object of intellect is found. For example, one might say that hearing is relatively nobler than sight, inasmuch as something in which there is sound is nobler than something in which there is color, though color is nobler and simpler than sound. For, . . . the action of intellect consists in this: that the idea of the thing understood is in the one who understands; while the act of will consists in this: that will is inclined to the thing itself as existing in itself. And therefore the Philosopher says (in the sixth book of his *Metaphysics*) that 'good and evil,' which are objects of the will, 'are in things;' but 'truth and error,' which are objects of the intellect, 'are in the mind.' When, then, the thing in which there is good is nobler than the soul itself which apprehends it ideationally, by comparison with such a thing, will is higher than intellect. But, when the thing which is good is less noble than the soul, then in comparison with that thing, intellect is higher than will. Wherefore, the love of God is better than the knowledge of God; but, on the contrary, the knowledge of corporeal things is better than the love thereof. Absolutely, however, intellect is nobler than will."

CHAPTER NINE

THE POWERS OF MAN

i

The Principle of Specification

Aquinas has given us a very simple ground plan for the study of man's powers. In view of all the misunderstandings that have arisen about the nature of our human abilities, this plan is particularly significant. It is, in fact, a very modern and scientific pattern of procedure because it is laid squarely upon an operational basis. Briefly, it amounts to this: that what a man can do is to be inferred from what he actually does; and further, that what he actually does is to be understood in terms of an objective world which sets his powers into motion. According to Aquinas, therefore, any thoroughgoing analysis of the powers of man must necessarily include some study of objective factors, since it is with objects that the acts of man are properly employed. Aristotle proposes the same technique when he says: "If we want to know what the power of thinking is, or what the powers of perception and nutrition are, then we must go farther back and give an account of the acts of thinking, perception, and nutrition. For, in the order of investigation, the question: what does an agent do? precedes the question: what enables it to do what it does? Moreover, if this method is correct, we must on the same grounds go yet another step back and get some clear notion of the objects of each power . . . *e. g.*, of what is edible, what is perceptible, what is intelligible."

Aquinas puts the whole problem of human powers in its proper perspective when he says: "We know the nature of a power from the act to which it is directed. Accordingly, the nature of a power is diversified as the nature of the act is diversified. Now, the nature of an act is diversified by the various natures of the objects. Not any difference, however, diversifies the powers of the soul, but only a difference in that precise thing to which the power is by its nature ordained." In fine: we know the nature of a power from the nature of its acts. We know the nature of its acts from the nature of the object of such acts. But several different acts may be engaged upon the same object. Consequently, it must be by virtue of formal, not material, differences of objects that acts are distinguished. We reach the position, then, that powers are proximately differentiated by acts, but ultimately differentiated by formal objects.

ii

The Connatural Object of Human Powers

The soul of man is wedded to a body. This psychosomatic union is no mere whim of chance, but a basic design of nature. It was intended from the beginning that the human spirit should have matter as its bedfellow. Matter, therefore, is part and parcel of the essence of man. Now, if the soul of man is so basically related to matter that union with it is necessary to his very entity as a man, there should be no surprise in the fact that all the powers of the human soul are similarly related to material things as their proper objects. Aquinas, at any rate, quite logically concluded that such is the case. In the psychology of the Angelic Doctor, every one of our human abilities is somehow exercised with matter. By matter, here, we mean corporeal substance. Now, corporeal substance—from inferior element to superior man—is composed of matter and form; and it is with this kind of substance that our powers are properly concerned. Our vegetative powers assimilate it; our senses register its measurable properties; our intellects strive to understand its nature. It is something connatural to our hylomorphic being. How, then, can it be anything but connatural to the powers of our hylomorphic being?

iii
The Distinction of Human Powers

We have already observed, with Aquinas, that man's soul virtually contains all the forms of corporeal substances which are inferior to it. Man, then, must be endowed with all the powers of plants and animals. Furthermore, he has sufficient understanding of his own nature to know these powers in their various distinctions. Now, there are three fundamental ways in which the powers of man may be distinguished: first, by *orders*, according to the grades of cosmic life which man represents within his own being; second, by *genders*, which are divisions within the orders; and third, by *species*, which are divisions within the genders. On a basis of these variants, it is possible to arrive at a complete enumeration of the powers of man.

iv
The Orders of Human Powers

The first division by orders is, of course, a hierarchical arrangement. It indicates how man, while human in his own rightful way, is also something of an animal and a plant. At the same time, it supplies the groundwork of all other divisions. It is reached by noting the results of man's efforts at various levels of operation. Thus, certain of his acts are concerned, properly, with the transformation of corporeal substance. In their performance, the soul is completely dependent upon bodily structures. They are *vegetative* in character, and accordingly must proceed from vegetative powers. Other acts of man are concerned, properly, with the qualities of corporeal substance. Again, in their performance the soul is entirely dependent upon bodily organs. The corporeal qualities, in this case, impinge upon the bodily organs, and so dispose them to function. Acts of this sort are *sensitive* in character, and accordingly must proceed from sensitive powers. Finally, certain of man's acts are concerned, properly, with the essences of corporeal substance. They do not require the instrumentality of bodily organs. They are rational in character, and accordingly must proceed from *rational* powers.

Of course, these distinctions of acts do not indicate all the differences on which the distinctions of orders are founded; but they are sufficient to produce an essential separation of one level of operation from another. Aquinas sketches out, in clear relief, the whole hierarchical plan of man's powers when he says: "The activity of the human soul can be related to its objects in three ways: first, as a natural operation which proceeds from vegetative powers, and which employs the active and passive qualities of matter . . .; second, as an operation which is not concerned with matter, as such, but with its conditions, and which manifests itself in the sensitive powers whose function is to receive forms or species without matter but with material conditions; third, as an operation which transcends both matter and material conditions."

v

The Genders of Human Powers

The second division of powers by genders is grounded on a generic relationship of the objects of powers to the acts of powers. This relationship may be one of two sorts, according to Aquinas: first, when the object is the principle of the act; second, when the object is the term of the act.

A. IN THE VEGETATIVE ORDER

In the vegetative order, there is no relationship of object as principle, since the object is always the term of the act of vegetation. Now, the term of the vegetative act is threefold: first, the nourishment of the body; second, the development of the body; third, the propagation of the body. Accordingly, there is a gender of vegetative powers.

B. IN THE SENSITIVE ORDER

In the sensitive order, the relationship is twofold: "One, by which the object is in the soul after the manner of the soul and not by its own rightful mode of existence; the other, by which the soul is brought to bear on the object as it exists in itself." The first is the relationship of cognition; the second is the relationship of appetition. This means that there is one gender of sensitive powers which is cognitive in character; and another gender of sensitive powers which is appetitive in character.

The second of these two relationships, by which the soul is brought to bear on the object as it exists in itself, may be regarded as two: first, "inasmuch as the soul is related to the extrinsic object as an end which is first in intention," this being the relationship which is proper to appetition; and second, "inasmuch as the soul is related to the extrinsic object as an end which is the term of operation and movement," this being the relationship which is proper to locomotion. Besides the cognitive and appetitive genders of our animal powers, therefore, we should have at least a species of locomotive power, modally irreducible to the cognitive and appetitive genders, and concerned with the spatial displacements of the body.

C. IN THE RATIONAL ORDER

In the rational order, which is the order of intelligence in man, the double relationship of object as principle and term of act is again present. Accordingly, there are powers of cognition and appetition on this level also. But, whereas the soul is cognitively related to its intelligible object in two ways, namely, as potentially understandable and as actually understandable, it is appetitively related to its intelligible object in only one way, which is simply as desirable. This means that there is one gender of cognitive powers, but no gender of appetitive powers, in the rational order. The appetitive power, therefore, is a single species.

There is an ontological separation of vegetative, sensitive, and rational powers in man, as we observe from the foregoing analysis. Because of this hierarchical arrangement, it is unlawful to group together, under the same gender, powers that belong to different levels of being: for example, a power of sensitive cognition and a power of rational cognition, or a power of sensitive appetition and a power of rational appetition. Consequently, there is no way, really, of constructing a gender for the power of rational appetition. It cannot be resolved into further divisions. It must be classified, then, under the heading of species.[a]

vi

The Species of Human Powers

If the division of powers by genders is based upon a generic or material relationship of object to soul, the division by species is founded upon a specific or formal relationship. Analysis of our human accomplishments reveals that some of our acts are concerned with one and the same object; others deal with different objects. We may turn this statement about and say that the same object may produce several kinds of acts; and several objects may produce only one kind of act. How is this possible? Simply because the same object may have different formal relationships to the soul; while different objects may have the same formal relationship to the soul. A fruit, for example, is colored, odorous, palpable. Or it is present, absent, past. Here are at least six formal relationships which the object bears to the soul. Accordingly, there must be at least six powers in the soul if it is to appreciate these six formalities in one and the same object. Again, all men are rational beings. Rationality, as a proper characteristic of all men, has but one formal relationship to the soul which apprehends it. Accordingly, it is sufficient to postulate a single power in the soul in order to appreciate this same formality in different men. And thus we reach the conclusion of Aquinas that "powers are not diversified according to the material distinction of objects, but by virtue of a formal distinction which is based upon the nature of the object as such." On this basis of formally distinct relationships, therefore, we can enumerate the powers of the human soul.

A. IN THE VEGETATIVE ORDER

In the vegetative order, the single gender is divided into three species, by virtue of the triple relationship of the soul to the body: first, as something to be nourished if it is to be developed; second, as something to be developed if it is to be propagated; third, as something to be propagated if the race is to survive. In the first instance, the relationship is expressed by the act of nutrition; in the second, by the act of growth; in the third, by the act of reproduction. Accordingly, there are three vegetative powers in the soul of man: the *power of nutrition;* the *power of growth;* and the *power of reproduction.* Because they operate only through the instrumentality of material organs, they are properties, not of body alone or soul alone, but of man, the synolon.

In the sensitive order, the cognitive gender is divided into several species. The object of each species is material or sensible, and is brought to bear on the power by virtue of certain corporeal qualities that it possesses. Thus, it is tangible, odorous, sapid, audible, visible. These are five ways it may appeal to the soul. The soul, then, must have at least five kinds of powers that can respond to such appeal. They are: *somesthesis* or body sense, *smell, taste, hearing,* and *vision.* We say, at least five kinds of powers, because somesthesis really covers a wide group of sensations that are distributed throughout the whole body, such as cutaneous, kinesthetic, equilibrial, organic, and so forth.

But, the sensible object exhibits several other characteristics besides those that we have just mentioned. It is related to the soul by certain spatial and temporal features, within whose dimensions, so to speak, its corporeal qualities are presented to the powers of sensation. These dimensional aspects of the object are described as motion, rest, number, measure, and magnitude. They represent, in their sum total, the object's common sensibility, just as tactual quality, odor, flavor, sound, and color represent the object's proper sensibilities. To perceive common sensibles and to apprehend, synthesize, and differentiate proper sensibles, the soul has the power of *common sense.*

Thus far, in our analysis, we have observed the effects upon the soul of formalities that are actually here and now present to it. But experience tells us that the qualities of corporeal substance, once perceived, may be imaged when they are absent, and remembered when they are past. Now, absence and past-ness are further formalities, the recognition of which demands two more powers in the soul: *imagination* and *memory*. Again, certain corporeal qualities of an object are related to the soul because of their biological significance: they are particularly useful or harmful to the organism. To appreciate such qualities, the soul must possess a *power of estimation*. In man, as we have noted elsewhere, the ability to estimate is called *cogitative power*.

The appetitive gender, on the sensitive level, is divided into two species: inasmuch as the soul is related to the corporeal object simply as desirable or repugnant; or as arduously so. Absence or presence of the difficulty factor, therefore, creates a formal distinction of objects to which the soul responds by acts of *concupiscible appetite*, in the first case, and of *irascible appetite*, in the second.

Finally, there is the *locomotive power* which accompanies appetite and executes its impulsions by various sorts of body movements. Theoretically, if the gender of appetition is speciated, we should expect to find a corresponding speciation of the locomotive apparatus. Actually, however, "the power of locomotion is not diversified except by a diversity of motions." The need here, as Aquinas implies, is not for multiple species, but for multiple modes of operation within the same species, since locomotive power is designed to move the animal as a whole. The diversity of motion characteristic of outer behavior is detected, first, in the different ways that animals move about from place to place, since some creep, others walk, others fly, others swim, and so forth; second, in the different ways that the same animal moves the members of its body. Thus, the lingual, manual, and pedal movements of man are diverse modes of his locomotive ability.

The important thing to remember about all the sensitive powers is the fact that they operate only through the instrumentality of organs. Like the vegetative powers, they are psychosomatic in nature. They belong, therefore, not to body alone or soul alone, but to the composite.

C. IN THE RATIONAL ORDER

In the rational order, there is one gender of cognitive powers, concerned with the essences of corporeal substance. As an object of understanding, such a substance presents itself to the soul under two distinct aspects: first, as something potentially understandable; second, as something actually understandable. Accordingly, two separate powers are required in the soul if it is to understand: *agent intellect*, whose object is the potentially understandable, and *possible intellect*, whose object is the actually understandable.

There is no gender of appetitive powers on the rational level. We have, however, a species of rational appetition called *will* whose proper object is, not the intellectually knowable, but the intellectually desirable. All the powers, in the rational order, operate without organs. They are, therefore, powers of the soul alone. But, because the soul is part of man's being, rational powers are properties of man, in the final analysis.[b]

vii
The Thomistic Classification of Human Powers

The accompanying diagram gives us a total picture of man's powers, arranged on a basis of the Thomistic principles of classification.

Several points of capital interest are suggested by the arrangement of Aquinas. In the first place, its basic ordering of powers is simply an application of the principle of immanence—a principle which states that a power is more perfect in proportion as its acts are less restricted by the contingencies of

DIAGRAM 7. THE POWERS OF MAN (AFTER AQUINAS)

Orders	Genders	Species	Acts	Objects
Vegetative	vegetative	nutritive power	nutrition	body to be nourished
		augmentative power	growth	body to be developed
		reproductive power	reproduction	body to be reproduced
Sensitive	cognitive	somesthetic sense	somesthesis	somesthetic qualities of bodies
		olfactory sense	smelling	odors of bodies
		gustatory sense	tasting	savors of bodies
		auditory sense	hearing	sounds of bodies
		visual sense	seeing	colors of bodies
		common sense	perceiving	body qualities actually present
		imaginal power	imagining	body qualities absent
		memorial power	remembering	body qualities past
		estimative or cogitative power	estimating or cogitating	body qualities useful or harmful
	appetitive	concupiscible appetite	love; hatred; desire; disgust; joy; sorrow	body goods and body evils
		irascible appetite	hope; despair; courage; fear; rage	difficult body goods and difficult body evils
		power of locomotion	movements of body	body to be spatially displaced
Rational	cognitive	agent intellect	abstracting	body essences potentially understandable
		possible intellect	understanding	body essences actually understandable
		will	volition	body goods understood as desirable

248

matter. By this criterion, the sensitive powers are more excellent than the vegetative, and the rational powers are more excellent than the sensitive. In nutrition, for example, matter is received without form. In sensation, form is received without matter, yet not without the appendages of matter, since the form is individualized. In intellection, form is received without matter and also without the appendages of matter, since the form is universalized.

In the second place, the object which is placed in opponency to a given power on the chart is, in every instance, the proper object. It is to this object that the power is primarily ordained. Thus, we may speak of being in general as the adequate object of intellect; or of good in general as the adequate object of will; yet, the fact remains that the object to which man's intellect is connaturally related is the being of corporeal substance; just as the object to which his will is connaturally related is the good of corporeal substance.

In the third place, the Thomistic classification shows how profound and far-reaching is the influence of the hylomorphic doctrine of Aristotle. Thus, objects are comparable to acts as form to matter, and acts also are comparable to powers as form to matter. Now, in the order of corporeal being, it is the particular office of form to determine and speciate matter. In the order of powers, therefore, it is the particular office of objects to determine and speciate acts, and of acts to determine and speciate powers; so that we may very correctly say that powers are speciated by acts and objects.

In the fourth place, the classification exemplifies the principle of continuity which is present in all the works of creation. The principle may be stated in broad terms by saying that "higher nature, in its lowest degrees, touches lower nature, in its highest degrees." On the vegetative level, the nutritive power is basic; but the power of reproduction is most perfect, because it has its effect, not in the parent body, but in the body of the offspring. On the sensitive level, somesthesis is basic; but the power of estimation is most perfect, because it functions like a particular reason. On the rational level, agent intellect is basic; but possible intellect is more perfect, because it actually understands. Looking at nature in its total perspective, we might say that the affinities of chemical substance border on nutritive power; the power of estimation borders on agent intellect; and possible intellect borders on angelic intellect.

In the fifth place, appetitive and locomotive powers are not reckoned in this hierarchical ordering because, as we have pointed out elsewhere, they are in function of something else. Within the scale of human powers, immanence of knowledge is the criterion of hierarchy; and knowledge is remotion from matter. Now, on the vegetative level there is no remotion from matter; on the sensitive level, there is partial remotion from matter; on the rational level, there is complete remotion from matter. From this criterion, therefore, we may infer to three orders of powers in man.

viii

The Thomistic Classification and Modern Research

A great deal of research work has been done in our modern laboratories which has an immediate bearing on the problem of human powers. The question arises: How has scientific investigation affected the Thomistic grouping of man's abilities?

A. THE VEGETATIVE POWERS

The vegetative powers have been repeatedly confirmed by biological studies which center, today, around the contrasted functions of metabolism and reproduction. The concept of epigenesis—referring to the special developmental properties of living substance—and the notion of equipotentiality—founded on the fact that an embryonic organism, in the early stages of epigenesis, is potentially several organisms—are both aspects of the augmentative power. To this same power, working in conjunction with the fundamental nutritive ability, we can attribute all the numerous adaptive responses which were described in the chapter on man's vegetative life. No essential changes need be made, therefore, in the Thomistic classification of vegetative powers.

<h3>B. THE SENSITIVE POWERS</h3>

The sensitive powers have received abundant analysis from the psychophysiologists. The five external senses, set down in the chart of Aquinas, have been recognized in all quarters. Modern investigators would appear to agree that proper object cannot be eliminated as a differential factor in the sensitive apprehension of corporeal qualities. Thus, out of a series of stimuli, that particular one is favored which provides appropriate excitation of the sense organ. Introspection shows a continuous shading between the phenomena of the same sensitive power; but it fails to discern any qualitative transition from one modality, such as vision, to another modality, such as hearing.

The four internal senses, formally distinguished in the chart of Aquinas, have not been recognized in all quarters. Some investigators argue, as a probable opinion, that there is only one central sense which is able not only to perceive, but also to imagine, remember, and estimate. Such a view, however, has no experimental basis; and since perceptual, imaginative, memorial, and estimative acts are differently related to the object which arouses them, they would seem to indicate a formal difference of internal senses.

The sensitive appetites in the classification of Aquinas have received substantial confirmation at the hands of the modern research worker, who divides the phenomena of animal orexis into mild and emergency factors. The power of locomotion, also, is readily admitted into the company of man's abilities. In a special manner, the behaviorist has appropriated this phase of human activity for investigation; and, although his technique has been fruitful in results, incautious and unwarranted generalizations from one level of human accomplishment to another have spoiled many of his programs. Certainly, Aquinas would never agree that thinking is nothing more than an exercise of locomotive power.

C. THE RATIONAL POWERS

The rational powers in the Thomistic classification are firmly established by the findings of specialists who have studied the phenomena of intellect and will. Such phenomena, to the scholar who analyzes them in detail, are irreducible contents of mind: which means that they cannot be explained in terms of sensitive products, being in a class by themselves. Accordingly, the powers that produce them must also be placed in a special category.

ix

Factors and Faculties

A. THE FACULTY THEORY

Although scientific research points to the existence of differentiated acts within the realm of human achievement, modern psychologists are not prepared, as a group, to admit the existence of differentiated powers. The faculty theory has been the subject, unquestionably, of more debate and misrepresentation than any other part of the Thomistic psychology. The name itself is sufficient to guarantee its rejection as something medieval, and to prohibit a fair hearing of its claims. The fact is, of course, that the modern disavowal of faculties is a renouncement in name rather than in reality. Thus, any investigator who uses the terms "property," "ability," "capacity," is signifying exactly what the medievalist meant by "faculty." Only, the medievalist very seldom used the word "faculty." He liked the names "power" or "capacity" or "property" better. He was, indeed, quite modern. The whole science of psychometrics, which is one of the best achievements of contemporary psychology, is really founded upon the Aristotelian concept of faculty. It is to the credit of Charles Spearman, father of the factorialists, that the faculty problem now rests on a sound experimental basis.

B. MEANING OF FACTOR

Nothing was wrong with the traditional doctrine, declares Spearman. Where things went amiss was when the modern investigator, undertaking to measure the abilities of man, falsely assumed that one faculty can adequately represent all the rest. The theory of factors is leveled squarely against any unwarranted hypothesis of the sort. To determine scientifically the relationship of our human powers, Spearman constructed his correlation coefficients. These are numbers that become unity when two compared abilities go together perfectly, but drop to zero when the compared abilities are independent. By actual tests, neither of these effects was achieved, although a surprising impression of regularity was revealed in the correlating process.

In the end, it was found that the correct reading of the scores of comparison depended upon two general principles: the first, *G factor*, or general intelligence, which always remains identical in all the powers of the same individual; the second, *S factor*, or special ability, which differs freely from one power to another. In time, other factors were added to the picture of man's powers, all the results of an enormous amount of experimental work. There is, for example, *P factor*, which manifests itself as a broad form of mental inertia, making it difficult for the subject to pass rapidly from one kind of psychological operation to another. Again, in what we may call the characterological dimension, there is an apparently independent principle which has been provisionally labeled *W factor*, or will. Those who possess it in high degree tend, as a rule, to act more on reasoned motive than on impulse. With regard to special abilities, investigators claim to have discovered moderately broad factors in the fields of mathematics, language, music, and mechanics.

C. MEANING OF FACULTY

The point about the broad factor, in all these cases, is its basic correspondence with the Aristotelian concept of faculty, that is, of *a power of performing certain operations which are grouped together in a class because they have some obvious connection with one another*. Visual phenomena, for example, are of many sorts; yet they are fundamentally related as acts of seeing. It is sufficient, then, to classify them under a single power of vision. Again, the operations of reason are highly diversified; yet they are fundamentally related as acts of understanding. It is quite enough, then, to group them under a single power of intellect. And so with the other abilities of man.

Another significant point about modern factorial analysis which accords well with the traditional psychology is the basic unity of man's powers—a unity, however, which does not exclude a relative independence of one ability from another. Thus, Spearman's work shows that no two human faculties are perfectly correlated or perfectly uncorrelated. Aquinas gives us the philosophic reasons for such a phenomenon when he declares, first, that all the powers of man are rooted in his soul as the ultimate principle by which he operates; second, that the powers of man are not only distinct from his soul, but also among themselves. The first proposition indicates the source of unity in man's operations; the second accounts for the fact of operational differences. Thus, if the acts of men are unified, it must be because the powers of man are unified, or, more ultimately, because man himself is a unit. On the other hand, if the acts of man are diversified, it must be because the powers of man are diversified, or, more ultimately, because man himself is a composite of diversified principles.

x

Facts of Psychometric Analysis

The orientation of the entire field of psychometrics towards an explicit recognition of the faculty theory is best seen when we examine some of the more important conclusions that emerge from mental measurements. Briefly, modern testers are agreed on the following points: first, that there are established differences in the way that man operates; second, that each difference represents at least a general tendency to act in a particular way; third, that all such general tendencies are native, and must be developed by actual practice and over a period of time before they reach their perfect stature; fourth, that in their progression towards maturity general tendencies show the results of environmental influences, education, and so forth; fifth, that native tendencies vary from one man to another. Now, a faculty is nothing more than a general tendency to perform a certain class of operations that are put together because of some natural relationship that exists among them, as we have already said. If, then, we substitute "faculty" for "general tendency" in the above inferences, we have five experimentally verified propositions that are in perfect harmony with the Thomistic notion of faculty. It might be well to repeat that Aquinas uses the word "power" rather than "faculty" in his analysis of human abilities. Further, because the powers of man are, in the strict philosophic sense, proper to man, Aquinas also refers to them as "properties." Thus, in the same way that the powers of matter are the natural properties of matter, or the powers of protoplasm are the natural properties of protoplasm, so "the powers of the soul are the natural properties of the soul."

xi

The Problem of Individual Differences

Among the important conclusions from psychometric experiment, just enumerated, the last is probably the one of deepest concern to modern scholars at the present moment. It is the problem of individual differences. As star differs from star, so one man differs from another in native endowment or in the gifts of nature. The memory or intellect of one individual, for example, is superior to the memory or intellect of another individual; and the superiority, in such cases, is a birthright, pure and simple. With this fact Aquinas appears to have been well acquainted; and it led him to conclude, most interestingly, to differences in the souls of men. Such differences, however, do not refer to the substantial nature of the soul, since all men are specifically the same, but only to its properties or powers. How do these accidental differences of nature arise? Through the soul's union with matter. Just as the capacity of a tumbler determines the amount of water that it will hold, so the capacity of matter determines the amount of perfection that its conjoined form will enjoy.

As a result of this fact, human nature is not shared by bodies in the same degree of nobility and freedom of exercise. On the contrary, "in each body, the soul possesses an existence that is determined strictly by the capacities of the body." Wherefore, "the more perfect the structure of the body, the more excellent is the soul infused into it; for, a receptacle always modifies what it receives by the degree of its capacity for receiving . . . and so, from a diversity in bodies, we have a diversity in souls." Thus we see that "intellect is more perfect in one individual than in another, because the body is better disposed." The same conclusion is reached when we analyze our sensitive powers, since these are psychosomatic in character and therefore rooted in the composite. Because intellect requires the services of these lower powers in the generation of its ideas, it follows that "those in whom the powers of imagination, cogitation, and memory are of better disposition, are better disposed to understand."

READINGS FROM AQUINAS

Summa Theologica, part I, question 77; question 78, article 1; question 85, article 7.

CLARIFICATIONS

(a)

The genders of human powers

From the logical point of view, man's cognitive powers may be regarded as a single gender which is speciated into senses and intellects; just as his appetitive powers may be similarly regarded as one gender which is speciated into sensitive appetites and will. But, from the ontological point of view, which is the basis of our classification in the text, the senses and sensitive appetites belong to one order of being, which is sensitive; while the intellects and will belong to another order of being, which is rational.

Further, in our diagram on page 248 we have shown only those genders which are strictly generic, that is, genders which include genuinely specific distinctions. Accordingly, no gender is found for locomotive power or rational appetite, since both these faculties are ultimately specific. One could, of course, find another way of enumerating man's powers by simply pointing out the irreducible modes of human operations, that is, modes which cannot be brought together under one category. Such modes would be enumerated as vegetative, sensitive cognitive, sensitive appetitive, locomotive, rational cognitive, and rational appetitive. Of these modes, four are genuinely generic because they subsume several species, namely, the vegetative, with three species; the sensitive cognitive, with at least five species of external sense and four species of internal sense; the sensitive appetitive, with two species; and the rational cognitive, with two species. The remaining two modes, namely, the locomotive and rational appetitive, are ultimately specific.

(b)

The species of human powers

Aquinas has given us a good summary of the powers of man in his *Treatise on the Soul*, which is one of a large group of essays known collectively as the *Disputed Questions:*

"To the end that an individual may be brought into being, the *reproductive power* is ordained; that it may attain to its proper size, the *augmentative power* is ordained; and that it may be conserved in being, the *nutritive power* is ordained. . . .

"For perfect sensitive knowledge, which is needful to the animal, five things are required:

"First, that the sensoria receive their species from sensible objects; and this pertains to the *proper senses* [of which there are five kinds].

"Second, that the animal make some judgment about the sensible objects which it perceives, and that it distinguish such objects, one from another—an office which is accomplished by the power to which all sensibles are referred, namely, *common sense.*

"Third, that the species of sensible objects which have already been experienced, be conserved. For, the animal must needs know things not only in their presence but also in their absence . . . and so it has another kind of power called *imagination*. . . .

"Fourth, that the animal know certain intentions, such as the harmfulness or usefulness of objects, and the like; which intentions the senses do not apprehend. Man possesses this sort of information as a result of inquiry and comparison; but animals acquire it by natural instinct, as the lamb, for example, naturally flees from the wolf as something obnoxious. To discern such things, therefore, the brute has a *power of natural estimation*, while man has *cogitative power*. . . .

"Fifth, that those things which were first apprehended by the senses and then internally conserved, be brought back again for actual consideration; and to this end the *power of remembrance* is ordained.

"Moreover, the sensitive appetite, which follows the knowledge of sense, is necessarily divided into two powers: since a thing is appetible, either because it is delightful and appropriate to the senses, for which reason there is *concupiscible appetite;* or because there is a kind of usufruct in regard to the things that are delightful to the senses, and even at times in regard to the things that are burdensome to the senses, as when the animal, by fighting and repelling obstacles, exercises a quasi-choice in respect to what is delectable; and to this end, *irascible appetite* is ordained.

"*Motive power*, from the fact of its being designed for movement, is not diversified except in respect to the different modes of local motion. Such movements may be different for different animals, since some creep, others fly, others walk, and others have still different modes of progression; or they may be different for different parts of the same animal, since the separate members of the body have their own special functions to perform.

"The grades of intellectual powers are similarly distinguished between cognitive and appetitive. Thus, the knowledge of intellect requires two powers, namely, *agent intellect* and *possible intellect*. . . . Besides sense and intellect, moreover, it is necessary that there be a *power of intellectual appetency*."

CHAPTER TEN

THE HABITS OF MAN

i

The Rôle of Habit in Human Life

Man is a creature of habit. He is born with a wide assortment of powers that open up limitless visions of future development. But powers, as such, are only the seeds of perfection. In order to grow and mature and bring forth fruit in abundance, they must be properly exercised. This is one of the fundamental laws of nature. Proper exercise for each power, however, is not always an easy task, especially at the beginning. Accordingly, the same provident nature which supplies us with powers to act also sees to it that, with each exercise of power, a special quality is produced which makes for ease and grace and pleasure of future action. This special quality is what we mean by habit. In the order of development, therefore, power gives birth to action, and action gives birth to habit.

Power is something essentially innate, a primitive endowment which is basically the same in all men. Habit, on the other hand, is something acquired. It has the stamp of personal initiative upon it; and, because of this fact, it is stronger in one man than in another. Further, though habit is genetically the offspring of action, it becomes itself a principle of conduct and a medium through which power operates. This is its proper function. For, unless it were a source of action, it would be of small service in the development of man. And how is habit a mainspring of action? By determining power to act. In the order of operation, therefore, it occupies a place midway between power and act.

Here, again, we are able to make use of our hylomorphic concepts to clarify the relationship. For, if habit determines power, then it is comparable to power in the same way that form is comparable to matter. Now, form is the perfection of matter. So, too, habit is the perfection of power. Moreover, form supplies to matter what is wanting to it in the order of existence. So, also, habit supplies to power what is wanting to it in the order of operation. But, no single form exhausts all the potentialities of the matter that it informs. Similarly, no single habit exhausts all the latent possibilities of the power that it perfects. Of course, all this is merely analogical; but it is the sort of analogy that is helpful in grasping the basic relationship between power and habit.

ii

The Function of Reason in Habit

Man is a microcosmos. Within the compass of his nature, the whole hierarchy of corporeal being is somehow represented. Not all his powers, however, are strictly proper to himself. Some are shared with the plants; and these are his vegetative powers. Others are common to himself and the animals; and these are his sensitive powers. Only his rational powers are distinctively his own. Reason, then, is the characteristic property of man. He is, as his taxonomic name declares, *homo sapiens*. Reason stands at the very apex of that vast array of human abilities which we enumerated in our previous chapter. From its position of eminence, it is able to wield its influence, in greater or lesser degree, over all the other powers that belong to human nature. Further, if the powers of man are to be integrated into the whole of human personality, it must be reason that performs the important offices of integration. But, integration implies exercise, development, and

maturation of powers; and powers are expanded and made
perfect by habit. Reason, therefore, must be behind the formation of every habit.

Do we condition our reflexes? Then reason must be the
ultimate conditioner. Do we cultivate our memories by mnemonic devices? Then reason must be the ultimate cultivator.
Do we modify our instincts and bring them into line with the
demands of social civility? Then reason must be the ultimate
modifier. Do we control our passions and sublimate their vast
energies into higher levels of operation? Then reason must be
the ultimate controller and sublimator. Do we exercise special
skill in the use of tongue, foot, hand, or any other organ of the
human body? Then reason must be the ultimate source of
proficiency in such behavioral movements. How is reason the
ultimate cause of all these achievements? By producing in
each power a disposition to act in accord with the patterns of
rational insight. From whatever angle we analyze it, therefore,
habit is the result of reason. It belongs properly only to creatures that have intellectual powers. It is an attribute of person
alone. If we speak, as one sometimes does, of the habits of
animals, or plants, or even inanimate matter, it can only be
because these infrahuman creatures sometimes fall under the
influence of human reason. This is the teaching of Aquinas, as
we shall presently see.

iii

The Notion of Habit

Habit, says Aristotle, is *a quality whereby a thing is disposed
either in itself or in relation to something else.* Etymologically,
it means *that which is had.* The derivation comes about in two
ways, as Aquinas points out: "First, inasmuch as man, or anything else, is said to have something; second, inasmuch as a

particular thing has a relation either to itself or to something else." Habits, broadly speaking, are of two sorts: *entitative*, when they modify the substance of a thing; operational, when they dispose the powers or accidents of a thing. Habits, strictly speaking, are of one sort, namely, *operational*. The so-called entitative habits, such as health or beauty of body, are really nothing more than the passible dispositions of a substance. We are interested here only in operational habits, since these are the qualities by which our acts and powers are made perfect.

iv

The Acquisition of Habit

The first thing that we note about an operational habit is its character of permanency. Because of its firm entrenchment in the power, it is not easily lost. This is quite as it should be, since, in most cases, habit is acquired only with laborious effort and frequent repetition. It requires solid effort. Only on condition that we are willing to expend such effort can it be established. In its formation it is like the starting of a pathway through a virgin forest. With each successive step, the track is beaten down, made deeper, smoother, surer. At first, the surface is scarcely scratched. Only by the constant passing of human feet is the earth impressed and modified. So, too, with the powers of the soul. Like the soil of the forest, they are plastic and impressionable. They can preserve the traces of past operations and profit by them in the future. They are able to achieve a lasting history because of their ability to fixate what has gone before. Such is their constitution that, with each specific performance, they gain something from the residue of previous performances.

The habits that enrich our powers, therefore, do not come into being in an instant. Neither do they vanish in an instant.

True, the habit of first principles appears at once, with no preliminary exercise. But the habit of first principles is more akin to nature than to habit, since to deny a first principle is to deny the very meaning of intelligence. With all our other operational habits, the rule is repeated action. As Aristotle puts it: "One becomes a mason only by laying bricks, and a sculptor only by handling a chisel." So, a power becomes informed with habit only by recurrent exercise with its proper object. There are such things as individual differences, however, in the number of performances required for the production of habit. One man has a stronger tendency toward certain acts than another. Like differences in the personal equation of powers, to which we referred in our previous chapter, differences in the personal equation of habits can be, and often are, the result of the human form's conjunction with matter. As Aquinas points out, some of our habits of intellect and will may exist in outline from the very beginning of life. One man's reason is more excellently inclined toward habit than another's, because the administrations of sense are more excellent. Or, again, one man's will is more readily disposed to virtue than another's, because the impulsions of concupiscent and irascible appetite are not so vehement. In both cases, it is quite obvious that the more perfect power would require fewer repetitions of act in order to acquire the habits appropriate to its nature.

v

The Characteristics of Fixed Habit

Once habit has been made part of man's permanent equipment, it displays other definite characteristics which Aquinas has summarized under three headings:

First, every established habit manifests a typical *uniformity* in the way that it functions and in the acts that it produces.

So smooth and regular are its operations, in fact, as to suggest the automatism of a machine. This trait appears all the more striking when we contrast the initial stumbling performances of a habit in formation with the stabilized products of a habit that is fixed.

Second, every established habit exhibits a *propensity* to act at the slightest provocation. As soon as an object is presented, it at once, and without effort, and often without consciousness of what is involved, begins to operate. So emphatic is this habitual impulse that it may require a special act of will to prevent our doing what we are accustomed to doing. For this reason habit has rightly been called *second nature*. Like nature at work, it is full of grace and ease and masterful action. There is artistry in the craftsman's skillful labor, in the painter's manipulation of colors, in the sculptor's handling of chisel and hammer, in the singer's exercise of vocal cords, in the thinker's clean-cut incision through the body of error to the soul of truth, in the saint's splendid mortification of sense and appetite. The task of habit, accordingly, is analogous to the task of the perfect servant: to make the work of the power wherein it dwells more lightsome and unobtrusive, more readily undertaken, more effectively accomplished.

Third, every mature habit is a *pleasure* to its possessor since its operations are so assured and well rounded and satisfying to the power thus accustomed to act. Without such pleasure as a reward for our efforts, the work of forming habits would be grievous and burdensome.

vi

The Proper Subject of Habit

As Aquinas points out, not all our powers are in need of habit, since some of them are disposed by their nature to operate well and successfully. Being determined to a single course of action or a single kind of stimulus, they are not in potentiality to many things. The eye, for example, sees light, and nothing else. Its action is confined to the visual field, and the mode of its operation is fixed beforehand. This sort of determination is found in all our psychosomatic powers, where activity is impossible except through a material organ. Obviously, then, it is in the intellectual dimension that habit is properly lodged. For, here our powers are not determined to one. Light and sound, odor and tangibility, accident and substance are all so many objects of human understanding, just as any conceivable kind of good may attract the human will. And so, because our rational powers can act in indefinite ways, they have need of habit in order to act well in definite ways. Sense, for example, is directed to concrete and singular entities. Intellect, on the other hand, is directed to abstract and universal entities. Similarly, sensitive appetite is ordained to particular goods. Will, on the other hand, is ordained to good in general. While sense and sensitive appetite, therefore, do not require habits for their perfection, intellect and will can reach the operational excellence that is possible to them only through the acquisition of habits.[a]

vii

The Extensiveness of Habit

Only a power that exhibits a potentiality to many objects, then, is properly the subject of habit. Does this mean that habits cannot be imposed on our lower powers? By no means, since many of these powers are subject to rational control. The possibilities of habit formation on the psychosomatic level are constrained only by the limits of mind's influence over matter. This influence is rather narrow in the case of our vegetative powers, though conditioning of reflexes has been achieved within certain areas. It broadens out considerably when we reach the level of our animal activities. The senses, both external and internal, are determinate by nature; yet, to the extent that their operations fall under the command of reason, they can be exercised upon different objects, in different ways, and with different results. The greater latitude of power, in all these cases, is explained by the proximity of sense to intellect.

From this point of view, imagination, memory, and cogitative power occupy positions of definite advantage. Accordingly, as Aquinas points out, these powers may be clearly improved by the cultivation of habit. The same fact applies to our sensitive appetites and powers of locomotion, all of which can be perfected by habit to the extent that they are subject to reason and will. Animals, too, as we remarked before, may be trained by man for special performances. Left to themselves they acquire no such skills, since instinct is sufficient to care for all their needs. It is only the creative vision of intelligence that can set up new goals for irrational creatures, and train the inferior powers of nature to serve the purposes of human life.[b]

viii

Recapitulation

To sum up, then: habit is a developed power. It is a mean between the ability to operate and actual operation. Accordingly, it has something of the character of both power and act. With respect to power, habit is as act. With respect to act, habit is as power. It is both a result of operation and a cause of operation. Habit is formed by acts of a specific nature, proceeding from a specific power. The power, thus informed by habit, is better enabled to perform further acts of the same specific nature. What we are able to do only with difficulty at first because our capacities are naked and undetermined by habit, we now can accomplish with grace and ease and celerity because our capacities have been perfected by the principle of habit. Habitual acts are pleasant because they are produced so readily by our powers. They have the sureness of touch that comes from constant practice and long familiarity with the objects upon which they are exercised. Acts of this sort approach the artistry of the acts of nature, and habit, which is the source of such acts, is rightly regarded as a second nature.

In the traditional teaching of Aquinas, the notion of habit is restricted to those permanent dispositive qualities of which rational powers are the immediate subject, or in whose formation the rational powers are immediately involved. Habit, as such, is distinguished from disposition. Both are species of quality; but, whereas the former is not easily changed, since it has a cause that is relatively unchangeable, the latter is quite easily altered. Just as one and the same body may be the subject of several dispositions, so one and the same power may be the subject of several habits.[c]

ix

Increase and Decrease of Habit

A. BY ITS OWN ACTS

A habit may be strengthened or weakened in two ways: either by its own acts, or by the acts of other habits. It is strengthened by its own acts in proportion as it is exercised more vigorously, and weakened in proportion as it fails in this regular and constant exercise. Increase and decrease of habit, therefore, are measured in terms of intensity of operation. "If the intensity of the act is . . . greater than the intensity of the habit, it will reinforce the habit . . . and in this manner, repeated acts cause an augmentation of the habit. If, on the other hand, the intensity of the act falls below the intensity of the habit, it tends to weaken rather than to strengthen the habit." To pit one's tennis skill against a superior player is to improve one's game; to exercise one's intellect on cheap fiction is to spoil one's taste for good reading. In the matter of habit, as in the matter of perfection, if we are not progressing, we are deteriorating. The only exception that Aquinas would allow for this rule is in the case of the habits of first principles, which are in no wise corruptible. Thus, in the speculative dimension, it would require an uprooting of human nature itself to deprive a man of the knowledge that being cannot be identified with nonbeing; just as, in the practical dimension, the same destruction of human nature would be necessary to eliminate the knowledge that right cannot be identified with wrong. Here, forgetting or self-deception is simply impossible.

B. BY ACTS OF OTHER HABITS

Further, habit may be strengthened or weakened by the acts of other habits. Thus, in the speculative order, a well-practiced memory is a definite asset to the habit of science. An ill-practiced memory, on the other hand, is a liability to the same habit of science. Again, in the practical order, the exercise of one virtue, such as prudence, tends to fortify the habit of another virtue, such as temperance. The vice of pusillanimity or moral cowardice, on the other hand, weakens or obliterates the habits of prudence and temperance. As Aquinas acutely observes, the seeds of opponent habits are sown in man's very nature by the opponency of reason to passion. Thus, "the habit of moral virtue makes a man ready to choose the happy mean in his acts and passions; so that, when one fails to employ such a habit in moderating his behavior, many of these acts and passions fall short of the happy mean, either because of the strong impulses of the animal appetites or because of some other external agency." In the last analysis, of course, it is always with reference to the act which is proper to the habit that we judge the status of the habit. Whatever contributes to the intensity of the act, whether it be intrinsic or extrinsic to the habit, tends to increase the habit. Similarly, whatever contributes to the remissness of the act, whether it be intrinsic or extrinsic to the habit, is likely to decrease the habit. Cessation from act would mean, in time, a complete extirpation of habit.

x

The Psychological Value of Habit

The habits of man are related to his nature in the same manner that accidents are related to substance. The kinship between habit and nature, therefore, is more basic than the kinship between habit and power. Just as the qualities of a material thing are ultimately rooted in its substance through the mediation of quantity, so, analogously, the habits of man are ultimately rooted in his nature through the mediation of his powers. The point is critical in judging of the suitableness or unsuitableness of habits. For, manifestly, some habits are good; others are bad. We are not speaking of their ethical value, as such; but simply of their agreement or disagreement with the total nature of man. It is chiefly with reference to his end that man's habits, like his acts, take on the aspect of morality. Here, we are referring to what may be called the psychological value of habits; and every habit has such a value, since it is definitely an asset or a liability to man as a whole.

This means that habit modifies not only the power which is the immediate subject of the habit, but also man who is the ultimate subject of the power. It further means that the dispositive quality which is produced by habit in a power is naturally good or naturally bad in exact proportion as it is good or bad for the total psychological organism which is man. Habit, in short, is not a matter of indifference. Rather, it definitely conveniences a man to have it; or it definitely inconveniences him. Having it, he is placed in a position of advantage or disadvantage, with regard to the perfection of his total nature. As Aristotle says: "Habit is a disposition whereby that which is disposed is disposed well or ill."

xi
The Ethical Value of Habit

A habit that is in conformity with the nature of man is obviously in conformity with right reason; and a habit that accords with right reason also accords with the ultimate end of man. To act in harmony with right reason, therefore, is to act in a manner that will bring us, finally, to supreme happiness. But, to act contrary to right reason is to act in a manner that will deprive us, eventually, of supreme happiness. Good habits, in relation to man's ultimate destiny, are called virtues. Bad habits, in relation to man's ultimate destiny, are called vices. A vice is nothing more than the negation of a virtue, or the deprivation of a good that man ought to possess. Aristotle has given us the classic definition of moral virtue when he describes it as "a quality which makes its possessor good and his work good." ❡

As we have already pointed out, the proper subject of an operational habit is a rational power, since only a rational power is undetermined to one. No particular truth limits man's intellect; and no particular good compels man's will. If we are searching, then, for the mainsprings of virtuous action, we must look first to intellect and will; for it is within the rational part of man's being that virtue primarily abides. But the lower powers, also, may develop habits, in the degree that they are subject to reason and will. This possibility is of prime importance in regard to the sensitive appetites, since the passions of man are fertile sources of action; and passions must be made conformable to reason if human nature is to reach its goal.

xii

The Intellectual Virtues

The intellectual virtues are habits of intellect. The moral virtues are habits of appetites. The first are concerned with knowledge, and perfect man only in part. The second are concerned with conduct, and perfect man as a whole. Aquinas, following Aristotle, enumerates five intellectual virtues: understanding, science, and wisdom, which are habits of speculative intellect; art and prudence, which are habits of practical intellect. In the first three intellectual habits, it is a question of knowledge for its own sake; in the second two intellectual habits, it is a question of knowledge for the sake of practice. Briefly: *understanding* is the habit of first principles. *Science* is the habit of proximate causes. *Wisdom* is the habit of ultimate causes. *Art* is right knowledge about things to be made. *Prudence* is right knowledge about things to be done.

The basis of all these habits is understanding. Without a knowledge of first principles no further development of intellect would be possible. Similarly, the basis of all the moral habits is prudence. Without a knowledge of how things should be done no further development of will or sensitive appetite would be possible. Because right moral action is simply out of the question without prudence, it is proper to say that prudence is a complete virtue. It makes the whole man good. It is the only one of the intellectual virtues, therefore, that perfects the entire man. In this respect it is an exception to the rule, since all the other intellectual virtues are incomplete, perfecting man only in part. The reason for this exception is easy to discover, since prudence is really a mixed virtue, having a formal aspect which is intellectual and a material aspect which is moral. It deals with human acts; and the acts of man are human precisely to the extent that they are elicited or commanded by his rational appetite.*

xiii

The Moral Virtues

Aquinas reduces all the moral virtues of man to justice, temperance, and fortitude. Theoretic knowledge is good, after its kind; but only moral rectitude is wholly good. A good scientist may be a bad church-goer. A good artist may be a moral leper. But a prudent man, or a just man, is entirely good. Life is lived successfully, and human nature is integrated perfectly, only by the moral virtues. The important thing is to lead a good life. No man is punishable if he is so ignorant as to be a poor scientist or a poor philosopher. But every man is punishable if he is so imprudent as to be an extortioner, so intemperate as to be a drunkard, or so cowardly as to be a deserter. We have already defined prudence as a habit of doing things according to right reason. With prudence as a foundation, man can develop his moral nature: first, by *justice*, which rectifies the impulsions of his will; second, by *temperance*, which moderates the passions of his concupiscible appetite; and third, by *fortitude*, which regulates the passions of his irascible appetite. Because of their position of pre-eminence in the development of moral behavior, the habits of prudence, justice, temperance, and fortitude are commonly referred to as *cardinal virtues*.

DIAGRAM 8. THE VIRTUES OF MAN

Gender	Power	Species	Object
Intellectual	speculative intellect	understanding	first principles
		science	proximate causes
		wisdom	ultimate causes
	practical intellect	art	things to be made
		prudence	things to be done
Moral	will	justice	human acts to be rectified
	concupiscible appetite	temperance	mild passions to be moderated
	irascible appetite	fortitude	emergency passions to be moderated

xiv

Habit in Modern Psychology

Any psychology of habit which is founded on the principles of sensism is irreconcilable with the basic analysis of Aquinas. Thus, if the acts of man are confined within the limits of vegetative or sensitive powers, the habits of man must be restricted by the same boundaries. For the behaviorist, reflex is the sole principle of human behavior. Habit, therefore, is nothing more than a concatenation of reflexes, a system that functions in serial order when the organism is confronted with certain stimuli. For the response psychologist, habit is simply a stamping in of physical associations, resultant upon the constant impinging of stimuli on the organism and the completion of sensorimotor arcs. For the Freudian, habit is part of the larger concept of instinct, and, like instinct, is determinate and compulsory in character.

Aquinas, of course, would agree with none of these interpretations. For him, habit is essentially a product of reason. It is the property of man alone. It resides in his intellect and will, as in its rightful dwelling place; and in his inferior powers, by virtue of their subjection to intellect and will. It is necessary only for man, since nature has provided, from the beginning, the determinate pathways along which the powers of the plant and animal kingdoms shall operate. In the final analysis, therefore, the necessity of habit is a necessity of man's immaterial soul. Because his soul is immaterial, his intellect and will cannot be determined by particular objects in the way that the powers of plants and animals are determined by particular objects. Now, the function of habit is to compensate for this lack of determination. Accordingly, man alone needs habits.

xv

A Guide for Habit-Building

Are there any practical rules that will help us in forming our habits? The question is difficult to answer, since the matter of molding habits is so intimately bound up with the problem of personal equation. Psychologists are agreed, however, on certain general requirements. In the first place, we must launch into our task with strong initiative and resolution. This means that we shall deliberately place ourselves in circumstances that are favorable to the growth of the embryonic habit. Once we have gathered momentum in our efforts, the danger of a breakdown becomes remote. Second, we must allow no exception in the constant exercise of the habit, until we are assured that it has struck deep roots within the power that it informs. Training must be continuous if the work of cultivating a habit is to progress in a satisfactory manner, and if the habit is really to become a second nature by the ease and alacrity of its performances. Third, every occasion must be taken to practice the habit. To repeat the advice of Aristotle: "One becomes a sculptor only by handling a chisel. Even so, one becomes possessed of virtue only by the exercise of virtuous acts."

READINGS FROM AQUINAS

Summa Theologica, parts I–II, questions 49–61; questions 71–75.

CLARIFICATIONS

(a)

The proper subject of habit

To be the proper subject of habit, in the teaching of Aquinas, a power must be: first, passive, since it has to have a potentiality for the reception of new qualities; second, intellectual, since it must be indetermined to one way of action or determinable to several ways of action. According to these criteria, therefore, it is impossible for agent intellect to acquire habits, since it is by its very nature always in act.

(b)

The habits of animals

Aquinas says: "The sensitive powers of the brutes do not act at the command of reason . . . and so in them there are no habits ordained to operation. . . . But because dumb beasts are trained by man's intelligence to do certain things in this way or that, one can admit that they have habits after a fashion. Thus Augustine says: 'We find the most untamed beasts deterred by fear of pain from that wherein they took the keenest pleasure; and when this has become a custom in them, we say that they are tame and gentle.' But the habit is incomplete in respect to will since they have no power either of using or of refraining from use, which seems to belong properly to the notion of habit."

(c)

Multiplicity of habits

Aquinas says: "Habits are dispositions of a thing that is in potentiality to something: either to nature; or to operation, which is the end of nature. As to those habits which are dispositions to nature, it is clear that several can be in one and the same subject: since in one subject we can distinguish several parts, according to the various dispositions of which parts there are various habits. Thus, if we take the internal secretions as being parts of the human body according to their disposition in respect of human nature, we have the habit or disposition of health: while, if we take other parts, such as nerves, bones, and muscles, the disposition of these in respect of nature is strength or weakness; whereas, if we take the limbs, that is, the hands, feet, and so on, the disposition of these, in proportion to nature, is beauty. And thus there are several habits or dispositions in the same subject.

"If, moreover, we speak of those habits that are dispositions to operation and belong properly to the powers, again there may be several habits in one power. The reason for this is that the subject of a habit is a passive power. . . . Now, a passive power is compared to acts of a specific kind as matter is compared to form: because, just as matter is determined to one form by one agent, so, too, a passive power is determined by the nature of one active object to an act specifically one. Wherefore, just as several objects can move one passive power, so one passive power can be the subject of several acts or perfections specifically diverse. Now, habits are qualities or forms inhering in a power, and inclining that power to acts of a determinate species. Consequently, several habits, like several specifically different acts, can belong to one power."

(d)

The meaning of virtue

A power is naturally disposed to act. Therefore, it is naturally disposed to acquire habit which comes from repeated action. Moreover, a power is naturally disposed to acquire virtuous habits, that is, habits which are in conformity with the nature and end of *vir* or man, as Cicero tells us. Aquinas defines virtue as an operational habit which is essentially good. Thus, virtue is distinguished from vice, which is an operational habit that is essentially bad. Good, here, means conformable to right reason; and bad means discordant with right reason. The intellectual virtues, as we have pointed out in the text, are good only in a restricted sense. They confer a power of well-doing, but not, necessarily, of well-using; for example, a good logician. The moral virtues, on the other hand, are good in every sense. They confer a power, not only of well-doing, but also of well-using; for example, a good judge. A man may act illogically, even though he is a good logician. But a man cannot hand down unjust decisions and still remain a good judge.

Interestingly enough, the thesis that good acts produce good habits was first promulgated, not by Plato, but by Aristotle, as Professor Jowett points out in the introduction to his translation of the *Republic*. This thesis, as Jowett further remarks, "is, perhaps, the greatest single principle in education." Socrates, as we remember, identified all virtue with wisdom. Plato defined it as the order, harmony, and health of the soul. But it was Aristotle who introduced us to the idea that moral virtue is the result of exercise—a fact that is also true in the case of art. "For, the things we have to learn before we can do them, we learn by doing them. Men, for example, become builders by building, and lyre-players by playing the lyre. So, too, we become just by doing just acts, temperate by doing temperate acts, and brave by doing brave acts." From the exercise of moral habits "states of character" arise, corresponding to our moral activities. Therefore, concludes the Stagirite, "it is not simply a matter of indifference whether we form habits of this or that virtue from our youth. On the contrary, it is a matter of great difference. In fact, it makes all the difference in the world."

(e)

Prudence and the moral virtues

"Other intellectual virtues can exist without moral virtue," as Aquinas points out, "but not prudence. The reason for this is that prudence is right knowledge about things to be done (and this, not merely in general, but also in particular); concerning which things actions are placed. Now, right knowledge demands principles from which reason proceeds to argue. And when reason argues about particular cases, it needs not only universal but also particular principles. As to universal principles of action, man is rightly disposed by the natural understanding of principles, whereby he understands that he should do no evil; or again by some practical science. But this is not enough in order that man may reason aright about particular cases. For, it happens sometimes that the aforesaid universal principle, known by means of understanding or science, is destroyed in a particular case by passion. Thus, to one who is swayed by concupiscence, when he is overcome thereby, the object of his desire seems good, although it is opposed to the universal judgment of his reason. Consequently, as by the habit of natural understanding or of science, man is made to be rightly disposed in regard to the universal principles of action; so, in order that he be rightly disposed with respect to the particular principles of action, namely, their ends, he needs to be perfected by certain habits, whereby it becomes connatural to him, as it were, to judge aright as to the end. This is done by moral virtue: for, the virtuous man judges correctly about the end of virtue. 'As a man is,' says Aristotle (in the third book of his *Nichomachean Ethics*) 'so does his end appear to him.' Consequently, right reason about things to be done, which is prudence, demands that a man have moral virtue."

CHAPTER ELEVEN

MAN: THE PERSON

i

The Peak of Cosmic Perfection

Man is a person. When we have said this much about him, we have paid him the highest possible tribute that can be given to a cosmic creature. He is, so to speak, the top rung on the ladder of corporeal substances. He is the most perfect being composed of matter and form. The reason he is most perfect, of course, is that his form is most perfect. His soul is a rational thing. It is gifted with the properties of intellect and will. If man is a person, therefore, it must be because he possesses powers of insight and volition. No other corporeal substance is a person. It is common to refer to a person as a self, or an ego. There is, really, no basic difference between any of these terms. All of them designate the same thing, in the last analysis: what a man is. They do not signify what a man does. What a man does is something accidental. What a man is, on the other hand, is something substantial.

Accidents require a proper subject. So, the acts of man must have a proper subject. Now, the person of man is the substance of man. Person, then, is the subject or carrier of all man's acts. It is not allowable, therefore, to say that man *has* a person. He *is* a person, just as he *is* a substance. Because he is a person, man enjoys the highest mode of existence that is possible to a corporeal being. Everything that is good and excellent in the visible cosmos points to the person of man as the crown of corporeal perfection, since everything is integrated in his person. He exists, with the elements. He lives and vegetates, with

280

the plants. He senses, feels, and moves, with the animals. But above all, he thinks and wills; and his thoughts and volitions are proper to himself. As a being that can think and will, he is a person, the only person in the material universe. To be a person, therefore, is to stand at the head of visible creation. Such is the exalted position of man. And because he enfolds within the bosom of his person the seeds of a world-perfection, there is cosmic joy in the full realization of his person, and cosmic grief and agony in its frustration.

ii

Etymology of Person

The etymology of the word "person" is a very interesting one. It seems, in its history, to have rolled along with wonderful bounds, striking right and left, and always leaving behind a cloud of controversy. Because of its tremendous significance and implications, it has always occupied a prominent place in both philosophic and religious discussion. Some scholars derive it from the Greek *prosopon*, which means a *mask*. Others find its origin in the phrase *peri soma*, which means *around the body*. The majority of authorities, however, trace it to the Latin *personare*, meaning *to sound through*. The reference, again, is to the mask, which was so constructed, with a large concave opening at the mouth, that the voice of the actor might be thrown toward his audience with more force and volume. The *persona* of the Roman stage, therefore, corresponds to the *prosopon* of the Greek stage. In time, it came to mean the external appearance of an individual, or the part one plays in life, or the assemblage of qualities that fit a man for his work in life, or the dignities or distinctions that he achieves.

It remained for Boethius, a writer of the sixth century, to fix the philosophic meaning of the term. Aquinas and most of the schoolmen of the Middle Ages adopted the explication of Boethius. The point to be noted, of course, is the fact that, whatever its philological history, the word "person" has come today to have a definite and unchanging significance for all philosophers who work in the tradition of Aristotle and Aquinas.

iii

The Definition of Boethius

Person, according to Boethius, is an *individual substance of a rational nature*. Let us examine the various parts of this definition.

A. SUBSTANCE

In the first place, person is a substance. In a general way, substance means something that requires no support. In this way, it is distinguished from accident. As something which underlies accident, substance is referred to as an hypostasis. This term is a direct Latin and English transcription of the Greek word *hypostasis* which means a *support*. Moreover, if substance is a support for accident, it is obviously a subject of accident. From this point of view, it is referred to as a *supposit*. There is no essential difference between the etymological meaning of these two words, since both connote a foundation of some sort—something that is placed under something else. Now, substance is placed under accident as its support and subject. Substance, therefore, is an hypostasis or a supposit. Further, as something that needs no support on which to lean and no subject in which to inhere, substance is also known as subsistence. It exists in itself and not in another. The Latin *subsistere* means *to stand firm against*. Thus, substance stands firm against invasion by another substance. It tends to preserve its own integrity. It is so sufficient unto itself that it does not require the aid of anything else, naturally speaking, in order to exist. When we say that person is a substance, we imply all these things: that it is a hypostasis, or support; that it is a supposit, or subject; that it is a subsistence, since it exists by itself and does not need anything else in which to inhere.

B. INDIVIDUAL SUBSTANCE

Moreover, person is an individual substance. It is undivided in itself and divided from everything else. It is a unit, or what Aquinas calls an *individuum*. As an individual substance, person is a first substance. First substance, we remember, is logically divided against second substance. The division, as the Angelic Doctor tells us, is not one of gender into species, since second substance covers nothing that is not covered by first substance; but a division of a gender according to different modes of being or existence. Thus, "second substance denotes the generic nature in itself, absolutely; while first substance signifies that nature as individually subsistent." Accordingly, person falls under the gender of substance, not as a species, but as defining a specific mode of existence: namely, a substance which neither inheres in any subject nor is affirmed of any subject. By this specific mode of existence, person is distinguished from second substance, which does not inhere in a subject but is predicated of a subject.

Peter, for example, is a first substance. He does not inhere in a subject, because he is, himself, a subject. He is not affirmed of a subject, because he is not Paul, or James, or anyone else, but Peter. A second substance, on the other hand, does not exist in a subject, yet is affirmed of several subjects. Man, for example, is a case in point. There is no such thing as man, in general, actually existent in a subject; nevertheless, man or rational animal is predicated of any number of subjects. From the logical point of view, therefore, which is the point of view of predicability, substance is divided between individually subsistent being, which corresponds to what exists in reality; and universally subsistent being, which corresponds to what exists only in the mind by way of an abstraction.

Now, to repeat, person is a first substance. It is, as Aquinas puts it, a singular in the gender of substance; just as second substance is a universal in the gender of substance. Further, when we say person is a singular in the gender of substance, we mean that its singularity or oneness is real and is not due to any grouping together by the mind into a unit. It is truly an *individuum*, a thing undivided in itself and separate from all other things. Moreover, as an individual substance, person is not a part of any substance. Obviously, Peter is not part of himself. Neither is the hand or foot of Peter the whole Peter, though each is an integral part of him. Similarly, the soul of Peter or the body of Peter is not the whole Peter, though each is an essential part of him. In brief, Peter, as an individual substance, is a complete substance. The soul of man, to be sure, can exist apart from his body, as we shall demonstrate in the next chapter; yet, the soul of man is not a complete substance, since it requires to be united with matter before it can constitute a human being. Only the synolon is a species. Only the synolon, then, is a complete substance or a person. Even after its departure from the body, the soul of man retains its natural inclination to be united once more with matter. Now, person has no such capacity. It is something incommunicable. Peter cannot be transformed into Paul. The actions of Peter cannot be the actions of Paul. The substance of Peter cannot be the substance of Paul. The substance of Peter cannot be conjoined to the substance of Paul. In short, the very concept of person, as Aquinas tells us, excludes the idea of its being communicated to something else or of its being assumed by something else.

C. RATIONAL NATURE

Further, person is an individual substance of a rational nature. There is a fundamental difference to be noted between person or individual substance, on the one hand, and essence or nature, on the other. Thus, an *individual substance* is something that is individually subsistent. It subsists in such wise that it neither inheres in a subject nor is predicable of a subject. It is substance in its most proper meaning, since, from the individually subsistent thing, for example, Peter, we derive our notion of second substance, for example, man or humanity. *Essence*, on the other hand, connotes the intrinsic constitutive principles of a thing, as expressed in its definition. Man, for instance, is said to be, essentially, a creature composed of body and soul. But, man, as a person or individual substance, is composed of this body and this soul, since he is something individually subsistent. Therefore, concludes the Angelic Doctor, "person adds the individual principles to the notion of essence." Hence, in creatures composed of matter and form, such as man, individual substance cannot be identified with essence. Finally, *nature* signifies any intrinsic principle of movement. In hylomorphic beings, it may refer either to matter or to form. Now, the end of nature is to generate the essence of the species; so that, when man is produced, he must possess a body and a rational soul if he is to have the nature of man. But, the nature of the species,—which, as signifying matter and form, is the same as the essence of the species—does not, *qua* nature, contain the idea of accidents and individual principles. Hence, in things composed of matter and form, "the nature and the supposit really differ; not indeed as if they were wholly separate, but because the supposit includes the nature, and, in addition, certain other things outside the notion of the species," namely, the individual principles and the accidents of the thing which is a supposit.

To sum up: when we think of man as a person, we think of him as an individually subsistent being, existing by himself, demanding no subject in which to inhere, and supplying a foundation for all the accidents that he possesses as well as an ultimate basis for all the actions that he performs. When we think of him as having an essence, we think of him as made up of body and soul, or, more properly, of matter and a rational form; for, of these two constitutive principles is his essence compounded. When we think of the nature of man, we think of his essence as endowed with powers of operation, since the nature of a thing is "the source of motion in that in which it is essentially," being nothing more than "the essence of the thing inasmuch as it is related to the thing's proper activity."

Man is a substance that is able to think and will. He is a person, therefore, because he is the subsistence of a being that is capable of knowing and loving in an intellectual way, and of deciding for himself the end of his actions. No animal or plant or other inferior supposit can be called a person, because it does not have a rational nature. Man is a free agent. He is, therefore, something sacred and inviolable, a being with special rights and special responsibilities. He has a destiny which he can share with no infrahuman corporeal creature. Still, he fulfills only the minimum requirements for admission into the noble ranks of person. He is an intellectual substance, but of the lowest sort. His person is only an analogue of the person of the angel. Least of all is he comparable to the person of the Godhead. Outside of his intuitive knowledge of first principles, he must grope through long and laborious reasoning processes before he can attain to anything like a complete idea of things. He is endowed with the power of election; but only too often his gift is exhibited to the world in the tattered garments of pride, passion, and ignorance. Yet, the fact remains that his nature is rational and that he is, therefore, truly a person. As

a person, he is a supposit. All individual substances are sup-
posits, but only those of an intellectual nature are persons, just
as all determining principles of matter are forms, but only
those of a living nature are souls. Because the person of man
belongs to the general category of supposit, it is sometimes
defined, more briefly, as the supposit of a rational nature.

iv

The Definition of Aquinas

The Boethian definition of a human person was accepted by
Aquinas, presumably because he found it already in possession
and recognized on all sides as a traditional formula. But I do
not believe that the Angelic Doctor was altogether satisfied
with it. The main difficulty arises with the meaning of the
word "individual" which needs so much clarification as to call,
really, for a new definition. Thus, as Aquinas points out, when
we say that a person is an individual substance, we imply three
things: first, that it is a complete substance; second, that it
subsists by itself; third, that it is separate from all else.

To say that person is a *complete substance* is to affirm that it
must have a complete nature. Person cannot be part of anything, either actually or potentially. The soul of man belongs
to man as part of his nature. It is not, therefore, a person, even
when it exists as an individual something in separation from
the body. Again, to say that person *subsists by itself* means that
it exists in and for itself. Thus, man, as a person, exists in his
own right. He is the ultimate possessor of his nature and of all
the operations of his nature. He is, further, the ultimate subject of predication of all his attributes. He cannot exist in another; for, what exists in another is not a person. Finally, to
say that person is *separate from all else* is to exclude the possibility of its being a second substance or a universal, since the

very notion of universal includes its predicability of several subjects.

From this explanation of Aquinas, it follows that person excludes three kinds of communicability: first, that of *part to whole*, since person is a complete substance; second, that of *assumption*, since person subsists by itself, and not only does not require a subject of inherence, but cannot, as such, be taken up by another subject; third, that of *universal to singular*, since person is a first substance, separate from all else. Person, then, is something essentially incommunicable and incapable of being assumed. The soul of man is a singular nature, capable of being communicated to the body. Accordingly, it cannot be a person. The body of man, or his material substrate, is also a singular nature, capable of being assumed, as a part of man, by the soul. Accordingly, it cannot be a person. In the nature of man, then, we do not find the threefold incommunicability that is demanded of his person. From this fact the followers of Aquinas are led to infer that the nature and person of man are really distinct; and, further, that the nature and supposit of all corporeal substances are really distinct. With the clarifications added by Aquinas to the formula of Boethius, we may now define the person of man as *a complete substance, subsisting by itself, separate from all else, and endowed with a rational nature.*[b]

v

The Ontological Basis of Person

What, precisely, is the ultimate determination of a nature which makes it a subsistence or a person? Or, more briefly, what is the ultimate ontological foundation of person? This is a problem which has been debated by the schoolmen for centuries. According to Scotus and his disciples, the final determining factor of person is a negation. Thus, any individual intellectual nature which is neither destined to be communicated nor is actually communicated is a person. To the teaching of Scotus it is objected that nature is not person, but that person possesses nature and all its attributes. Man, for example, is a person who has a rational nature. It is difficult to accept the view that person, as possessor, is distinct from nature, as possessed, only by a negation.

Accordingly, the traditional followers of Aquinas, after Cajetan, hold that there is a positive determination of nature which makes it a person. This positive determination is referred to as a mode of subsistence. In the language of Aquinas: *"Persona significat quamdam naturam cum quodam modo existendi"*: that is to say, person signifies a certain nature with a certain mode of existence or a certain mode of subsistence. It is the function of the mode of subsistence proper to person: first, to prepare the nature to receive its own existence; second, to render the nature incommunicable; third, to make the nature terminated in itself. *Subsistence, therefore, adds the final determination to nature and thereby constitutes it a person.* Some Thomists simplify the whole explication by saying that person is nothing more than the actual existence of an intellectual substance. The very fact that a thing subsists with its own rightful existence makes it incommunicable. The supposit is a supposit, then, and the person is a person, because it is a being endowed with existence in the strictest sense of the term.

vi

Recapitulation

To sum up: the person of man is the very center of the cosmos. The ultimate ontological determination of person is subsistence, which presupposes a substantial nature that is individual and singular. By the fact that it is endowed with subsistence, this nature cannot communicate with any other substantial nature, either in the act of existing or in the act of operating. Person exists before action. It possesses its existence, like its nature, in an incommunicable manner that is absolutely its own. Not only is it singular and individual, but it so possesses the existence which actuates it that it cannot share it with another.

Man is a contingent being; and in contingent being, nature or essence does not imply existence. Consequently, if the existence which a particular created nature receives is to be incommunicable, belonging to it alone, and unable to actuate another nature at the same time, it is necessary that this nature be terminated in itself by an additional act of subsistence. Thus determined, it becomes a closed whole, a subject which appropriates to itself the act of existing which it receives. The notion of subsistence, as the final determination which makes nature a supposit, imposes itself immediately once we have grasped the master distinction of Aquinas between essence and existence. All the determinations of essence have the aspect of potency in regard to the act of existence. Now, essence is complete in man by the union of body and soul. When this essence, which is a human nature, is able to possess itself in an immaterial way, when it can take itself in hand through the instruments of intellect and will, in short, when it belongs to the order of spirit and liberty, it is ready to be a person. All that is required is to receive the final perfection of subsistence. Once subsistence gives to nature the power of appropriating existence to itself, by that very act it renders existence incommunicable. If the existence of an individual and singular nature is incommunicable, for all the stronger reason the operations of that nature are also incommunicable.[c]

vii

Empiriological Person

A. ONTOLOGICAL AND EMPIRIOLOGICAL PERSON

When we say that the person of man is the supposit of a rational nature, we are defining it in its ontological meaning. There is another way in which the problem of person may be approached, namely, from the point of view of its empiriological significance. The ontological person is the foundation of the empiriological person. The empiriological person is the manifestation of the ontological person. The ontological person is permanent, static, immobile. It remains the same, essentially, throughout man's whole existence as man. The empiriological person, on the other hand, is changing, dynamic, mobile. It may differ, accidentally, from one man to another, and even in the same man. The ontological person we shall call simply person. The empiriological person we shall call personality or character.

B. PERSONALITY

Person has reference to the substance of man. Personality has reference to the properties of man, his acts, powers, and habits—all of which are accidents. The person of man does not grow in stature; but the personality of man develops and enlarges itself according to the pattern of his actions, the matured use of his powers, and the schema of his habits. Personality, therefore, is something compounded of the acts, powers, and habits of man; just as person is something compounded of the essence and existence, or the nature and subsistence, of man. But, whereas person is entirely a gift and a birthright, personality is largely a matter of one's own achievement. There is no such thing as the cultivation of person; but there is such a thing as the cultivation of personality. One individual is not more of a person than another; but one individual has more of a personality than another. If we are to give a satisfactory account of man's personalistic differences, therefore, it must be within the dimension of his acts, powers, and habits that the measure of such differences will be discovered. Now, the acts, powers, and habits of man not only vary from one individual to another, but also are subject to change within the same individual. It is true that our powers are part of our native equipment. But, powers must be exercised if they are to develop; and the important thing, in the genesis of personality, is not what we are able to accomplish, but what we actually do accomplish, what use we make of our capacities, and what kind of habits we form. Integration of personality means the gathering together and proper arranging of parts into a whole. The parts, in this case, are the acts, powers, and habits of man. The whole is a well-developed, well-rounded principle of human behavior.

C. CHARACTER

When this principle of human behavior is regarded in its moral aspects, it is known as character. If personality is a *psychological* entity, character is an *ethical* entity. We do not say that a man has a good or bad personality, but we do say that a man has a good or bad character. Thus, if personality is a principle of rational action, character is a principle of moral action. Personality might be defined as the sum total of all our rational habits grouped around the axis of intellect. Character might be similarly defined as the sum total of all our moral habits grouped around the axis of will. Character, like personality, is something empiriological. Also, like personality, it presupposes the abiding ontological reality of person. Man must exist before he can possess anything. Now, from the first moment of his existence, he is a person. But only with time and industry and enterprise, only with the maturation of his body and the unfolding of his powers, only with the acquisition of psychological habits and moral virtues, can he be said to have developed either a personality or a character.

viii

Person in Modern Psychology

Psychologists today may be conceded to have a fairly wide acquaintance with person in its empiriological aspects. But the same cannot be said of their knowledge of person in its ontological aspects. This is most unfortunate, especially since Aquinas and the schoolmen have resolved the concept of person in such clarifying detail. First of all, let us note that the modern terms "self" and "ego" may be used synonymously with "person," provided we make the proper distinctions between the empiriological and the ontological meanings of these words. It is scarcely necessary to add that the scientist is primarily interested in the empiriological content of person, whereas the philosopher is primarily interested in its ontological content. When James, for example, speaks of person as a stream of consciousness, he is referring to the phenomenal self. When Leibniz, on the other hand, speaks of person as a substance gifted with understanding, he is referring to the noumenal self.

With these basic distinctions in mind it is quite a simple matter to evaluate the modern attempts at a definition of person, self, or ego. Even the most cursory glance through the writings of the post-Cartesians reveals a wide variety of opinion and theory. Thus, for Wolff, person is something that remembers itself. For Locke, it is an intellectual substance that can consider self as itself. For Hume, it is a succession of conscious thoughts and feelings. For James, it is the thought of the moment, the passing state of consciousness. For James Mill, it is a series of conscious states, aware of itself as a series. For Cousin, it is will. For Bergson, it is a flash of intelligent being. For Whitehead, it is a projection of mind. For the emergent evolutionists of the idealistic sort, it is a development of thought. For the emergent evolutionists of the mechanistic sort, it is a development of matter. Obviously, some of these definitions contain a partial truth. But none of them provides a really satisfactory analysis of person in its ultimate ontological aspects. All of them exhibit a definite Cartesian influence, manifest in the gradual surrender of the concepts of mind and person as something substantial, and in the final resolution of these concepts into nothing more than states of consciousness, or special organizations of matter.

ix

Person and Consciousness

The fact is, of course, that consciousness or rational insight has an immediate relationship with person, since it is by acts of intellectual consciousness or by the operations of reason and will that we become aware of the existence of person. Further, unity of consciousness is the empiriological basis of unity of person. Now, empiriological person, as we have seen, is made manifest by motion of different kinds. Man feels, remembers, thinks, wills. These are acts of a conscious nature. But, no movement can be apprehended without some sort of knowledge of the thing that moves. So, no act of consciousness can be apprehended without some sort of knowledge of self as the subject of such action. Thus, introspective analysis of empiriological person must issue in knowledge of ontological person, that is, of the ultimate foundation or carrier of man's acts, powers, and habits. For, acts, powers, and habits are accidents. As accidents, they must have a subject of inherence. The subject of inherence is, by definition, a substance. And when we have arrived at the notion of self as a substance, the carrier of all our actions, the support of all our powers, the subject of all our habits, we have struck the ultimate roots of our being, which is the ontological person.

But, analysis of the phenomena of consciousness does not stop short at the recognized existence of ontological person. It further reveals that this ontological person is something stable and enduring, even though change is going on constantly at its periphery. Every act of memory implies a knowledge of the fact that I, presently remembering, am the selfsame person who experienced the events that are being recalled. The events themselves are past and gone. But I, the experiencer, am still perduring, though influenced by all the mutations of time and place to which every cosmic being is liable. From this permanence, fully recognized, springs the consciousness of self as a unitary principle. The one to whom all the variations of state belong is apprehended as an entity complete in itself and distinguished from all other entities. Unity of consciousness does not constitute, but manifests unity of being, unity of individual substance, unity of ontological person.

In hylomorphic creatures, the reason for unity of consciousness is the unity of substantial form which, in conjunction with matter, makes a single corporeal substance. This does not mean that substantial form, which is one, is identical with supposit or person, which is one; but that substantial form is the source of unity in composite creatures whose material substrate is regularly undergoing change. It is quite obvious that the body of man, for example, is the subject of constant metabolic activities. Does this fact challenge the permanency of his ontological person? Not at all! The difficulty was foreseen by Aquinas, and he meets it with his usual clearness of distinction.

Thus, if we regard the body of man simply as matter, then, like all matter, it is bound by the laws of change, always building up and breaking down its protoplasmic contents. If, however, we regard man's body as a definite species of matter, then it constantly retains its identity, because it is always a *human* body.

There is the further consideration that, regardless of age and the changes that are wrought by time, the body which a man possesses is always *his* body because it is informed by *his* soul. To the permanency of his soul, in the last analysis, is due the abiding unity of man, and, therefore, the abiding unity of his ontological person. In his body we have the principle of the soul's individuation. In his soul we have the principle of his body's speciation. Each has a function to perform for the other. Each is a natural complement of the other. Only in the union of matter and form do we find the perfection of complete substance. Only in the action of substance do we find the perfection of complete nature. Only in the subsistence of nature do we find the perfection of complete person. Moreover, the person of man is one, the nature of man is one, and the substance of man is one, ultimately, because the soul of man is one.

x

Multiple Personality

A. VARIATIONS OF EMPIRIOLOGICAL PERSON

The empiriological person, as we have already pointed out, is something dynamic. It is, therefore, subject to change. It grows and extends itself as acts are multiplied, as powers are developed, and as habits are formed. It is something accidental, springing from the depths of the ontological ego, in which it is rooted. We have agreed to call it personality in its psychological aspects, character in its ethical aspects. From the laboratories of the scientists, from the clinics of the analysts, and from the broad field of everyday life, there is abundant evidence to show that, in the same individual, personality frequently undergoes metamorphosis of a rather strange sort. Some of these transformations are not beyond the range of normal experience. They are due to partial change in the contents of consciousness. Others are definitely in the category of the abnormal. They are due to complete changes in the contents of consciousness. Let us briefly examine each of these types of aberration.

B. PARTIAL CHANGES

All of us are more or less familiar with the continuity of our sensations, and with the regular succession of affective states, consequent on our cognitive processes. The experience of such continuity, together with our empiriological consciousness of self and of its identity in time, accounts for the fact that personality does not change with each new cognition and affect. Yet it is surprisingly easy to change this situation. Suppose that we are reading a gripping story, or looking at some sublime scene of nature, or probing the depths of an intricate problem. It is easy to see how the unusual pattern of this sort of experience should thrust the accustomed sensory and affective states of awareness far into the background. Under the altered conditions of consciousness, one may really "feel like a new person."

The impression of change gathers strength when physiological causes are at work to modify an otherwise normal constancy in the succession of body sensations. Such ordinary disturbances as buzzing in the ears, light-headedness, water in the auditory passages, and so on, may also lie at the roots of this notion of a changed personality. But, whatever its physical or mental contributing factors, the fact remains that, whenever the constant mass of our sensations and feelings becomes unfamiliar, or whenever the regular flux of consciousness is partially broken, we appear, to that degree, to have altered our personality.

C. COMPLETE CHANGE

Complete change in the contents of consciousness means that the condition of the individual is pathological. Phenomena of this kind are described in terms of multiple personality, split personality, and so forth. Here the situation may involve change of character as well as change of personality. In cases of this description, the revival of earlier experiences is seriously interfered with and sometimes entirely suppressed. Should an individual retain part of the old and familiar contents at the same time that new and strange ones are experienced, a schizophrenia or division of personality will result, characterized by partial loss of memory. If the past is recaptured, the individual may become quite conscious of the alteration. Should the process be repeated with recurrent lapses of memory, a veritable host of personalities may ensue. Presumably, in each case where the smooth and uninterrupted current of body sensations and body affects is changed, the subject enters into a new field of conscious experience.

This adoption of several personalities by one and the same individual is comparable to the artistry of the actor who is able to portray several different rôles on the stage; with this difference, however, that, whereas the actor can at any moment become aware of his offstage life, the subject of multiple personalities cannot retrace his pathway to a normal existence, but is condemned to face the world with the particular personality or character which his presently evolved mental constellations and emotional patterns have imposed upon him. Yet it is noteworthy that, even in the most extreme pathological cases, there is no scientific evidence which would cause us to suspect the unalterable identity of the ontological ego.

READINGS FROM AQUINAS

Summa Theologica, part I, question 29.
———————— part III, question 2, articles 1–3.
De Potentia Dei,   question 9, articles 1–4.
Contra Gentiles,   book IV, chapter 38.

CLARIFICATIONS

(a)

Distinction of person from essence or nature

Person is denominated by various terms. As the support of accidents and the subject of actions, it is called a supposit or an hypostasis. Thus, "to the hypostasis alone are attributed the operations and the natural properties, and whatever belongs to the nature in the concrete; for, we say that this man thinks, and is risible, and is a rational creature. So, likewise, this man is said to be a supposit, because he underlies whatever belongs to man and receives its predication." Moreover, inasmuch as it is a subject which exists in itself and not in another, person is called a subsistence. It is scarcely necessary to add that every individual substance is a supposit, or hypostasis, or subsistence; and that only the individual substance of an intellectual nature is a person.

On the other hand, person is emphatically not the same as essence or nature, and therefore should not be used synonymously with these two terms. The following are the complete texts from the Angelic Doctor, bearing on the distinctions: "Strictly speaking, the essence is what is expressed by the definition. Now, the definition comprises the principles of the species, but not the individual principles. Hence, in things composed of matter and form, the essence signifies not the form alone, nor the matter alone, but what is composed of matter and the common form, as the principles of the species. But, what is composed of this matter and this form, has the nature of an hypostasis and person. For, soul, flesh, and bone belong to the nature of man; whereas, this soul, this flesh, and this bone belong to the nature of this man. Accordingly, hypostasis and person add the individual principles to the idea of essence; nor are these identified with the essence in things composed of matter and form."

Again: "The Philosopher says (in the second book of his *Physics*) that 'nature is the principle of motion in that in which it is essentially and not accidentally.' Now, this principle is either form or matter [in things composed of form and matter]. Hence, sometimes form and sometimes matter is called nature. And because the end of natural generation, in that which is generated, is the essence of the species, which the definition signifies, this essence of the species is called a *nature*. And thus Boethius (in his *Treatise on the Two Natures*) defines nature as 'that which informs a thing with its specific difference,' *i.e.* that which perfects the specific definition."
But, "*person* has a different meaning from *nature*. For nature, as we have just said, designates the specific essence which is signified by the definition. And, if nothing were found to be added to what belongs to the notion of species, there would be no need to distinguish the nature from the supposit of the nature, that is to say, from the individual subsisting in this nature, since every individual subsisting in a nature would be altogether one with its nature. Now, in certain subsisting things, we happen to find what does not belong to the notion of the species, namely, accidents and individuating principles. This is very obviously the case in things that are composed of matter and form. Hence, in such as these, the nature and the supposit really differ; not indeed as if they were wholly separate, but because the supposit includes the nature, and, in addition, certain other things outside the notion of the species. Accordingly, the supposit is understood to be a whole which has the nature as its formal part to perfect it. Wherefore, in such beings as are composed of matter and form, the nature is not predicated of the supposit, for we do not say that this man

is his manhood. If, however, a being exists in which there is nothing outside its species or its nature, as in God, the supposit and the nature are not really distinct in it, but only in our way of thinking, inasmuch as it is called a *nature* as it is an essence, and a *supposit* as it is subsisting. And what is said of a supposit is to be applied to a person in rational or intellectual creatures, since a person is nothing else than 'an individual substance of a rational nature' according to Boethius. Therefore, whatever exists in a person is united to it in person, whether it belongs to its nature or not."

(b)
The formal and material significance of person

Aquinas tells us that "a thing is signified in two ways: formally, and materially. Formally, a term signifies that which it is chiefly intended to signify; and this is the definition of the term. Thus, *man* signifies something composed of a body and a rational soul. Materially, a term signifies that which is requisite for the definition. Thus, *man* signifies something that has a heart, brain, and such parts as are required in order that the body be animated with a rational soul. . . .

"Now, the term *person* signifies nothing more than an individual substance of a rational nature. And since under an individual substance of a rational nature is contained every individual substance, that is to say, every substance which is incommunicable and distinct from other things, (whether we are speaking of the substance of God, of men, or of angels), it follows that a divine person must signify something subsistent and distinct in the divine nature, just as a human person signifies something subsistent and distinct in human nature; and this is the formal signification of person, whether divine or human.

"Since, however, that which is distinct and subsistent in human nature is nothing else than something individualized and differentiated from other things by individual matter, it follows that this is the material signification when we speak of a human person."

(c)

Essence and existence

To say that man is composed of essence and existence is not the same as saying that he is composed of matter and form. The distinction between essence and existence is really the first application of the most fundamental dichotomy of created being, namely, the distinction between potency and act: what a thing can be, and what a thing is. Thus, essence is related to existence as potency is related to act, because existence is the perfection of essence. Similarly, nature is related to subsistence as potency is related to act, because subsistence is that perfection of nature which makes it a supposit.

Essence and existence together, as Cajetan points out, yield a composition *with* two principles. Matter and form together, on the other hand, yield a composition *from* two principles. Man, for example, is a composite being *with* essence and existence in his makeup. Man is a composite being made *from* matter and form. Thus, it is true to say that from matter and form a third entity is compounded, which is neither matter alone, nor form alone, but a combination of both. But, quite obviously, it is not true that from essence and existence a third entity is compounded, which is neither essence alone, nor existence alone. Here are the words of Cajetan: "The composition of matter and form is a composition *from* these two things: and, therefore, from such a composition is made a single third thing. The composition of essence and existence, on the other hand, is a composition *with* these two things. Nothing, properly speaking, is compounded of essence and existence, in the way that a thing is compounded of matter and form. Rather, essence goes along with existence, and existence goes along with essence. Wherefore, essence and existence are said to be conjoined by themselves (*per se*); but they are not said to compose a third thing."

CHAPTER TWELVE

THE SOUL OF MAN

i

Substantial Nature of the Human Soul

At the beginning of our book we said that there are two ways of looking at the soul of man: *entitatively*, as the form of his body; and *operationally*, as the root of his powers. As the form of his body, man's soul is part of his essence. As the root of his powers, man's soul is the ultimate principle by which he lives, senses, and thinks. Now, our human powers are divided into two general classes: those that belong to body and soul together; and those that belong to soul alone. The first are psychosomatic; the second are purely psychic. It is by his psychic powers, or by his intellect and will, that the soul of man is distinguished from all inferior forms. Moreover, psychic powers are identical with mind; and mind, by extension, is identical with soul. To ask, then: is the mind of man a substance? is really to ask: is the soul of man a substance?

The answer to the query is abundantly revealed from our analysis of the nature of man, as well as from our study of his acts, powers, and habits. Thus, man is a hylomorphic creature. He is made up of two basic principles: matter and form. Each is a necessary part of his essence. As parts, each is incomplete without the other. Each belongs to the category of substance, though neither, alone, is a complete substance, because neither, alone, is a complete species. The point is that, entitatively speaking, the soul of man, like all souls, is a substantial form of matter. This means that it demands a material substrate as a coefficient of its very being, in conjunction with which it establishes the complete corporeal substance that we call man.

Further, the soul of man is the immediate subject of his rational powers. As a subject, it does not require to be possessed by anything else. It exists, in short, by its own rightful title, which means that it is a substance. For, obviously, acts suspended in a vacuum are inadmissible. Thinking demands, not only a power that thinks, but also a substance in which the power to think is rooted. Similarly, willing demands, not only a power that wills, but also a substance in which the power to will is imbedded. Now, thinking and willing are acts proper to the soul alone, since the soul alone is the ultimate principle of such operations. As a basis of rational processes, then, the soul of man must be a substance. What we said about the soul of man is also true of his mind, since his mind is operationally identified with the essence of his intellectual soul.

ii

The Notion of Soul in Modern Psychology

The notion of soul as a substance declined when the notion of mind as a substance began to decay. After the entrenchment of Descartes's philosophy, mind and matter were no longer regarded as conjoined in a substantial union. Some psychologists became intrigued with the study of mind in isolation from matter; and these were the extreme idealists. Others were fascinated with the study of matter in isolation from mind; and these were the extreme materialists. But human nature, it seems, is more easily seduced by the tangibilities of matter than by the intangibilities of mind. The importance of matter grew; the importance of mind waned. Phenomenalism made its appearance. Its great leaders, like Hume and Taine, stoutly maintained that the mind of man is nothing more than a series of conscious acts. Associational psychology came into being, defended by scholars like James Mill, Spencer, and James. Mind is now definitely reduced to consciousness.

This type of theory was in the ascendency when Wilhelm Wundt and Gustav Fechner separated the science of mind from the philosophy of mind. The first investigators in the field of scientific psychology all show unmistakable evidences of the influence of associationism. It was an influence destined to survive down to our contemporaries. Functionalism, in the theory of Dewey and his followers, is simply a disguised associationistic doctrine or, more fundamentally, a disguised phenomenalism. Mind is an historical event wherein change overrides stability. It is simply part of the larger complex of events that go under the name of "nature." Mind, therefore, is a process rather than a subject of processes; so that the concept of it as a substantial nature is meaningless and unpragmatic.

One of the early defenders of the functional idea was Watson. But not for long! Dissatisfied with the notion of mental events as the subject matter of psychology, Watson began anew on a strictly objective basis. Behavior is substituted for consciousness. External observation is exchanged for introspection. Reflexes take the place of sensations. And the principle of conditioning supplants the principle of associationism. Now man is without soul, without mind, and without consciousness, with nothing left except the physiological functions of his nervous system.

But the end is not yet; and the pendulum is turning back to a moderate position. As we pointed out before, certain groups of investigators—notably the factor psychologists, the psychoanalysts, and the personalists—appear to be operating on a basis of the whole-making approach to man. Such an approach is founded, of course, on the principle of a hylomorphic union between body and soul. And just as we cannot deny the substantiality of man's body, so we cannot deny the substantiality of his soul. Otherwise, we must commit ourselves to the view that the proper acts of the human soul have no support or carriage to sustain them. The soul of man, therefore, must be a substance.

iii

Immaterial Nature of the Human Soul

A. HISTORICAL APPROACH TO THE PROBLEM

What kind of substance is this mind or soul of man? From his ultimate analysis of its acts and powers, Aquinas replies that the human soul is essentially immaterial. To say that it is immaterial is to say that it is *incorporeal:* that it is not a body. Further, to say that it is immaterial is to say that it is *subsistent:* that it is not intrinsically dependent on a body. Obviously, any system in modern psychology which is founded on sensistic principles is committed to a denial of an incorporeal and subsistent soul or mind. Such, for example, is the school of Watson and its behavioral interpretation of thinking processes as minute movements of the laryngeal mechanisms. Such, too, is the school of Titchener, and its structural interpretation of thought as a refined image, feeling, or sensation. Such, moreover, is the school of Köhler and its gestaltic interpretation of thought as a sensory process, determined by patterns in cortical or cosmic matter. Such, finally, is the school of Freud and its psychoanalytic interpretation of higher intellectual processes as emergences from *id* or instinct. In the end, theories of this sort are bound to bring the highest levels of human achievement down to the dimensions of the material.

Philosophic schools, on the other hand, working in the main traditions set by Socrates, Plato, and Aristotle, and even by earlier writers than these—barring, of course, the followers of

Democritus—have always consistently held for the immaterial nature of the human mind. In fact, this point of view is one that is common to several thinkers whose theories, in other respects, are widely divergent: for example, Augustine, Aquinas, Descartes, Leibniz, Kant, Hegel, and their successors, and, more modernly, Bradley, Croce, and Bergson. A conviction so steadfast and consistent, even though arrived at by different routes, gains weight and momentum as the phenomena of private experience and introspection are examined and properly evaluated. That there are realities which are essentially immaterial, that intellectual operations, intellectual powers, and intellectual substance fall within this category, becomes increasingly clear as philosophic reflection is carried to its ultimate conclusions.

B. HUMAN SOUL NOT A BODY

The line of reasoning which Aquinas employs in establishing the incorporeal and subsistent character of man's soul rests, mainly, on an analysis of its cognitive operations. Knowledge is a vital experience, wherein object and subject are intentionally united. Its perfection, as a living function, is judged by the degree of its remotion from matter. In the cognitions of sense, there is semidetachment. In the cognitions of intellect, there is complete detachment. In the first instance, the form is separated from matter, but not from the conditions of matter. In the second instance, the form is separated from matter, and also from the conditions of matter. This is simply another way of saying that the form of sense knowledge is particular and concrete; while the form of intellectual knowledge is universal and abstract. We speak of the detachment of form from matter, in the act of human knowledge, because hylomorphic substances are the proper and connatural objects of the human mind.

Now, let us suppose, with Aquinas, that the human mind is not incorporeal: that it is, in fact, a corporeal entity, a body. In such a case, the particular kind of body that it is would prevent it from becoming, and therefore from knowing, all other bodies. Yet, introspection tells us that the human mind does know bodies indifferently; that there is no limitation to the number or kind of bodies that it can know; that it is everything, to the extent that it can become everything through its knowledge. The point is that no corporeal substance is incapable of being grasped by it. For, of whatever sort it is, man's mind can recognize it as a substance of a specific nature.

Observe that when we say the human mind *can* know all bodies, we do not thereby imply that it actually *does* know all bodies. Neither does it follow that, because the nature of a body is known, it is therefore known completely, by the ultimate specific difference whereby it is distinguished from every other body. What the intellect of man can and does grasp is the fact that here, in its presence, is a corporeal substance which, by certain ascertainable properties, is distinct from other corporeal substances. In addition, it can and does grasp the fact that some corporeal substances, like elements and compounds, are essentially distinct from other corporeal substances, like living organisms. Even further, it discerns that some living organisms are plants, others animals, others men. In short, the mind of man apprehends a hierarchy of cosmic beings, wherein one order of reality is separated from another. The point of the argument is simply this: that because the mind of man is able to understand the determinate nature of all corporeal substances, it cannot, itself, be a corporeal substance.

C. HUMAN SOUL NOT SUBJECTIVELY DEPENDENT ON A BODY

Moreover, the mind of man does not and cannot function by a body organ. Why? Because the fixed and determinate nature of the organ would prevent it from knowing all bodies. The eye, for example, sees everything as colored or bathed in light. It knows nothing about the other properties of matter. Now, if intellect were like sense, it would be constricted by material structures. In such a case, it could not know bodies in themselves, but only in relation to the determinate character of the organ which would mediate its knowledge. But, introspection testifies to the fact that, in every act which it performs, the human mind knows corporeal substances precisely by abstracting from the accidents that make them concrete and individual, removing them out of the dimensions of space and time, and considering them according to their forms, absolutely and universally. Its act of understanding, therefore, must be subjectively free of the body.

Such freedom, of course, does not exclude the need of the administrations of sense. It is the teaching of Aquinas that, in the natural course of man's life, no ideas are produced without conversion to phantasms. It is proper to say, then, that the human mind exhibits an objective dependency on sense, since the data of sense furnish it with the objects of intellection. But in the subjective order, that is, in the act of abstracting and understanding, the intellect of man is completely devoid of matter and the appendages of matter. But if it is immaterial in its intellectual operations, it must be immaterial in its intellectual nature.

D. HUMAN SOUL KNOWS BEING AS SUCH

The foregoing arguments are based on an analysis of the proper object of human intellection, which is corporeal being. They gain additional force when we consider its adequate object, which is being as such. We might state the difference here involved by saying that the proper object of human understanding belongs to man, as man; but that its adequate object is common to all intellectual agents. Outside this adequate object, nothing really can be understood, since it includes everything that is intelligible. Such an object must be *being:* first, because nothing is understandable unless it is a being of some sort; second, because being, as being, is the only object which is inclusive of all the objects of intelligence. Every new factor added to being limits it, and thus transforms it into a particular kind of being. Thus, all the objects of intelligence agree in the notion of being, even if they do not agree in anything else.

Every thought of the human mind, therefore, must be finally resolvable into the concept of being. If we ask, for example: what is man? the ultimate reply is, a rational animal. If we further ask: what is an animal? the ultimate reply is, a substance that has life and feeling. If we ask, at the end: what is substance? the ultimate reply is, a being to whose nature is due existence in itself and not in another. So with all other things that we know: analysis always leads us eventually to the notion of being. Even accidents are "beings of being," as the ancients said.

Now, the mind of man is able to apprehend all the various kinds of being in one single notion of being precisely because it can abstract from the concreteness of this or that particular being. Its vast sweeping vision of reality sees something basic to the whole ordered sequence of perfections in existence: rising from the cogencies of inert matter, through plant, animal, and man, to the sphere of angelic substances; stopping, in fact, only when it has reached the center of all being, the uncreated and unparticipated reality of God. If corporeal essence, then, does not escape the intelligence of man, or if the body does not prevent the flight of human understanding from the pure potentiality of primary matter to the pure actuality of ultimate being, must it not be because matter has no part in the operations of the human mind? Again, we reach the conclusion that the principle of man's intellection, which is his soul, is an immaterial substance.

iv

Simple Nature of the Human Soul

A. ABSENCE OF ENTITATIVE AND QUANTITATIVE PARTS

From the fact of the soul's complete lack of matter we are able to infer to its absolute simplicity. We say that the soul is simple, first, because it is not made up of entitative parts, in the manner that a corporeal substance is composed of matter and form; second, because it is not made up of quantitative parts, in the manner that matter is composed of discrete or continuous units. That the soul of man is not made up of entitative parts is obvious from the fact that it is, itself, a form of matter, that is, a form which, in conjunction with matter, makes the composite substance of man. That the soul of man is not made up of quantitative parts may be concluded from its incorporeal nature. Its lack of quantitative parts may also be deduced from empirical analysis. For, introspection tells us that a thought has no extended components dwelling side by side in space. It has no arrangement comparable to the local position of protons, electrons, atoms, or molecules, in a given quantity of matter.

B. TOTAL REFLECTION OF MIND ON ITSELF

Further, the human mind can reflect on itself. It is able to understand that it understands, surveying both its action and itself in one complete, wholly immanent movement. In such self-reflective attitudes, it grasps itself, not as to part, but as to whole. Matter, on the other hand, is never moved by itself except in respect to part, in such wise that one portion of it is the mover and the other is the thing moved. Matter, indeed, contains nothing except by quantitative commensuration. The mind of man, on the contrary, is enriched with ideas precisely by freeing itself from the contingencies of matter. The goal of its operations is to comprehend the universe and all its parts: and the perfect idea would be one which, from the depths of its utter simplicity, would picture the whole schema of cosmic reality in a single act of understanding. We can conceive of a point by point correspondence between a given material object and our singular image of it; but we are unable to conceive of any point by point correspondence between the same material object and our universal idea of it. Indeed, it is the sheerest futility to attempt an application of the criteria by which we rule and measure matter to an intellect or mind or soul that offers no basis for such quantitative commensuration.

v

Manner of the Soul's Presence in the Body

How, it may be asked at this point, is the human soul present in the body? If it is immaterial by nature, it cannot be conjoined to matter in a material way. This means that its mode of habitation is not circumscriptive—as water is in a tumbler or a hand is in a glove. Because it is immaterial, it has no quantitative parts and no extension, and, therefore, no dimensional contact with the body. It is present in the organism *definitively*, being limited by matter and material organs only in the exercise of its faculties. For, while it has no parts outside of parts, it does have powers outside of powers; and its powers are exercised within definite areas. Because it is the form of the organism, it is present everywhere throughout the organism. Not only is the whole of it present in the whole body, but the whole of it is also present in every part of the body. To repeat: though everywhere present, the soul of man does not exercise its powers everywhere, since certain of these are dependent on material structures and are operative only in and through such material structures.[a]

vi

Origin of the Human Soul

The body of man is essentially material. His soul, as we have concluded, is essentially immaterial. The fact of its immateriality is immediately connected with the problem of its origin, because, as an incorporeal and subsistent entity, it cannot have its inception in matter. Further, the soul of man is essentially simple. The fact that it has no parts and is indivisible is also immediately connected with the problem of its origin, since its birth cannot be ascribed to the division of another soul. It must, therefore, as Aristotle said, come into existence "from without."

First of all, let us note that the soul of the animal, unlike that of man, is so completely immersed in matter that it can neither exist nor operate apart from a body. Its dependency on matter is, in fact, absolute. In accounting for its origin, therefore, one need not go outside the realm of material structures and material processes. The case of man, however, is quite different, since the thing reproduced is a being which, so far as the body is concerned, is material in nature; but, so far as the soul is concerned, is immaterial in nature. Now, the soul of the animal can be educed from the potentialities of matter. Is it possible that the soul of man, too, should be brought forth from the bosom of matter? Is it a product of the body of the parents, or an emergence from the cosmic elements of the uni-

verse, or an effect of the constant and all-pervading developmental tendencies of nature?

In answer to these questions, let us note, in the second place,
that a thing is said to be made when it is brought into existence. Further, it must be made in a way that is suitable to its
mode of existence. If the soul of the animal is utterly dependent on matter for its existence, then material generation is
sufficient to account for its origin. If the soul of man is independent of matter for its existence, then material generation is
not sufficient to account for its origin. Strictly speaking, the
term of any reproductive process is neither matter nor form in
isolation, but the entity compounded of both. In human generation, through the fusion of sperm and egg, an organism is
brought into being which is fitted to receive a human soul. To
say that parents produce their own offspring does not mean
that they generate a human soul, but simply that they produce a body which is able to act as the receptacle of a human
soul.

What mode of origin, then, is suitable to the immaterial
mode of existence which the human soul enjoys? Certainly,
not to be made out of matter, as Aquinas points out: otherwise,
it would have a corporeal nature, which is incompatible with
its immaterial manner of existence. Certainly, also, not to be
made out of another soul: otherwise it would have a divisible
nature, which is incompatible with its simple manner of existence. Since neither of these alternatives is allowable, we are
forced to conclude, with Aquinas, that it cannot exist at all except *by a special act of creation.* It is produced from nothingness
by the hand of God, from Whom it comes, not as an emanation
of the divine being, since God is pure act; but as a substance
"which is sometimes in potency to know, which acquires its
knowledge somehow from things, and which is equipped with
a multiplicity of powers."

vii

Time of the Human Soul's Origin

A. THEORY OF PRE-EXISTENCE

Although there is a definite point in time when the human soul begins to exist, it is quite impossible to fix this time except within very general limits. Some philosophers, like Plato and his disciples, have held that the soul of man antedates his body. According to Aquinas, any theory of pre-existence is purely gratuitous. More than this, it is devoid of reasonable foundation. Thus, the very concept of the human soul as the form of the body, created precisely in order to be linked with matter, must preclude its having any history before it is conjoined to matter. Without a body, it would be unable to function; and without a function, it would have no reason for being. This inability to operate before its union with matter is quite obvious in the case of the psychosomatic powers, which manifest an absolute dependency on material organs. It is also true, however, in the case of the purely psychic powers, since the ideas of intellect are born of experience; and experience is acquired only through the operation of the senses. Hence, for Aquinas, a theory of pre-existence would automatically imply the presence of a defect in the soul from the beginning. But, this is out of the question, because the soul originates from the hand of the Creator, and the Creator "made the first things in their perfect natural state, as their species required."

The whole argument, here, rests on the proposition that the soul of man, by an intrinsic design of its nature, is intended to inform matter. It would be a violation of this intrinsic design, then, were it created without a body. Its condition would be one of frozen immobility, since it could perform no single operation; and a nature that is unable to operate is not only a futile and empty thing, but also a contradiction in terms. The case is somewhat different after the separation of the soul from the body, for then possible intellect has already acquired a number of intelligible species; so that it can "understand what it understood formerly . . . not by turning to phantasms, but by a mode suited to a soul existing apart from the body," as we shall see in a later section of this chapter.

B. THEORY OF TRANSMIGRATION

Closely related to the Platonic teaching is the theory of metempsychosis, which maintains that the human soul successively inhabits several bodies. This has always been a favored doctrine with the Indian philosophers. Even today it is quite widespread among the followers of theosophic systems of thought. Plato himself was intrigued with the idea, which he probably picked up in the writings of Pythagoras. Aquinas stoutly rejects any theory of the sort, for much the same reason that he rejects the theory of pre-existence: it is a violation of human nature. Thus, man is a hylomorphic being, composed of body and soul. His material substrate and rational form constitute a single unified essence. This being the case, his soul must be related to his body in such a manner that it cannot acquire an essential relationship with another body. The fact of essential relationship means, in the concrete, that every individual soul is so intimately conjoined to the particular body which it inhabits that it cannot become ordained to another body without parting with something intrinsic to its nature. According to the laws of its very being, therefore, it is bound to continue its relationship with one body and one only—even after its separation from matter.

The transcendental character of this relationship really works in two directions: since, from the material point of view, the body of man is specifically human because it is united to an intellectual soul; and, from the formal point of view, the soul of man is an individual entity because it is possessed by a particular body or by a particular quantity of matter. As Aquinas points out, the distinction of human souls does not follow from a difference in essential properties or from a difference in kind between one soul and another, but from the fact that this soul is adapted to this body, that soul is adapted to that body; and so on. This coadaptation, which is the transcendental relationship of which we spoke above, "remains in the soul even after the body has perished; just as the soul's substance remains, because it is independent of the body in the act of existence." While, then, the doctrine of transmigration may be reconciled with the Platonic theory of accidental union between soul and body, it is basically opposed to the hylomorphic principles on which Aquinas grounds his position.

C. THEORY OF SUCCESSIVE FORMS

Aquinas's own theory regarding the time of the soul's origin is highly interesting. According to his account, the material substrate, which eventually becomes a human body through the infusion of a rational soul, is previously informed by a number of infrahuman souls. Thus, the fertilized egg or zygote first exists as a simple vegetative organism, then as an animal, before it actually becomes human through the presence of a created intellectual soul. As the vegetative form disappears by reverting back to the potentialities of matter, its place is immediately taken by a sensitive form, which, in turn, becomes extinct upon the advent of the rational form. The theory of Aquinas postulates a certain intrinsic proportion between matter and form—which proportion, it is contended by those who hold the theory, is not to be found between the first matter of the zygote and the rational soul.

In favor of the position of the Angelic Doctor, the following evidence is adduced: first, the successive structural development of the growing organism from plant body, to animal body, to human body; second, the successive operational development of the organism from vegetative acts, to sensitive acts, to rational acts. A difficulty arises with regard to the appearance of the animal soul. According to Aquinas, it succeeds upon a plant soul. How? As an effect of what he calls a "formative virtue" in the seminal fluid. Such an hypothesis, however, is unconfirmed by our present-day knowledge of the fluid media of reproductive cells. The only other agent that might plausibly explain the emergence of the animal soul is the vegetative principle. But a vegetative form is confined by its nature to the production of vegetative phenomena. A way out of the difficulty is proposed by modifying Aquinas's original theory to hold that the first form in the zygote is a sensitive soul. Accordingly, it is to a primitive animal form that the rational soul succeeds.

D. THEORY OF ONE FORM

The theory of one form states that the human soul, and it alone, is present in the organism from the instant of conception. Such a view, it is maintained by the proponents of the theory, does not violate any principle of proportion which demands that there be a certain ratio between matter and form in the generation of a corporeal substance. Thus, even in the zygotic stage of human ontogenesis, the fertilized ovum has all the potentialities of a perfect human body. This means, of course, that from the moment in which the pronuclei of ovum and sperm are fused, to become a single organism, the human soul is present—entitatively constituting a human being by its union with first matter; and operationally supplying the principle of human epigenesis. The material receptacle of the rational soul is adequately prepared for the reception of such a form by the very fact that it results from a reproductive act which is human.

That a highly specialized material system is not necessary to the presence of a rational soul may be inferred from the fact that thought and volition, the specific functions of the rational form, actually do not manifest themselves until long after birth. Their absence is due to the circumstance that there has not yet been a sufficient maturation of sensitive organs to allow for the operation of man's rational powers. Nevertheless, man is identified as a human being long before he makes his appearance in the cosmic world, wherein his senses gradually unfold. Just as an infant is born a human being and does not metamorphose into one, so the fertilized egg, resultant upon the act of human reproduction, is actually a human being, and is not, by the successive stages of gestation, transformed into one. The genetic evolution of man, therefore, has nothing to do with a change of nature, but merely with the gradual manifestation of his powers, all of which are present from the beginning because the rational soul is present from the beginning.

E. EVALUATION OF THE POLYMORPHIC AND MONOMORPHIC THEORIES

As to the relative merits of the foregoing arguments, I should like to stress the point that neither the theory of successive forms, which Aquinas defended, nor the theory of one form, which most of his modern disciples uphold, enjoys more than a probable certainty. Thus, the notion of a successive development of organic structures and a successive manifestation of vegetative, sensitive, and rational functions is not intrinsically repugnant to the idea of a rational soul being present from the time of conception; and so the second position may be the correct one. On the other hand, the operations of a being follow its nature and are a legitimate clue to the kind of form possessed by the being. In this particular case, the acts of the organism are successively vegetative, sensitive, and rational; and so the first position may be the correct one. Neither the special experience of the scientist nor the common experience of the philosopher avail to give us more than a probable opinion regarding the time of the human soul's advent. Accordingly, we are bound by the laws of logic to have some misgiving about the position which we hold, since the alternative position may be the true one.

viii
Immortality of the Human Soul

A. POSITION OF THE MATERIALISTS AND IMPERSONALISTS

The status of the human soul after death has always been a topic of prime importance in philosophic circles, for manifest reasons. We are not interested in the views of those who take refuge in the negative attitude that we can know nothing about the problem. There are only two possible answers that can be made to the question: what is the ultimate destiny of the soul of man? Either it is extinguished with the corruption of the composite, or it continues to exist after its separation from the body. The first of these two alternatives represents the position of the materialist. It holds, briefly, that when the human body is disintegrated and returns to dust, the human soul also disintegrates and disappears with it. As far back as the time of the Epicureans, this sort of philosophy had attained a completely systematized exposition. Indeed, no modern writer on materialism has added anything noteworthy to the arguments which Lucretius proposed for the demise of the soul with the corruption of the body.

Committed by implication to a theory of extinction are those who hold: first, that all the operations of man, without exception, are finally explained in terms of physico-chemical events, or as phenomena of a purely mechanical system; second, that thought and volition, the products of man's intellectual powers, are resolvable into sensory elements; third, that human consciousness or its principle, the mind, is the product of the general emergent tendencies of cosmic nature. For, it must be quite clear that whatever is explicable in terms of purely mechanical processes, or whatever is circumscribed by the limitations of the particular and the concrete, is material in character, and must, therefore, be subject to the same laws of disintegration that control all matter.

On the other hand, if it is allowed that there is some survival of the human soul after death, this does not signify that philosophers are all agreed about its nature. In particular, there is a difference of opinion as to whether such survival is personal or merely the impersonal sort of existence wherein the soul loses its identity in some vague and indefinable absolute. The latter is a Buddhistic interpretation, and may be said, roughly, to represent the point of view of those who declare for survival, but not in the personalistic sense.

B. POSITION OF AQUINAS

Firmly opposed to any form of materialism, on the one hand, and to the doctrine of an impersonal survival, on the other, is the Angelic Doctor's well-reasoned position which holds that the soul of man is by nature incapable of destruction; and further, that its survival is not conditioned by its activities on earth. Moreover, since it is also an individual form, it must continue to exist as such. Absorption into the bosom of the absolute is, therefore, abhorrent to its very essence. Strange to say, the doctrine of human immortality is developed at great length in the writings of Plato, but is treated very cursorily by Aristotle; yet, it is on a basis of the Stagirite's hylomorphic teaching that Aquinas establishes his thesis of a personal survival of the soul of man.

The main argument of the Angelic Doctor rests on an analysis of the intrinsic nature and extrinsic cause of the human form.

First, with respect to its *intrinsic nature*, the soul of man is not a body, as we have already established. In its essential constitution, therefore, there can be no movement of opponent and warring elements. Moreover, the soul of man is not dependent on a body. This fact we demonstrated from a study of his intellectual acts which, though objectively in need of the administrations of sense, are nevertheless subjectively free of matter and its contingencies. But, if the human intellect does not, absolutely speaking, require a body in order to think, the human soul does not, by the same token, require a body in order to exist. In this truth we discern the basic difference between man's form, which is subsistent, and all other corporeal forms, which are merely informing. The point about the distinction is this: that whereas every infrahuman form is corrupted with the corruption of the composite, man's form is essentially free of any force or element that might destroy it.[b] Neither by the corruption of itself, nor by the corruption of the body of which it is intrinsically independent, is it able to lose its existence.[c]

Second, in regard to its *extrinsic cause*, the human soul is created with a nature that is incorruptible. This does not mean that it can exist apart from its Creator. Indeed, without His supporting hand, it would instantly revert to nothingness. Annihilation of man's soul is not impossible, therefore, in view of God's supreme dominion over all His creatures. Nevertheless, the exercise of this absolute power is excluded by the essential wisdom and benevolence of the First Cause, since it is incredible that an all-wise and gracious Being should deprive the soul of the existence which He has given to it as a natural endowment. Moreover, a suggestion of this sort is particularly repugnant to the scientific mind, whose training and background commit it to the principle of inviolability so far as the laws of nature are concerned. To deprive a human soul of life, after it has been gifted with natural immortality, would be inconsistent, therefore, with human logic and divine wisdom.

D. PSYCHOLOGICAL PROOF OF SURVIVAL

The proof of survival from the subsistent nature of the human soul is a metaphysical type of argument. From an analysis of human thought and volition and the goal of these rational activities, Aquinas has built up another strong demonstration of immortality. Thus, the pivotal point from which we make our ultimate judgment on the nature of a thing is the end toward which it tends. This motion toward an end is spoken of, by Aquinas, as a natural desire. Such desires or innate impulsions cannot be fruitless or incapable of satisfaction: otherwise, nature, which is founded on the wisdom of the Creator, would manifest inane dispositions. Now, there are two kinds of natural desire in man which have an immediate bearing on the immortality of his soul: first, the natural desire of his intellect to know universal truth; second, the natural desire of his will to be united with universal good. Supreme truth and supreme goodness, then, must be the final goal of all man's rational strivings. But, the basis of the appetitive union is knowledge. Hence, the ultimate felicity of man must be found in a complete intellectual vision of limitless reality.

In his *Compendium of Theology*, Aquinas speaks of this fundamental urge to know, not particular truths, but all truth: "When the ultimate end is reached, natural desire is appeased. Thus, it makes no difference how far we progress in experiential forms of knowledge: we still have the urge for further knowledge. There are many things that our senses cannot know and of which we have very scant information by means of our abstractions from the data of sense. We may understand *that* certain things are: but we do not understand *what* they are. Such, for example, is the case when we attempt to grasp the essences of immaterial beings which completely transcend the essences of material beings. And even in the province of sensible reality, there are many things whose natures we cannot know with certitude, some of which we do not comprehend at all, and others only slightly.

"The desire to know and to have perfect understanding is always present with us. Because it is inborn, it cannot be vain or aimless. We shall reach our ultimate end, therefore, only if an agent higher than our natural faculties actualises our intellect and fills to repletion our natural desire for knowledge. Such is the character of this cognitive impulse that when we know effects, we also want to know their causes. Thus, no matter how much we learn about the phenomenal aspects of a thing, our minds are not content until they have apprehended its very essence. Indeed, our natural desire to know cannot be appeased until we know the First Cause—not in any haphazard way, but in its very essence. Now the First Cause is God. Hence, the ultimate end of intellectual creatures is to see God in His essence."

By the faint and illusive ideas which his mind has of supreme truth, man is borne toward the goal of a complete knowledge of reality. So, too, by the imperfect impulsions of his intellectual love, he is carried toward the goal of a complete union with goodness. For knowledge without love is fruitless and irrational. Yet, the attainment of supreme reality, in the union of knowledge, and the attainment of supreme goodness, in the union of love, is manifestly impossible under the imperfect conditions of this life. Consequently, the desire to know reality without limit, and to possess goodness in all its fullness, necessarily implies a state of perpetual existence, without which it would be impossible to satisfy the natural impulses of man's intellect and will. And because desires of this sort cannot be futile or vain, since they are grounded on the very nature of man's rational powers, they argue for the continued existence of the possessor of such powers, which is the intellectual soul.[d]

E. MORAL PROOF OF SURVIVAL

Aquinas does not make formal use of what is called the moral argument for survival, though he does hold, of course, for the necessity of an eternal sanction of the moral law. The argument may be stated briefly by saying that the whole structure of the ethical life, as we recognize it, with its absolute claims, forces us to acknowledge survival as the only condition under which the conflict of rights and duties, and the correct apportioning of rewards and punishments, can be ultimately adjusted. Indeed, the entire concept of moral law, of conscience, of the distinction of right and wrong, is meaningless unless the individual soul persists after death.

ix

Mode of Being of the Separated Soul

What, precisely, is it that survives the cleavage of the bond which weds a man's body to his soul in this life? Plato, and those who followed in his tradition, could say that it is a complete being which endures: a spirit, sufficient unto itself, now delivered from its tormentor, matter: a soul, leaving behind a corporeal shell, to which, in life, it had merely an accidental filiation. For Aquinas, on the other hand, only man is a complete being; and man is made up of both body and soul. Accordingly, in the Thomistic psychology, it is incorrect to speak of the continuance of person beyond the grave. Personal survival, true; but not survival of the person!

This may seem somewhat paradoxical; but Aquinas explains his meaning quite clearly. The human soul, like every cosmic form, is individuated by matter: not any matter, but matter earmarked with quantity. This soul is adapted to this body, that soul to that body, as we have already seen; and such coadaptation remains in the soul even after death. Observe, however, that the individuality of the soul depends on the body only so far as the principle of the individuating process is concerned, and not in respect to its term. In short: the *source* of individuation is quantified matter; but its *end* is not quantified matter. This means that the commensuration of man's soul with the body which he has in life remains in his soul when the body perishes; so that personal survival is a basic demand of the human spirit.

The teaching of the Angelic Doctor is further developed by his observations on the acts of the man's soul. Those operations alone endure into the next life which are not exercised through the instrumentality of material organs. Such, of course, are the functions of intellect and will. As long as the human soul is united to the body, its rational operations are conditioned by the data of sense, as experience attests. But when it is separated from matter in death, it takes on a new mode of operation, which accords with its new mode of existence. Under the altered conditions of its being, the functions of agent intellect are also altered. Then, says Aquinas, the task of agent intellect will be, not to abstract intelligible speci from phantasms, but to supply the *virtus intelligendi* or nec sary stimulant which pushes possible intellect into action— action that results in understanding, through the medium species which the latter power has received from the angels

soul of man," explains Aquinas, "is on the boundary
between corporeal and incorporeal being. It dwells, as it
the fringes of time and eternity. It approaches the
receding from the lowest. When, then, it shall have
separated from the body, it will be perfectly assimilated
to the [angelic] substances that exist apart, and will receive influence abundantly. And so, though the mode
of which we presently employ, according to the
conditions of our earthly life, is destroyed with the destruction
of the body, it will be replaced by another and more perfect
mode of understanding."

x

Origin and Destiny of the Human Body

There is the further problem of the origin and destiny of
man's body, which can be treated here only in the briefest
fashion. The problem has its scientific and philosophic aspects.

A. ORIGIN OF MAN'S BODY

With regard to its origin, the human body has a double history: the one ontogenetic or individual; the other phylogenetic
or racial. There is really no difficulty about its ontogenetic
origin. It is the story of the organism's development *in utero*,
and it begins with the act of conception. The difficulties arise
when we come to discuss its phylogenetic beginnings. The
scientist tells us that there are evidences which point to the
evolution of the human body from a lower type of animal body.
These evidences are found, notably, in the fields of anatomical
analogues, genetics, embryonic recapitulations, and fossil remains. Their cumulative force is strong enough to establish a
presumption of the truth of evolution. The philosopher, especially if he is working in the tradition of Aristotle, finds no
inherent repugnance in this view. The modern Thomist, for

example, may cite the position of Aquinas who holds for the possibility of an evolution within the dimensions of matter—in which the bodies of animals could be included—leading up to and preparing for the creation and infusion of the human soul.

It is certain that matter antedated the appearance of the first rational form. It is also certain that a whole series of animal organisms antedated the appearance of the first man. Accordingly, it is possible that nature may have acted in a dispositive way—easily understood to include an evolutionary process within the animal kingdom—tempering and modifying matter so as to make it a suitable subject for the first human soul. Whether or not such a process actually took place remains for the scientist to say. In any case, its establishment as an historical fact can in no wise impugn the Thomistic principle of dispositive action on the part of nature. On the contrary, such a principle favors the idea of evolution. To be sure, Aquinas had no scientific evidence that man's body evolved; and so he committed himself to the theory that the body of the first human being was produced immediately by God. Nevertheless, the Thomistic principle which we have just cited would certainly allow us to accept the notion of an animal history for man's body.*

B. DESTINY OF THE HUMAN BODY

Regarding the human body's final destiny, science has little to say beyond the general proclamation of matter's essential indestructibility. The law of conservation presents no obstacle to the idea of a future reorganization of elements such as the human body requires. All this, however, is merely negative, so far as our corporeal resurrection is concerned, since there is nothing in the nature of matter which demands that it be reinformed with a principle of life. The account which philosophy gives us of the soul, on the other hand, is quite different, since there is something in the nature of the human entelechy which cries out for a reunion with the body.

The arguments are already familiar to us, though they have been employed in another direction. First, the human soul requires a body for its full perfection, that is, for the complete exercise of all its powers; and this requirement is born of its very nature, being rooted in the essence of the soul. Second, the body is the natural instrument of the soul in the accomplishment of good and evil. It should, therefore, share in the rewards and punishments which will be alloted to the soul in the life to come. Third, man is a microcosmos, a creature of two worlds. He is the natural link between the universe of matter and the universe of spirit, a link which would be missing from the total chain of reality if there were no resurrection of the body. The ultimate destiny of the human body, then, must be found in a future reunion with the human soul.[c]

READINGS FROM AQUINAS

On the subsistent nature of the human soul:
   Summa Theologica, part I, question 75, article 2.
On the simplicity of the human soul:
   Contra Gentiles,   book II, chapter 49.
On the manner of the human soul's presence in the body:
   Contra Gentiles,   book II, chapter 72.
On the origin of the human soul:
   Summa Theologica, part I, question 90, articles 1–3.
   Contra Gentiles,   book II, chapters 85–87.
On the time of the human soul's origin:
   Summa Theologica, part I, question 90, article 4.
   Contra Gentiles,   book II, chapters 81, 83, 84, and 89.
   De Potenia Dei,   question 3, articles 9 and 10.
On the destiny of the human soul:
   Summa Theologica, part I, question 75, article 6.
   Contra Gentiles,   book II, chapters 55 and 79.

On the separated soul's knowledge:
   Summa Theologica, part I, question 89.
   Contra Gentiles,   book II, chapter 81.
On the origin of man's body:
   Summa Theologica, part I, question 91, article 2.
On the destiny of man's body:
   Contra Gentiles,   book IV, chapters 79 and 86.

CLARIFICATIONS

(a)

Manner of soul's presence in the body

"Since the soul is united to the body as its form," says Aquinas, "it must necessarily be in the whole body, and in each part thereof. For, it is not an accidental form, but the substantial form of the body. Now, the substantial form perfects not only the whole, but also each part of the whole. Because a whole consists of parts, the form of a whole which does not give existence to each of its material parts, is a form consisting of composition and order, such as the form of a house; and a form of this kind is accidental. But, the soul is a substantial form; and so it must be the form and actuality, not only of the whole, but also of each part. Therefore, on the withdrawal of the soul, we do not speak of an animal or a man unless equivocally, as we speak of a painted animal or a stone animal; and the same is true of the hand, eye, tissues, bones, and so on, as the Philosopher says in the second book [412 b] of his *Treatise on the Soul:* so that, on the withdrawal of the soul, no part of the body retains its proper action; although that which retains its species, retains the action of the species. But actuality is in that which it actuates: wherefore, the soul must be in the whole body, and in each part thereof.

"That it is entire in each part thereof may be concluded from this, that since a whole is that which is divided into parts, there are three kinds of totality, corresponding to three kinds of division: first, the whole which is divided into quantitative parts, as a whole line, or a whole body; second, the whole which is divided into logical and essential parts, as a thing defined is divided into the parts of a definition, and a composite into matter and form; third, the whole which is potential, or divided into virtual parts.

"Since, however, the soul has no quantitative totality, either essentially, or accidentally, it is enough to say that the whole soul is in each part of the body, by a totality of perfection and of essence, but not by a totality of power. For, it is not in each part of the body with regard to each of its powers; but with regard to sight, it is in the eye; and with regard to hearing, it is in the ear; and so forth. We must, moreover, observe that since the soul requires a variety of parts, its relation to the whole is not the same as its relation to the parts; for to the whole it is compared primarily and essentially, as to its proper and proportionate perfectible; but to the parts, secondarily, inasmuch as they are ordained to the whole."

(b)

Brute souls are not immortal

"Sensations and the consequent operations of the sensitive soul," as Aquinas says, "are evidently accompanied by change in the body. Thus, in the act of vision, the pupil of the eye is affected by a reflexion of color; and so with the other senses. Hence it is clear that the sensitive soul has no *per se* operations of its own, and that every operation of the sensitive soul belongs to the composite. Wherefore, we conclude that, as the souls of brute animals have no *per se* operations, they are not subsistent. For, the operation of anything follows the mode of its being."

(c)

Simplicity and immortality

I have made no reference in the text to the proof from simplicity which is sometimes cited in establishing the immortality of the human soul. Such an argument, strictly speaking, is of value only as a corollary of the argument from subsistence. Thus, one might say that all substantial forms are simple, in the sense that they lack quantitative and entitative parts. All that would follow from the simple nature of man's soul, then, is this: that if it were to vanish from the sum total of the actual, its disappearance would be strictly instantaneous. The fact is, of course, that it cannot cease to exist, but is obliged, by a law inherent in its very being, to go on living after its separation from the body.

(d)

The desire to live forever

As Aquinas tells us: "Everything naturally aspires to existence after its own manner. Now, in things that have knowledge, desire ensues upon knowledge. The senses indeed do not know existence, except under the conditions of here and now, whereas intellect apprehends existence absolutely, and for all time; so that everything that has an intellect naturally desires to exist forever. But, a natural desire cannot be in vain. Therefore, every intellectual substance is incorruptible."

(e)

Endowments of man's resurrected body

According to Aquinas and the teaching of all Christian philosophers, the bodies of the just will have four special gifts after the resurrection: first, *impassibility*, so that they will no longer be subject to suffering or animal wants; second, *subtlety*, so that they will be able to penetrate other bodies; third, *agility*, so that they will act swiftly and surely at the command of the intellectual powers; fourth, *clarity*, so that their whole mass will be lighted up with a kind of spiritual splendor.

BOOK THREE

THE MODERNS

CHAPTER THIRTEEN

EPILOGUE

MODERN PSYCHOLOGY AND THE THOMISTIC SYNTHESIS

i

Introduction

My purpose in writing an epilogue is not to give a history of modern scientific psychology. That has already been done in several excellent manuals. Rather, I should like to suggest that the principles of the Thomistic synthesis provide a basic set of tools for working over and measuring the value of the data of experimentation and scientific observation. More specifically, I have in mind to show how the fundamental views of Aquinas on the nature of man can be linked up organically with the work that is being done today in our psychological laboratories and clinics.

To accomplish this end, it is necessary to point out, at least in a general way, the different lines of research that have been developed in the schools of modern psychology. By this method I believe it can be shown that the philosophic outlook of the Angelic Doctor has a real bearing on the problems investigated by the experimenter and the clinician. This bearing or relationship is established at two points in the programs of scientific psychology: first, at the beginning, where the philosophic approach furnishes certain directive principles as to how investigative work shall be prosecuted; second, at the end, where the same outlook supplies further criteria as to how the results of investigation shall be interpreted.

To illustrate: it should be clear to the scientist *preinvestiga-tively* that man is an essential composition of soul and body. By this we mean that the relation which obtains between the psychic and somatic parts of human nature, or, more simply, between soul and its material substrate, is substantial in character. Acceptance of this principle will give the true perspective not only on the scope and content of scientific analysis, but also on the proper methods of attacking the phenomenal area of human nature. Similarly, it should be obvious to the scientist *postinvestigatively* that human thinking and human willing are irreducible to purely sensitive acts. Acceptance of this principle will save him from the error of identifying the abstract insights and volitional impulses of man with the sensations and passions of the animal.

ii

Relation of Thomistic Psychology to Modern Scientific Psychology

A. THE BIRTH OF PSYCHOLOGY AS A SCIENCE

In his monumental work on the *Origins of Contemporary Psychology*, Désiré Mercier indicated, once and for all, the position which philosophy must occupy in reference to contemporary psychology. This book is indispensable to one who would understand the philosophic milieu in which the science of psychology was born. Mercier was admirably equipped to write such a book. He was thoroughly familiar, through long years of study, with all the fields of the traditional philosophy. He was also equally at home in the experimental laboratory and the intricate techniques of psychological investigation. No one could better discern, therefore, the various philosophic tendencies that manifested themselves in the systems which divided scientific psychology from the beginning.

The pioneer work of Wilhelm Wundt and Gustav Fechner, some three quarters of a century ago, laid down the general lines along which psychological investigation was to advance. These men not only applied the methods proper to physiology, but invented other methods more adequate to the analysis of conscious phenomena. They constructed a new discipline to which the somewhat equivocal name of "psychophysiology" was attached. How significant the title was of clashing philosophic tendencies, Wundt himself perhaps did not realize. But in it Mercier saw the ancient conflict of two irreconcilable points of view: first, extreme positivism, which sought to make a god of matter; second, extreme idealism, which apotheosized spirit, and was bound to put in its appearance in answer to the claims of pure natural science. With a genius tempered by the common-sense philosophy of Aquinas, Mercier could clearly distinguish between the fruits of objective analysis and the subjective interpretation which Wundt put on his own experimental findings. Thus, the great Louvain scholar could accept the data of the laboratory and at the same time proclaim a definition of psychology that was strictly in accord with his Thomistic training.

B. ESTABLISHMENT OF THE WUNDTIAN TRADITION

The very philosophic nature of the perennial psychology furnishes a framework of synthesis and an ultimate point of reference for the factual offerings of the scientist. Its balanced dualistic view of man, deriving from the principle of substantial relationship between body and soul, is the only satisfactory norm by which to investigate, set in order, and pass final judgment upon the results of scientific research. How, except on a basis of such intimate union, are we to account for the demonstrable connections between mind and matter? Despite its factual value, the work of Wundt was vitiated by false philo-

sophic prejudices. The strange wedding of incompatible tendencies, manifest in his writings, was possible only to a period
that had been heavily impregnated with a long tradition of
idealism, but which was pulled just as strongly in a positivistic
direction by the enormous development and successes of the
experimental sciences.

Such was the background against which Wundt projected
his vast programs of research in psychophysiology. If, as
Mercier points out, he could have disengaged his mind from
the grip of false metaphysical premises, inherited from his
Cartesian forebears; if he could have rid himself of his Kantian
notions of substance, and freely followed the implications
which his own researches imposed upon him, he would have
been led logically to the hylomorphic position of the Aristotelians. Certainly, he never could have limited the subject matter of psychology to the investigation of the facts of consciousness. Moreover, there is little doubt that he would have
accepted, in all its richness and exuberance of meaning, the
traditional notion of soul as the first actuality of living matter,
the ultimate source of all man's vegetative, sensitive, and
rational operations. This is the only empirically evolved concept which can give shape and substance to the phenomena of
human life. But Wundt was never quite able to master the
idea. In spite of its unsound metaphysical bias, however, the
psychology of the eminent Leipzig investigator represents a
definite counterattack on the position that one must commit
oneself either to a philosophy of pure matter or to a philosophy
of pure mind—as though no other interpretation of human
nature were admissible. Indeed, the Wundtian psychology
may be said to have inaugurated a movement which, con-
sciously or unconsciously, is decidedly sympathetic toward a
revival of Aristotelianism.

C. MAJOR PHILOSOPHIC TRENDS IN PSYCHOLOGY

Perhaps it will not be out of place at this juncture to make an observation on the significance of the important philosophic trends in psychology since the beginning. These are, mainly, three: idealism, positivism, and a critically moderate realism. The first represents the spirit of Plato; the second, that of Democritus; the third, that of Aristotle. In their final analysis, all three positions are epistemological attitudes. According to the idealist, only mind is real. According to the positivist, only matter is real. Only mind, therefore, or only matter, are valid objects of knowledge. In terms of the philosophy of nature, and more particularly, the philosophy of human nature, man is nothing but mind, or man is nothing but matter. In the first case, we have extreme formalism, which is the position of the idealist. In the second case, we have extreme materialism, which is the position of the positivist. Now, there are two ways in which the elements of idealism and positivism can be combined, so far as the philosophy of human nature is concerned: first, by the Platonic doctrine of accidental union between mind and matter; second, by the Aristotelian doctrine of substantial union between mind and matter. The modern Cartesian, with his insoluble problem of the body-soul relationship, is a sample of our Platonic heritage. His psychology is grounded on the principles of psychophysical parallelism. The modern Thomist, on the other hand, represents the Aristotelian tradition. His psychology is founded on the principles of hylomorphism. Both Fechner and Wundt, it should be noted, were psychophysical parallelists.

D. PSYCHOLOGY A STUDY OF HUMAN NATURE

Far from being invalidated by the work of the scientist, the basic principles on which Aristotle and Aquinas framed their analysis of man are emerging with new depth and vigor when confronted with the data of phenomenal investigation. More than ever before, we realize today that the observed facts of consciousness must be correlated with the physiology of human life if they are to be correctly understood. Furthermore, from serious reflection on the content and meaning of these same experimental data, it is obvious that the mechanistic concept of the soul as a property of cortical substance, or the Cartesian notion of it as an immaterial entity whose whole nature is to think, must be ruled out. Ideas of this sort simply will not fit the facts. If any solid advance is to be made in the field of psychophysical analysis, it must proceed on the principle that the soul of man, like the first actuality of all other cosmic creatures, is a form immersed in matter.

This being the case, psychology cannot limit itself to the phenomena of consciousness, but must extend its technical observation to the *whole man:* his acts, his powers, his habits, and his entire personality. It must be a science of human nature if it is to be a science at all. It must be a science of man as man if it is to contribute to the advance of knowledge by its investigation of a special area of reality. Assured against both excess and defect by the correctness of its methodological principles, it need set no boundaries to the daring of its plans for research. With its subject matter accurately fixed upon, it can proceed with assurance to the construction of proper techniques for attacking its special problems. In addition, it can so divide the labor of research as to secure, from all sides, a real coöperative analysis, and thus a balanced development, of all its particular problems. From this point on it is the task of philosophy, utilizing the data of scientific experience as well as common-sense observation, to establish the ultimate *ratio* of human nature, and to show forth the fixed ontological principles that underlie man's mobile and sensible being.

iii

The Evolution of Modern Psychology

A. THE PSYCHOPHYSIOLOGISTS

Even before Wundt's long and industrious career was closed, a movement was noted among certain of his followers which foreshadowed a new way of envisaging the field of psychology. The secret ambition of the Leipzig experimentalist was to construct a science of mind which would have as exact a pattern of measurement and classification as any other natural science. He left no stone unturned, no avenue unexplored, to accomplish his end; and, in collaboration with his pupils, was able, finally, to arrange the results of his enormous researches into something like a systematic whole. The goal of the Wundtians was twofold: first, to determine the laws of all the complex phenomena that either condition or accompany mental life; second, to investigate the structural contents of consciousness itself.

The first part of the program was really nothing more than applied physiology. Here, as might be expected, the effects of scientific inquiry were extremely gratifying. The second part of the program, on the other hand, proved unusually barren and inadequate. Here the data seemed peculiarly rebellious to methodic treatment. Wundt concluded that it was not possible to know, directly and by positive technique, the higher processes of conscious life. Thus, the meaning of intellect and will and their nonquantitative acts remained for him a closed book.

B. THE INTROSPECTIONISTS

It was the classical work of Hermann Ebbinghaus on memorial functions that paved the way for new researches, showing how the immediate introspective analysis of the operations of consciousness provides us with a wider range of data, and more complete information about man's rational nature, than the indirect study of physiological correlates. From this strategic point of departure, the road was short to a scientifically controlled method of self-analysis. Hence, when Oswald Külpe and his Würzburg school developed a systematic way of recording the facts of introspection, and demonstrated its empirical use within the area of conceptual and volitional processes, psychology had made a distinct advance in its claims for scientific recognition.

One thing Külpe made abundantly clear: that the investigation of the subject matter of psychology could not continue along the same lines on which sciences like physics and chemistry had been built. It must occupy its own special position in the world of knowledge. This position it can share with no other branch of natural science: first, because of the uniqueness of its method, which allows for the employment of an introspective technique; second, because of the character of its subject matter, which falls partly in the field of science and partly in the field of philosophy.

Of course, the use of self-observation must be exact and experimentally governed if its records are to have a universal value. To deny, however, the validity of these records and of the conclusions drawn from them is to make psychology simply a history of individuals. Indeed, if introspection is illegitimate as an investigative method, then psychology cannot possibly be anything more than an offshoot of physiology. It can hope for little or no enlightenment, for example, on the problems of human thinking and human willing—problems of capital importance for the analysis of human nature. Moreover, if the subject matter of psychology is simultaneously scientific and philosophic in kind, then the science of mind must be more closely related to philosophy than is any other natural science.

Wundt was a naturalist in psychology. Deeply immersed in his physiological studies, he was prone to undervalue the significance of mental functions for the life of man. He was more interested in somatic correlates than in the conscious acts with which such correlation takes place. In fact, he was willing to abandon altogether the idea that psychic processes, such as volition, can be causally connected with bodily acts, rather than disturb the order and rigidly determined economy of physical operations. Külpe, on the contrary, exhibited a decided preference for the psychic features of man's life. For him, thinking was a purely psychological phenomenon, something to be studied in and for itself and described, if possible, in purely psychological terms. To secure this end, the naïve *Selbstbeobachtung* of Wundt—simply having an experience and later recording it—was not sufficient. In the hands of Külpe and his pupils, self-observation became controlled observation. The fertility of the method has been proved over and over again by the work of the Würzburgers. It is sufficient to mention here the splendid researches of Karl Bühler on ideational processes, and of Narziss Ach on the determining tendencies of the will-act.

C. THE PHENOMENALISTS

The third dominant strain to be noted in the development of modern psychology is phenomenological. It appeared very strongly in the work of Carl Stumpf. Now the attention of the investigator is directed toward an analysis of conscious experiences, precisely as these experiences occur to the subject in their virginal immediacy and without implications. This method, it may be said, is a propaedeutic to all the natural sciences, but especially to the science of mind. Because of its demands on pure consciousness, phenomenology is closely related to introspectionism. It owes a great deal to the intentional psychology of Franz Brentano who was the first to bring out forcibly the important distinction between the contents of consciousness and its functions. Edmund Husserl, whose name is intimately linked with this phase in the evolution of the science of mind, describes phenomenological psychology as a study of the types and forms of intentional psychology.

iv

Contemporary Trends in Scientific Psychology

A. HISTORICAL APPROACH

Significantly enough, most of the story of modern psychology thus far related has been confined to the ranks of German scholars. In France and America, the Wundtian concept of psychology as a pure science, on a par with any other positive science, continued to have its vigorous supporters. But, whereas the naturalistic phase encountered no serious obstacles from the early American investigators, it was destined to meet the sternest sort of opposition from the French. Thus, Henri Bergson and Alfred Binet were its avowed enemies from the start. The work of Binet, in particular, was noteworthy because of its basic resemblance, both in content and in spirit, to the labors of Külpe in Germany. With the exception of Charles Spearman's efforts in England, no outstanding contributions were made by the British psychologists to the researches of Wundt and Külpe.

The accomplishments of Spearman in the field of factorial analysis, like those of Binet on intelligence, are more in the temper and tradition of the Würzburg school than in the Wundtian manner. Spearman is significant especially for his recognition of the need of building up a science of mind on a basis of sound philosophic principles, a feeling shared by the American, Thomas Verner Moore, who has done much to promote the ideas of Spearman in the United States. The factorialist, whether he admits it or not, is really a faculty psychologist. This is true of every investigator in the field of psychometrics. He is working in the best Aristotelian and Thomistic tradition, since the ground he covers is concerned with the acts and powers, or the performances and abilities, of man.

The early history of scientific psychology in Italy reveals no marked originality of views. Federico Kiesow followed the methods of his teacher Wundt with marked fidelity and with no better results. Sante de Sanctis likewise organized huge amounts of research work on the principle that psychology is as objectively scientific as any other natural discipline. Vittoris Benussi was a student of the Austrian school of Graz, and his experimental programs were designed to clarify the different classes of elementary mental experiences, according to the ground plan drawn up by Alexius Meinong, founder of the school. Most important of all, Agostino Gemelli defended the legitimacy and value of the experimental method in psychology, recognized introspection as an indispensable tool in the analysis of mental phenomena, and insisted on the need of rehabilitating the Aristotelian concept of soul if one is to arrive at a complete doctrine of psychological life.

B. POSTWAR DEVELOPMENTS

What we have said up to this point is a fairly comprehensive summary of the trends in scientific psychology before 1914. After the first World War (during which research was directed, in the main, toward practical ends) we witness a lively resumption of interest in psychological studies. The outlines of three distinct systems now make their appearance: the gestalt school, whose principal exponents were Max Wertheimer, Wolfgang Köhler, and Kurt Koffka; the eidetic school, represented by Erich Jaensch; and the behavioristic school, with John B. Watson at its head. Aligned historically with the behaviorists is the Russian school of reflexology, with which the names of Vladimir Bechterev and Ivan Pavlov are prominently associated.

A great deal of experimental research has been done under the aegis of these three systems, but the systems themselves, as theoretic constructions, have shown innumerable weaknesses and partialities. Other schools, voicing their dissatisfaction with the present modes and areas of investigation, and particularly with the restricted character of such investigation, have begun to put forward claims for admittance into the circle of psychology's official family. The personalistic doctrines of William Stern, for instance, seem to be gaining ground in several quarters. They are significant for the reason, already alluded to, that they would orientate the researcher once more toward a whole-making concept of the subject matter of psychology. The same observation may be made on the totality school of Felix Kruger and Otto Klem, and on the *Verständnispsychologie* or understanding psychology of Eduard Spranger and his teacher Wilhelm Dilthey. Such views, however, may turn out to be holistic in name rather than in fact.

v

The Contemporary Schools of Experimental Psychology

A. THE GESTALT SCHOOL

If there is one psychological system in the contemporary milieu which may be said to occupy a position of pre-eminence over other systems, it is the gestalt school. How long this superiority will endure is difficult to predict; yet, its birth could have been foretold as a logical reaction to the excessive associationalistic tendencies in the theories of Wundt and his followers. In outlook, gestaltism is squarely set against two false attitudes in psychology: first, the presumption that a science of mind can be founded simply on the analysis of conscious states; second, the pretense that conscious life can be conceived of as a mosaic of elementary sensations, images, and feelings. The first position is defended in the content psychology of Wundt; the second, in the structural psychology of his pupil, Edward B. Titchener.

The present successes of the gestalt theory can be understood only if we remember that, before the beginning of the present century, psychological phenomena were theorized about and interpreted mainly in terms of physiology. Quite naturally, much was said and written about the quantities and types of sensations, since it is within this fertile area that psychology makes its closest observable contact with physiology. The experimental work of the gestaltists changed all this by shifting the axis of analysis from sensations to perceptions.

Out of the bosom of long and tedious inquiries, especially on the processes of vision, was born the idea that the very first datum of psychological experience is that of *Gestalt* or form. Conscious life is primitively patterned into wholes, each whole having its own degree of configuration. This awareness of form or of patterned experience is an immediate datum, and nothing antedates it in the psychological order. Accordingly, sensations do not exist. Neither is there any need for postulating an active attention whereby the discrete units of sense experience are brought together, selected, and organized. This is all accomplished by the *Gestalt* which is fitted upon experience natively.

One thinks at once, in such an explication, of the a priori forms of Kant; but the promulgation of another complementary principle eliminates, theoretically at any rate, the prospect of making the form-school an offshoot of Kant's idealism. This second principle states that psychological processes are isomorphic with physiological processes, which means that they have the same construction as the processes in the central nervous system. Going a step further, it is likely, according to Köhler, that neurological processes are patterned on a similar configuration of events in physical nature. If this is so, it is hard to see how the gestalt theory escapes the charge of out-and-out materialism, since perceptual functions are reduced, in their final analysis, to a schema of purely cosmic forces.

B. THE EIDETIC SCHOOL

In spite of the vigorous efforts of its founder, the eidetic psychology of Erich Jaensch and his Marburg school has very much declined in general appreciation. Eidetic imagery is an undoubted phenomenon of youthful experience. The fact that it is of such wide incidence to childhood makes it of great interest, of course, to the psychologist. *Anschauungsbilder* are both spontaneous in origin and rich in the delineation of detail. Their reproduction is always easy and immediate. An eidetic individual is one who possesses the ability to project unusually lifelike images of the eidetic sort. Such an ability represents an excessive form of phantasmal function. Its unusualness becomes more pronounced as the individual grows into adulthood.

On a basis of observed facts in the eidetic field, Jaensch has constructed a whole system of psychology. He is concerned, especially, with the determination of personality types which he has arranged in two categories, to correspond with the types of eidetic image manifested by the subject in his perception of the external world. These are: basedowoid or B type, related to Basedow's disease, which is a toxic condition of the thyroid gland; and, tetanoid or T type, related to tetany, which is a dysfunction of the parathyroid gland. In the first grouping, the eidetic image is amenable to control, behaving like the ordinary products of imagination and memory; in the second, the eidetic image has more permanent features, since its form cannot be changed at the command of will.

There is a rough resemblance, in these two classifications, to Jung's introverts and extroverts. It is, perhaps, too early to predict what may be the final value of such distinctions. In any event, the Jaenschian typology has gained no very wide recognition among students of mind. Even the author himself does not appear to have overmuch faith in its ultimate survival. Its wholesale reduction of psychological phenomena to terms of imagery is a weakness that is bound to prove fatal. From a philosophic standpoint, it is nothing more than a refined form of materialism on a par with the deterministic concepts of the gestaltists and the positivistic notions of the Wundtians.

C. THE BEHAVIORISTIC SCHOOL

As its name indicates, the behavioristic school makes external conduct the object of psychological investigation. It is founded on the principle that, for a complete analysis of human nature, one need simply know how man responds to the presentation of stimuli. Accordingly, the less stock set on consciousness the more possibility there is of a completely objective and scientific record of human behavior. The best material for research, therefore, is not the activity of the human adult, but that of the child or the animal. Here the subject is not conscious of being conscious, and the pattern of behavior is not so likely to be twisted and distorted out of normal shape.

In practice, behaviorism is simply a physiological discipline. It is closely related, in its origins, to the functionalism of John Dewey, who was the first American to insist on the rôle of reflex arcs in the adjustment of the organism to its surroundings. Man himself, according to Dewey, is just a function or a process. Concepts of this sort are at once suggestive of the phenomenalism of Hume. Also linked up with the behavioristic position is the response psychology of Edward L. Thorndike and his associates, for whom the operations of human learning are explained in terms of stimulus-response bonds. Walter S. Hunter, Karl S. Lashley, Edward C. Tolman, and Albert P. Weiss are some of the better known experimentalists who have carried on the work of Watson. Animal studies, pursued by Köhler, Lashley, Robert M. Yerkes, and Joseph A. Gengerelli, have contributed to the development of comparative psychology. The fundamental outlook of all the behavioristic schools, so far as the analysis of human nature is concerned, is simply a masked materialism, resulting in either the rationalization of the animal or the derationalization of man.

We might add, here, that the field of research for the gestaltists is also largely given over to animal psychology. In this respect, they are very much like the behaviorists. The two groups are further alike in their mutual rebellion against the overtechnical kind of introspection which was practiced by Titchener and the structuralists. But, most important of all, both schools find a kinship in their mutual assumption, either explicit or implicit, of a mere difference of degree between the achievements of man and beast. Thus, the behaviorist applies his concept of conditioned reflexes to the explication of human and animal conduct without distinction. Similarly, the gestaltist employs his theory of perceptual wholes to resolve the intricacies of human and animal learning alike. The two systems differ to this extent: that the behaviorist appears to be primarily interested in the sensorimotor foundations of human behavior and in the biological rôle of the emotions, whereas the gestaltist is mainly concerned with configurations in the visual field and with problem solving. The latter is more ingenious in devising his experiments, more refined and elaborate in constructing his neurological hypotheses, than the former. Yet the physiological bases of the two schools would seem to be the same. Köhler, for example, recognizes the studies of Lashley on neural mechanisms as basic to his own theories.

D. RÉSUMÉ

These, in the main, are the leading systems of psychological research. Even so brief a survey as we have made is sufficient to indicate the distressing difficulties under which the science of psychology, as a whole, is laboring. The root of the trouble, as I think, lies in the failure of the investigators to appreciate the proper scope of their discipline. They cannot agree on the subject matter of psychology. Apparently, they have overlooked or forgotten the fact that, in order to build up a true science of mind, one must study, not this or that particular function of consciousness to the exclusion of other data, not somatic processes as a substitute for psychic processes, not the evolutionary tendencies of the organism or its motor responses to stimuli, but *man*, in all his various manifestations.

I would go a step further and say that the failure of the investigators is also due to their inability to appreciate the true nature of the subject matter of research. On what grounds, for example, does the behaviorist proceed *as if* man were merely an animal? Or by what antecedent evidence does the structuralist or the gestaltist proceed *as if* all man's conscious activities were reducible to a complexus of sensations or perceptions? ich methodological principles may be quite legitimate for the hysiologist, or even for the animal psychologist; but, for the tudent of human nature, they are wholly false and unwarranted.

If it is admitted, as I think we can admit, that psychology has the potentialities of becoming a well-established science, this does not mean that it can do so without the aid of philosophy, or in spite of such aid. Aristotle could have foretold the confusion and polemic of modern psychology had he known the false metaphysical premises with which the majority of investigators begin their studies, or the equally false metaphysical conclusions with which many end their labors. Mere acquaintance with the facts of the laboratory does not warrant the making of philosophic pronouncements on the nature of man; yet acquaintance with the nature of man is required if the observer of the facts is to understand them properly, even in their scientific aspects, and if he is to exercise the correct perspective upon them in their relation to the whole of psychological knowledge.

vi

The Contemporary Schools of Nonexperimental Psychology

A. THE PSYCHOANALYTIC SCHOOL

The leading criticism of the official systems of psychology has come from the psychoanalytic school. Now we step from the laboratory into the clinic; and while the method of gathering data is no longer experimental in character, yet it is employed over a field of observation that is wider and better calculated to give us the synolistic or whole-making approach which psychology needs today. The great merit of Sigmund Freud and his school is that of having shown the real importance of unconscious mental processes and their influence on conscious activities, particularly in the orientation of the individual toward a normal goal of life. Of course, other psychologist had made investigative studies of these unconscious phenomena. Jean Charcot, for example, and his disciples, Pier Janet and Theodule Ribot, contributed several valuable yses on obsessions and hysterias. But Freud was the first to show the intrinsic meaning of unconscious processes for psychological pattern of individual life.

In order to clarify the associations between the manifest

and latent contents of mind, it was necessary to study a wide expanse of pathological data. The abnormal, in mental phenomena, had been decidedly neglected by the official psychologists. Freud found it a fertile region for exploration. On a basis of certain observed facts, he built a psychological system which, in its roots, is simply a revival of the old associationistic doctrine, with instincts or instinctive urges supplying the rôle once played by sensations and images. Freudianism, however, is not merely a theory of instincts, or a branch of psychiatric science, or a method of probing the depths of the unconscious. More seriously, it is proposed as a philosophy of life, and a philosophy of the grossest materialism. In fact, toward the end of his career, the writings of Freud show little or no concern with psychological data, as such.

Psychoanalysis has had its ardent defenders, but it has also given rise to dissident schools. The foremost of these latter are the systems of Carl Jung and Alfred Adler. Jung's name is linked up with the beginnings of type psychology, just as Adler's name is prominent in the development of character psychology. The very existence of psychoanalysis and its derivative disciplines is proof that the official psychologists have been too narrow in setting the boundaries of investigation, either within the area of consciousness exclusively, or within the dimensions of objective behavior exclusively.

B. THE CRITERIOLOGICAL SCHOOL

Obviously allied to the theories of Freud, Jung, and Adler is the rising science of individual differences, which some investigators, like Emil Utitz and Ernst Kretschmer, regard as a completely established and autonomous discipline. It is sometimes referred to as the psychology of individual criteria, or, more simply, as criteriology. The study of such criteria has been given great impulse in the writings of Ludwig Klages and

Eduard Spranger, both of whom have attempted to set up a philosophic superstructure on their scientific work. The results represent a rather unsuccessful adventuring into the realms of idealism. They are interesting, nevertheless, as symptomatic of a basic need, which investigators generally are showing, of an ultimate interpretation for the phenomena of human nature.

The point about the whole matter is not that a science of psychology cannot be integrated with a philosophy of psychology, but that the science of psychology is one sort of discipline, and the philosophy of psychology is something entirely different. To neglect this distinction is to fall either into a materialistic position, like that of the behaviorist or the Freudian; or into an idealistic point of view, like that of the criteriologists, Dilthey and Spranger; or into an exaggerated dualism, like the phenomenalistic attitude of Husserl, Meinong, and their followers. On the other hand, to say that scientific psychology has no organic connection with the philosophy of psychology is to picture the former as a mere summary of facts, or an enumeration of accidental relationships. But man, who is the proper object of psychological investigation, simply cannot be studied in this unreal manner.

vii

Present Position of the Scientific Schools

A. VALUE OF THE INVESTIGATIVE METHOD

So multiple and changing are the manifestations of human life that it is impossible to trust to a single method or a single system for an analysis of these manifestations. The techniques of psychophysiology can still be employed to advantage and yield new results, especially in determining more explicitly the profound intercommunications between psychic and somatic activities. The methods of direct experimentation, wherein the introspective tool is cautiously used, also will yield further insights, particularly in the field of purely psychic processes, such as thought and volition. Again, phenomenal observation of the type practiced by the gestaltist can, if properly developed, widen our knowledge of perceptual functions, as a point of departure for the investigation of conceptual functions. The objective methods of the behaviorist, too, will extend our grasp of the mechanisms of external reaction, of reflex movements, and of the patterns of motor conduct. Finally, the study of the unconscious by the clinical techniques of the psychoanalyst will clarify more and more the import of man's carefully concealed mental abnormalties. The thing to bear in mind, always, is that no single group of experiments, no analysis of individual operations, no exclusive use of one method, will give us a complete picture of human nature. Moreover, it must be remembered that no amount of factual information which is not properly ordered and integrated with a true philosophic concept of man can ever serve its final purpose of being built up into a permanent science of psychology.

B. CONSTRUCTION OF A THEORETIC PSYCHOLOGY

As we examine, in retrospect, the work of the investigators, one significant point strikes us immediately. It is the fewness of the generalizations that have emerged from inductive studies. We have no theoretic psychology, in the sense that we have a theoretic physics or a theoretic chemistry. Perhaps the situation can be best expressed by asking: where are the universally recognized laws to cover such processes as sensation, perception, imagination, memory, learning, intellection, attention, association, emotional response, and volition, in the same way that universally recognized laws cover the phenomena of matter? Of course, there is an abundance of specialized information about the acts and powers of man. But, the need here is not so much for more data as for the establishment of laws on a basis of such data—laws that will be recognized in all quarters. Johannes Lindworsky, for example, has made a very commendable attempt to formulate a theoretic psychology without appealing directly to philosophic concepts. The attempt, however, does not satisfy the demands of strict theory, and the conclusions are too abstract to be of value to a humanistic science like psychology.

Indeed, the most significant generalizations that have been achieved thus far are nothing more than common-sense records of matters of public experience, to attain which no expert knowledge or instrumental technique is required. We have learned a great deal about the structure and functioning of the sense organs. The rôle of the nervous system in the activation of conscious processes is better known. The significance of the cortex in the conditioning of reflexes is better understood. The part played by body resonances in the operation of the animal appetites has been clarified. The effects on mental acuity of fatigue, glandular secretions, and drugs of different sorts, have been carefully studied. But, in the last analysis, these are all topics of physiological investigation. Few, if any, purely psychological descriptions have been contributed by the investigator to the content of scientific psychology, just as few, if any, successful attempts have been made to formulate a system of theoretic principles as a working basis for future psychological research.

C. NEED OF THE ANTHROPOLOGICAL APPROACH

Where the schools have erred, of course, is in extending to the whole of man's psychological life what is demonstrably true of only a part of it. We have already noted how, for the behaviorist, reflex action explains everything; for the gestaltist, perceptual patterns, with isomorphic structures in the nervous system, tell the whole story of man's conscious life; for the disciples of the Marburg school, the eidetic image is the supreme fact in the development of human personality; for the Freudian, the interplay of instincts is the final principle of all human achievement. But, reflexes, percepts, images, and instincts are only particular problems in the whole of man's psychological life. What we need today, as Aquinas would indicate, is really less of psychology and more of anthropology, using the term "anthropology" in its traditional meaning to signify the study of man. For that is what psychology should be: the study of man, as man, not as a concatenation of reflexes, or a sum of perceptual configurations, or a series of imaginal processes, or a complexus of instinctive responses. Such things are simply isolated events in the history of human nature, and they have no meaning except in relation to the whole nature. Further, the study of man, as man, means the study of man as a besouled organism, or as a creature composed of matter and spirit, whose operations fall within the dimensions of scientific analysis, but whose fundamental nature is the proper study of philosophy.

Just as there is no one idea deep enough to exhaust the contents of reality, no one term or proposition which completely describes it, so there is no single formula to express, in all its richness of meaning, the notion of human nature. One representation of it is, however, more full and more exact than another. If we are looking for an idea that expresses the central aspect of philosophic psychology, then the concept of man as a creature composed of body and soul is as faultless as any. Of course, such a concept is really very complex. Accordingly, it is allowable, for the sake of clear understanding, to consider its different facets as though they were separate realities. In this way, we are justified in studying the acts, powers, and habits of man, one by one, as though they were discrete properties or accidents of human nature; but all such peripheral entities derive their significance from the fact that they are rooted in the substance of man. All, therefore, must be analyzed and interpreted, eventually, in terms of this central substance which is, itself, a composition of matter and form. From the principle of a substantial union between body and soul, therefore, as from a fountainhead, spring all the peripheral truths that complete our phenomenal analysis of man. These truths, from their position of dependency on the central principle, can touch only the accidents of man. We may designate them truths of the structural order, in the sense that powers are accidental parts of a nature; or we may call them truths of the operational order, in the sense that the movements of powers are accidental manifestations of a nature.

The point is that structures and operations do not constitute a nature but presuppose it. This being the case, it is of capital importance that we understand the fundamental constituency of man's nature before we theorize about the meaning of his attributes. Understanding his essence, we can understand the arrangement and distinction of the acts and powers that flow from his essence and exhibit it, phenomenally, to scientist and philosopher alike. Thus it becomes as wrong for the scientist as for the philosopher to say or imply that man does not share some of his acts and powers with the plant and animal kingdoms, or that he is not essentially distinct, by other acts and powers, from both these orders of being. Putting the matter more concretely, I should say that it shows greater conformity with the demands of scientific evidence to regard man as the proper subject of vegetative, sensitive, and rational functions, and to look upon his soul as the basic operational principle by which he lives, feels, and thinks, than to attempt a monistic or falsely dualistic solution of the problems of human psychology. The investigator who recognizes the human person as a substance compounded of mind and matter will find no difficulty in grasping the significance of the data which he studies in the laboratory or the clinical chambers. For one who shares with Aquinas the view that man is a synolon, made up of contrasted psychic and somatic elements, there can be no idealistic fear that psychology will end by materializing the spirit of man, just as there can be no positivistic fear that psychology will vanish into the realm of the unknowable by dematerializing the body of man.

viii

Separation of Scientific Psychology and Philosophic Psychology

A. ADVANTAGE OF SUCH A SEPARATION

Despite the fact that it was born in an atmosphere of positivism, scientific psychology has profited by its separation from the field of philosophy, just as philosophic psychology has found it to its advantage to have its phenomenal area studied by the investigator. Thus, science is kept within proper bounds, at the same time that it is supplied with principles by which to interpret its data and formulate its laws. Similarly, philosophy is restricted to the goals and methods that are appropriate to its speculative nature, at the same time that it is compelled to re-examine its teachings in the light of experimental evidence, to extend the application of its principles, and to explore the possibilities of clarifying its doctrines by modern instance and example. Every perennial philosophy has a twofold life: the eternal life of its spirit, and the temporal life of its body. Its eternal life is, of course, unchangeable, because it is the very essence or truth of it, the thing that sets it apart, at once, from all false interpretations of reality. Its temporal life, on the other hand, is changeable. It grows with the growth of time, with the slow grandeur of centuries, with the discovery of new information. This is the life that enriches itself with the achievements of science, with the creations of art, with the history of nations. Psychology, as a philosophic discipline, has such a dual life. It faces time and eternity. It looks to the metaphysician in order to see the supreme ontological meaning of the truths which it proclaims; but it also looks to the work of the investigator in order to clarify its knowledge of the principles on which it is grounded.

B. ATTITUDE OF THE PHILOSOPHER TOWARD THE SCIENTIST

Nor need the philosopher have any fear of the results of scientific inquiry. It is true that the positivists in psychology have laid their trust in the methods of empirical investigation to free their science from the incubus of the soul; but positivism is simply a mental attitude which cannot change the intrinsic character of the findings that the investigative organ brings to light. There is really no substance to the shadows that cling to the materialist's laboratory or clinic. The diffidence which some philosophers have exhibited toward the experimental method in psychology is due, not to their alarm at its being applied to immaterial phenomena like thoughts and volitions, but rather to the fact that the experimental tool is manipulated only too often by those who have no philosophic training or insight, and who, therefore, are unqualified to recognize the existence and meaning of the immaterial accomplishments of man.

ix

Final Evaluation of Modern Scientific Psychology

In concluding, let us summarize the results of our examination of the modern systems in psychology. And since we are interested primarily in correcting false attitudes, let us indicate once more, briefly, just where things have gone awry.

A. THE PROBLEM OF SUBJECT MATTER

The first mistake is in the point of view that the sole subject matter of scientific psychology is either consciousness and its phenomena, or behavior and its phenomena. Obviously, the Cartesian wedge is still doing its work effectively when it can divide investigators into such widely opposed camps. A dichotomy of this sort not only fails to recognize the difference between the psychological, as such, and the physiological; but it also fails to see that man reconciles both within the depths of his human nature. And even in the field of consciousness alone, or of behavior alone, there is the further failure to distinguish between phenomena that are rational in kind and phenomena that are simply sensitive or vegetative in character.

B. NEED OF PHILOSOPHIC CRITERIA

The second mistake is in the investigator's complete abandonment of philosophic criteria for his work. Out of this abandonment comes the loss of the precious concept of soul, and its ensuing loss of the concept of human nature. Of course, I do not mean to say that it is the scientist's business to investigate the soul or the nature of man, for these are philosophic problems. But surely, if the scientist cannot successfully prosecute his work and build up his science without a truthful knowledge about human nature, then such knowledge must be presupposed to his investigations. At any rate, he must not theorize in a way that would negate the correct philosophic analysis of man. This, however, is just what he has too often done. We are forced to conclude, therefore, that the sad state of affairs in the science of psychology today must be due, in no small measure, to bad philosophic influences. Such can be shown to be the case, historically, I believe. Thus, under the influence of Kant, on the one hand, and of Comte, on the other, the scientists have been completely bogged down by their special preferences, either for the informations of subjective consciousness alone, or for the data of objective behavior alone. And so we witness a convergence, from idealistic and positivistic streams, of concepts that mark the investigator as a false dualist, if he is not already an out-and-out materialistic monist.

With the disappearance of the notion of substance, the notion of soul vanished out of reality. This made it relatively easy to discard the idea of consciousness in favor of the idea of behavior. Without a soul, psychology is like a temple without a deity, or a home without a family spirit. Of course, phenomena constitute the proper area of investigation for the scientist, in psychology as in any other discipline. But concentration on phenomena alone, as events have shown, tends to reduce psychology to the level of pure physiology. This is true in the case of the Wundtian as well as the behaviorist, of the gestaltist as well as the response psychologist.

Moreover, the prejudice created by the extraordinary progress of the experimental sciences, as contrasted with the sterility of philosophic discussion at its worst, has filled the minds of scholars with a distrust of speculation. This attitude has been strengthened by the fact that nonpsychological sciences depend on a method that is strictly objective, whereas psychology must fall back on the data of introspection in order to resolve its major problems. The latter circumstance has led men gradually to think that the temper of psychological investigation is at basic loggerheads with any kind of external observation; with the result that they either have concentrated too much on the phenomenally conscious aspects of their subject matter, or else have given themselves up exclusively to the study of objective behavior.

C. THE HYLOMORPHIC INTERPRETATION OF HUMAN NATURE

Finally, let us urge once more the point that not every philosophy is useful to the science of psychology, but only that analysis which expounds the truth of human nature. Such, I take it, is the analysis which was formulated over two thousand years ago by Aristotle, which was subsequently taken over, refined, and developed by Aquinas, and which presently is known as the traditional psychology. This is the position which denies the idealistic creed that psychology is nothing but a philosophy of spirit; and, with equal vigor, denies the positivistic position that psychology is simply a physiological discipline. Every investigator, at some time or other, is confronted with the task of passing judgment on his work. His research programs can be marred and distorted and his conclusions invalidated by wrong philosophic premises which, wittingly or unwittingly, he has accepted as a basis of his inductive procedures.

Now, the psychologist is a student of human nature; and human nature fairly bristles with problems that require the combined efforts of the scientist and philosopher, if adequate solutions are to be reached. It is difficult to see, then, how the investigator can avoid assuming some definite philosophic attitude toward the subject matter which he is studying. In this case, the subject matter is man, regarding whom there can be but one satisfactory attitude. It is the position which recognizes in every human being, regardless of race or age, a creature possessed of soul and body; a cosmic entity made out of spirit and matter; an organism quickened with a principle of rational life; a corporeal substance that not only vegetates with the plants and senses with the animals, but also, and more importantly, reflects on its own intellectual nature, and stretches out, by its faculty of divine love, toward a Good that is supremely perfect.

READINGS

Mercier, D., *The Origins of Contemporary Psychology* (translated by W. H. Mitchell), London, Washbourne, 1918.

Müller-Freienfels, R., *The Evolution of Modern Psychology* (translated by W. Béran Wolfe), New Haven, Yale University Press, 1935.

BIBLIOGRAPHY

In citing the works of Aristotle, the divisions of the Berlin Academy edition have been used.

Captions, diagrams, and suggested readings are not to be counted in reckoning the lines of *Thomistic Psychology*.

The following abbreviations have been employed in referring to bibliographical sources:

S. T. = *Summa Theologica*
C. G. = *Contra Gentiles*
Q. D. = *Quaestiones Disputatae*
    in = commentary on
    a. = article
    b. = book
    c. = chapter
    d. = distinction
    l. = lecture
  obj. = objection
    p. = part
p. I–II = first part   of part two of *S. T.*
p. II–II = second part of part two of *S. T.*
    q. = question

CHAPTER 1: *THE PSYCHOLOGY OF ARISTOTLE*

The soul is defined as ἐντελέχεια ἡ πρώτη σώματος φυσικοῦ δυνάμει ζωὴν ἔχοντος: the first entelechy of a natural body that is potentially alive. *Entelechy* here means εἶδος (μορφή) or form; *natural body that is potentially alive* means ὕλη or matter. Just as the soul is ἐντελέχεια ἡ πρώτη in reference to matter, so matter is ὕλη ἡ πρώτη in reference to the soul.

There are three species of souls, corresponding to the three kinds of ἔμψυχα or besouled organisms: first, ψυχὴ ἡ θρεπτική or the vegetative soul; second, ψυχὴ ἡ αἰσθητική or the sensitive soul; third, ψυχὴ ἡ διανοητική or the rational soul. The rational soul is δυνάμει a sensitive soul and a vegetative soul.

The rational or dianoetic soul is defined, in its operational nature, as ᾧ ζῶμεν καὶ αἰσθανόμεθα καὶ διανοούμεθα πρώτως: that whereby we primarily live and sense and think.

Because the final purpose of vegetative life is to reproduce the parent stock, the principle of vegetative life is very properly referred to as a ψυχὴ γεννητική.

αἴσθησις means either the power or the act of an external sense. As a power it is described as τὸ δεκτικὸν τῶν αἰσθητῶν εἰδῶν ἄνευ τῆς ὕλης: a faculty

PAGE	LINE	
		capable of receiving sensible forms without their matter.
12	10–20	*De Anima:* 425b.
		In the process of sensation ἡ δὲ τοῦ αἰσθητοῦ ἐνέργεια καὶ τῆς αἰσθήσεως ἡ αὐτὴ μέν ἐστι καὶ μία: the act of the sensible object, as it impinges on the sense, and the act of the sense, as it responds to such stimulation, are one and the same reality.
12	21–25	*De Anima:* 424b.
12	25–31	*De Anima:* 418a.
		The proper object of an exterior sense is known as an ἴδιον αἰσθητόν or proper sensible.
13	1–16	*De Anima:* 413b; 421a; 422b; 423a; 434b; 435a.
		The proper objects of ἀφή or somesthetic sense are τὰ ἁπτά: the tangible qualities of bodies.
13	17–24	*De Anima:* 414b; 422a—423b; 434b.
		De Sensu et Sensato: 441a—442b.
		The proper objects of γεῦσις or gustatory sense are οἱ χυμοί: the sapid qualities of body.
13	25–29	*De Anima:* 421a—422b.
		De Sensu et Sensato: 442a—445a.
		The proper objects of ὄσφρησις or olfactory sense are τὰ ὀσφραντά: the odorous qualities of bodies.
13	30–	
14	–9	*De Anima:* 419b—420b.
		De Sensu et Sensato: 437a.
		The proper objects of ἀκοή or auditory sense are τὰ ἀκουστά: the audible qualities of bodies.
14	10–15	*De Anima:* 418a—419a.
		De Sensu et Sensato: 437a.
		The proper objects of ὄψις or visual sense are τὰ ὁρατά: the visible qualities of bodies.
14	16–	
16	–13	*De Anima:* 418a; 425a; 426b—427a.
		De Sensu et Sensato: 449a.
		De Memoria et Reminiscentia: 450a.
		De Somno et Vigilia: 455a.
		De Juventute et Senectute: 467b.

PAGE	LINE	
		The root of all the exterior senses is κοινὴ αἴσθησις or common sense. The objects of common sense are divided as follows: first, ἴδια αἰσθητά or proper sensibles; second, κοινὰ αἰσθητά or common sensibles; third, αἰσθητὰ κατὰ συμβεβηκός or incidental sensibles, *i.e.* objects that fall under the senses only *per accidens*.
16	14–	
18	–18	*De Anima:* 425b; 427b—429a; 433a—434a. *Rhetorica:* 1370a. *De Somniis:* 460b—461b. φαντασία is the power of forming φαντάσματα. It is related, etymologically, to the word "φάος" or "light." Two kinds of imaginal function are found in man: the first an act of φαντασία αἰσθητική or sensitive imagination; the second an act of φαντασία λογιστική or dianoetic imagination.
18	19–	
20	–3	*De Memoria et Reminiscentia:* 449b—453b. *Analytica Posteriora:* 99b—100a. *Metaphysica:* 980a—981a. μνήμη is properly a sensitive power, since its object is a past experience apprehended *as past*. Like his imagination the memory of man is both αἰσθητική or sensitive; and συλλογιστική or dianoetic.
20	4–	
21	–14	*De Anima:* 431a; 433b—434a. *Historia Animalium:* 588a—638b. *De Partibus Animalium:* 648a; 650b. *Physica:* 199a. *Ethica Nichomachea:* 1141a. The explanation of the purposive behavior of animals is to found neither in τέχνη or art; nor in βουλή or deliberation; nor in νοῦς or understanding; but in φύσις or nature. Such purposive conduct results from a kind of δύναμις προνοητική or power of foresight. It is also referred to as σύνεσις αἰσθητική or sensitive prudence.

PAGE	LINE
21	15–
23	–33

De Anima: 414b; 432b—434a.
Ethica Nichomachea: 1102b; 1139b; 1153b; 1174b; 1175b.

ὄρεξις αἰσθητική or sensitive appetite is divided between ἐπιθυμητική which generates concupiscible impulsions; and θυμική which gives rise to the passions of irascibility. Oretic phenomena are always determined by knowledge of some sort: τὸ ὀρεκτικὸν δὲ οὐκ ἄνευ φαντασίας. The power of locomotion is τὸ κατὰ τόπον κινητικόν.

PAGE	LINE
24	1–
27	–11

De Anima: 427a; 429a—433a.
Analytica Posteriora: 87b.

Poietic intellect is what it is by its power to make all things: πάντα ποιεῖν. Receptive intellect is what it is by its power to be made all things: πάντα γίνεσθαι. Thus, intellect is truly described as πως πάντα: everything, as it were. The *adequate* object of intellect is τὸ τί ἦν εἶναι: the being or essence of what a thing was, thus indicating not only its present actual existence, but also its eternal and essential constitution. The *proper* object of intellect is τὸ σακρὶ εἶναι: the essence of corporeal substance. This immediately distinguishes intellect from sense whose proper object is ὧν λόγος τις ἡ σάρξ: the concrete determinate qualities of corporeal substance. We might indicate the object of intellect in another way by calling it σὰρξ οὐκ ἄνευ τῆς ὕλης: substance free of all the contingent determinations of matter. The transformation of the phantasm from a νοητὸν δυνάμει into a νοητὸν ἐνεργείᾳ is accomplished by poietic intellect. The intelligible in act is identical with intellect in act: τὸ αὐτό ἐστι τὸ νοοῦν καὶ τὸ νοούμενον. The soul never understands without converting to phantasms: οὐδέποτε νοεῖ ἄνευ φαντάσματος ἡ ψυχή. Since phantasms arise only from experience, therefore at the beginning man's intellect is

PAGE	LINE	
		like γραμματεῖον ᾧ μηθὲν ἐντελεχείᾳ γεγραμμένον: a tablet on which nothing is actually written. αἴσθησις or sense knowledge is always dependent on a material organ; but ἐπιστήμη or intellectual knowledge is intrinsically free of such dependence. This means that νοῦς or intellect is χωριστὸς καὶ ἀπαθὴς καὶ ἀμιγής: separable, impassible, and not mixed with any bodily instrument.
27 28	12– –2	De Anima: 431b; 432b; 433a. Ethica Nichomachea: 1140a—1140b; 1141b; 1147a. The function of νοῦς θεωρητικός is to distinguish τὸ ἀληθὲς καὶ τὸ ψεῦδος: the true and the false. The function of νοῦς πρακτικός is to distinguish τὸ ἀγαθὸν καὶ τὸ κακόν: the good and the evil. The knowledge of practical intellect is concerned either with ποίησις: the making of things; or with πρᾶξις: the doing of things.
28	3–19	De Anima: 414b; 433a—434a. Ethica Nichomachea: 1139b; 1141b. Will is denominated in two ways: first as ὄρεξις διανοητική or dianoetic appetite; second as νοῦς ὀρεκτικός or appetitive reason. The act of will is ἡ βουλή or ἡ βούλησις. Just as αἴσθησις is essentially distinct from ἐπιστήμη in the cognitive order, so the movements of sensitive appetite, namely, ἐπιθυμία and θυμός, are essentially distinct from βούλησις, in the orectic order.
28 29	20– –6	De Anima: 414a; 415a. The acts of man are to be studied before his powers: πρότεραι γάρ εἰσι τῶν δυνάμεων αἱ ἐνέργειαι καὶ αἱ πράξεις κατὰ τὸν λόγον. The three orders of powers in man are: first, αἱ θρεπτικαί concerned with τρόφιμα or digestible objects; second, αἱ αἰσθητικαί, concerned with αἰσθητά or sensible objects; third, αἱ διανοητικαί, concerned with νοητά or intelligible objects.

PAGE	LINE
29	9–
31	–27

Ethica Nichomachea: 1098a; 1100a; 1100b; 1102a— 1103b; 1105b—1108b; 1110a—1145a.
Metaphysica: 1022b.
Categoriae: 8b—9a.
ἕξις or habit is *something had*. As a species of quality it is distinguished from σχέσις or disposition. Some habits are διανοητικαί or intellectual; others are ἠθικαί or moral. The intellectual habits are: νοῦς or understanding; ἐπιστήμη or knowledge; σοφία or wisdom; τέχνη or art; and φρόνησις or prudence. The moral habits are: δίκη or justice; σωφροσύνη or temperance; and ἀνδρεία or fortitude.

| 31 | 28– |
| 32 | –31 |

Categoriae: 2a—4b.
Metaphysica: 1028a—1032a.
οὐσία or substance is distinguished from συμβεβηκός or accident. Substance is logically divided into οὐσία ἡ πρώτη and οὐσία ἡ δευτέρη.
First substance neither is said of any subject nor exists in any subject: μήτε καθ' ὑποκειμένου τινὸς λέγεται, μήτ' ἐν ὑποκειμένῳ τινί ἐστιν.
Second substance does not exist in any subject, yet is said of a subject: μήτ' ἐν ὑποκειμένῳ τινί ἐστιν, ἀλλὰ καθ' ὑποκειμένου λέγεται.
The distinctive marks of every first substance (which is substance in its most proper signification) are as follows: first, not to be in a subject nor to be said of a subject, as already noted; second, to signify "this something": τόδε τι σημαίνειν; third, to be receptive of contraries: τῶν ἐναντίων εἶναι δεκτική: fourth, to be something that has no contrary: τὸ μηδὲν ἐναντίον εἶναι; fifth not to be susceptible to more and less: μὴ ἐπιδέχεσθαι τὸ μᾶλλον καὶ τὸ ἧττον.

| 32 | 32– |
| 33 | –12 |

Physica: 192b—193b; 199b.
Metaphysica: 1014b—1015a; 1070a.
De Caelo: 301b.

PAGE	LINE	
		φύσις or nature, as an intrinsically spontaneous and uniform principle of operation, is distinguished from τέχνη or art and τύχη or chance. It is τὸ τέλος τῆς γενέσεως: the final and perfect cause of all development.
33	13–	
34	–7	*De Anima:* 408b; 413b; 430a.

De Anima: 408b; 413b; 430a.
De Generatione Animalium: 736b; 737a.
Ethica Nichomachea: 1177a; 1177b.
Metaphysica: 1070a.

The soul of man comes into existence θύραθεν or from without. In its origin no ἐνέργεια σωματική or material force is involved. When it departs from the body, it continues to exist, since it is ἀθάνατον καὶ ἀΐδιον: something immortal and eternal.

34   8–27   *Ethica Nichomachea:* 1113b—1114b.
Topica: 112a.

The human will is a δύναμις βουλευτική or faculty of choice. Therefore it enjoys a basic freedom in its acts.

The soul of every man is his own destiny: ταύτην γὰρ ψυχὴν ἑκάστου εἶναι δαίμονα.

35   11–

38   –18   *In Librum Boetii de Trinitate Expositio:* q. 5.

42   3–13   *S. T.:* p. I, q. 79, a. 11.

42   14–15   John of St. Thomas points out that Aristotle may have had some intimation of the difference between person and nature though he never developed the idea. Thus, in his *Physica* (193b 5) the Stagirite says: "The combination of the two [principles, namely matter and form], for example, man, is not *nature* but *by nature.*" (*Cursus Philosophicus Thomisticus: Phil. Nat.,* p. I, q. 9, a. 2.)

43   16–28   *Categoriae:* 1a—1b.

44   1–3   *De Anima:* 408b 18–19: ὁ δὲ νοῦς ἔοικεν ἐγγίνεσθαι οὐσία τις οὖσα, καὶ οὐ φθείρεσθαι: *quod intellectum spectat, videtur innasci tamquam specialis substantia neque corrumpi.*

PAGE	LINE	
44	3–7	*De Anima:* 413b 24–27: περὶ δὲ τοῦ νοῦ καὶ τῆς θεωρη-τικῆς δυνάμεως οὐδέν πω φανερόν, ἀλλ' ἔοικε ψυχῆς γένος ἕτερον εἶναι, καὶ τοῦτο μόνον ἐνδέχεται χωρί-ζεσθαι, καθάπερ τὸ ἀΐδιον τοῦ φθαρτοῦ: *at quod intellectum et facultatem speculativam attinet, res nondum clare apparet, nisi quod videtur esse aliud animae (vegetativae et sensitivae) genus atque hoc solum posse distingui sicuti res aeterna a re corruptibili.*
44	11	*De Generatione Animalium:* 736b 27 ff.

CHAPTER 2: *THE PSYCHOLOGY OF AQUINAS*

47	1–3	*Ethica Nichomachea:* 1105b.
47	3–12	*In Ethica Nichomachea:* b. II, l. 5.
48	11	*The Treatise on Man* is found in the *Summa Theologica*, p. I, qq. 75–102. This is volume 4 of the English edition.
49	6–16	Aristotle: *De Anima:* 412a—413a.
		Aquinas: *In de Anima:* b. II, ll. 1–4.
50	3–22	*In de Anima:* b. II, l. 6.
61	24–	
62	–18	Maritain, J. *The Degrees of Knowledge:* pp. 38–49; 248–55. New York, Scribner, 1938.

CHAPTER 3: *MAN: THE INTEGER*

65	1–	
67	–21	Aristotle:—
		Physica: 184a—267b.
		De Caelo: 298b—313b.
		De Generatione et Corruptione: 314a—338b.
		Metaphysica: 1013a—1052a.
		Aquinas:—
		Commentaries on the foregoing.
		De Ente et Essentia (opusculum).
		De Substantiis Separatis (opusculum).
68	25–	
69	–2	*De Anima:* 412b 6–9.
69	13–21	*S. T.:* p. I, q. 76, a. 1.

PAGE	LINE	
70	3–12	*S. T.:* p. I, q. 75, a. 4.
70	19–26	*C. G.:* b. II, c. 57.
		Cf. S. T.: p. I, q. 75, a. 3.
71	9–32	*Q. D. de Veritate:* q. 26, a. 10.
72	4–5	*S. T.:* p. I, q. 76, a. 1.
72	26–	
73	–26	*S. T.:* p. I–II, q. 5, a. 3; p. II–II, q. 164, a. 1.
73	28–	
74	–3	*S. T.:* p. I, q. 76, a. 4.
74	3–5	*Q. D. de Spiritualibus Creaturis:* a. 3.
74	13–19	*S. T.:* p. I, q. 76, a. 4.
74	20–	
75	–11	*S. T.:* p. I, q. 76, a. 3.
76	10–	
77	–22	*C. G.:* b. II, c. 57.
		Q. D. de Anima: a. 1.
77	23–	
80	–23	Gruender, H. *Problems of Psychology:* pp. 132–64. Milwaukee, Bruce, 1937.
82	14–	
83	–10	*C. G.:* b. II, c. 67.
83	17–19	*Q. D. de Veritate:* q. 10, a. 1, reply to obj. 2.
83	20–22	*S. T.:* p. I, q. 75, a. 2.

CHAPTER 4: *THE VEGETATIVE LIFE OF MAN*

85	2–7	*In de Anima:* b. I, l. 8.
85	14–	
86	–16	Rousselot, P. L'Esprit de St. Thomas. *Etudes*, volume 28, 1911, pp. 627–34.
86	21–	
106	–24	Carrel, A. *Man the Unknown:* chapter 3. London, Hamilton, 1935.
106	25–	
108	–29	*C. G.:* b. IV, c. 11.
		Q. D. de Veritate: q. 4, a. 8.
		S. T.: p. I, q. 18, aa. 1–2; q. 75, a. 1; q. 78, aa. 1–2.
		Brennan, R. E. *General Psychology:* problem 5. New York, Macmillan, 1937.

PAGE	LINE	

CHAPTER 5: *THE SENSITIVE KNOWLEDGE OF MAN*

111	24–	
112	–2	*In Librum de Causis:* l. 18.
112	8–	
113	–2	*Q. D. de Veritate:* q. 2, a. 2.
113	28–	
114	–3	John of St. Thomas: *Cursus Philosophicus Thomisticus: Phil. Nat.,* p. IV, q. 4, a. 1: *Cognoscentia autem in hoc elevantur,* etc.
114	4–	
115	–16	*S. T.:* p. I, q. 78, a. 3; q. 79, a. 3.
116	5–8	*S. T.:* p. I, q. 14, a. 1.
116	12–16	Cajetan: *In Summam Theologicam Thomae de Aquino Commentarium:* p. I, q. 14, a. 1: *Cognoscens est ipsum cognitum actu vel potentia,* etc.
116	17–22	*S. T.:* p. I, q. 14, a. 2.
		In de Anima: b. III, ll. 2 and 12.
117	15–18	*In de Anima:* b. II, l. 24: *alterius modi esse habet forma,* etc.
117	26–	
118	–3	John of St. Thomas: *Cursus Philosophicus Thomisticus: Phil. Nat.,* p. IV, qq. 4–8.
118	16–31	*S. T.:* p. I, q. 78, a. 3.
		In de Anima: b. II, l. 14; b. III, l. 2.
		Brennan, R. E. *General Psychology:* Problems 11–14. New York, Macmillan, 1937.
119	1–13	*In de Anima:* b. II, l. 13: *sensibile proprium est,* etc.
119	14–30	*De Anima:* 418a—426b.
		De Sensu et Sensato: 437a; 441a; 444a.
120	1–7	*In de Anima:* b. II, l. 24: *sensus est susceptivus,* etc.
120	13–17	*In Libros Sententiarum:* b. I, d. 40, q. 1, a. 1, reply to obj. 2 (Parma edition).
120	22–	
121	–9	*In de Anima:* b. II, l. 10.
		S. T.: p. I, q. 78, a. 3.
121	17–27	*In de Anima:* b. III, l. 7: *sensus efficitur impotens,* etc.
		S. T.: p. I, q. 75, a. 3, reply to obj. 2.

PAGE	LINE	
121	28–	
122	–23	*In de Anima:* b. III, l. 3.
122	24–	
123	–18	*In de Anima:* b. II, l. 13: *sensibilia communia sunt ista quinque,* etc.
		De Potentiis Animae (opusculum): c. 4: *Non enim sensus proprius,* etc. Note: The authenticity of this opusculum has been questioned by Mandonnet, who describes it as "a composition of extracts from St. Thomas, or a digest of different passages from his writings." Thus, though not written by Aquinas, it nevertheless represents the genuine doctrine of the Thomistic psychology. (*Cf. S. Thomae Aquinatis Opuscula Varia,* tome I, p. xiv. Paris, Lethielleux, 1927.)
		Brennan, R. E. *General Psychology:* pp. 188–97. New York, Macmillan, 1937.
123	22–25	*In de Anima:* b. II, l. 13: *Sensus enim communis est quaedam potentia,* etc.
124	7–13	*In de Anima:* b. II, l. 13: *dicimus quod Diarus vel Socrates,* etc.
124	14–30	*De Potentiis Animae* (opusculum): c. 4: *Ista autem potentia est animali necessaria,* etc.
125	1–10	*S. T.:* p. I, q. 78, a. 4, reply to obj. 2.
125	22–27	*S. T.:* p. I, q. 84, a. 8, reply to obj. 2.
126	1–	
127	–26	*In de Anima:* b. III, ll. 5–6.
		S. T.: p. I, q. 78, a. 4.
		De Potentiis Animae (opusculum): c. 4: *Secunda vis interior est phantasia,* etc.
127	27–	
128	–4	*In de Anima:* b. III, l. 15: *ita tamen quod* etc.; and l. 16: *Phantasia etiam habet,* etc.
128	4–12	*In Librum Boetii de Trinitate Expositio:* q. 6, a. 2.
129	5–7	*In de Anima:* b. III, l. 4: *Passio phantasiae est in nobis,* etc.
129	11–	
131	–19	*In de Memoria et Reminiscentia:* ll. 1–8.

PAGE	LINE	
		Q. D. de Veritate: q. 10, a. 2: *memoria secundum communem usum,* etc.
		Q. D. de Anima: a. 13: *requiritur quod ea quae prius,* etc.
		Brennan, R. E. *General Psychology:* problem 18. New York, Macmillan, 1937.
130	4–10	*S. T.:* p. I, q. 78, a. 4.
130	16–21	*In de Memoria et Reminiscentia:* l. 8.
131	1–19	*In de Memoria et Reminiscentia:* l. 5.
131	20–	
132	–2	*S. T.:* p. I, q. 78, a. 4.
		C. G.: b. II, c. 66: *Alia autem animalia ab homine,* etc.
		De Potentiis Animae (opusculum): c. 4: *Licet quantum ad formas sensibiles,* etc.
		Brennan, R. E. *General Psychology:* problem 17. New York, Macmillan, 1937.
132	5–15	*S. T.:* p. I, q. 83, a. 1.
133	1–28	*S. T.:* p. I–II, q. 13, a. 2, obj. 3 and reply.
134	3–7	*S. T.:* p. I, q. 78, a. 4.
134	25–27	*In Analytica Posteriora:* b. II, l. 20.
		In Metaphysica: b. I, l. 1: *Supra memoriam autem in hominibus,* etc.
134	28–	
135	–13	*Q. D. de Veritate:* q. 10, a. 5, *corp.* and reply to objections 2 and 4.
135	21–	
136	–16	*Quodlibetum Quintum:* a. 9, reply to obj. 2.
		S. T.: p. I, q. 27, a. 5; q. 85, a. 2, reply to obj. 3.
		Q. D. de Veritate: q. 8, a. 5: *Est enim aliqua cognoscitiva potentia,* etc.; a. 7, reply to obj. 2 (last series).
		John of St. Thomas: *Cursus Philosophicus Thomisticus: Phil. Nat.,* p. IV, q. 6, a. 4.
136	16–18	*S. T.:* p. I, q. 85, a. 2: *Sed contra.*
136	28–	
137	–9	*C. G.:* b. II, c. 73.
		Q. D. de Veritate: q. 8, aa. 5–6.
139	22–	
140	–12	*Cf.* reference page 116, lines 12–16.

PAGE	LINE	
140	13–	
141	–3	*S. T.:* p. I, q. 78, a. 3, reply to obj. 2.
142	22–	
143	–6	*S. T.:* p. I, q. 78, a. 4.
143	22–	
144	–3	*S. T.:* p. I–II, q. 94, a. 2.
144	4–	
146	–2	*Cf.* references page 134, lines 25–27.
145	15–16	*Analytica Posteriora:* 99b—100a. According to Aristotle, sense impressions persist in certain animals while in others such impressions do not extend beyond the actual perception of things. Man is able to store up the data of exterior sensation in the form of images. He is also capable of systematizing such data, with the result that memory is born. Moreover, out of frequently repeated memories ἐμπειρία or *experience* is begotten, since experience is the fruit of much remembering: αἱ γὰρ πολλαὶ μνῆμαι τῷ ἀριθμῷ ἐμπειρία μία ἐστίν. From experience, in turn, originate the skill of the craftsman and the knowledge of the scholar: ἐκ δ' ἐμπειρίας . . . τέχνης ἀρχὴ καὶ ἐπιστήμης.
145	27–	
146	–2	*In Analytica Posteriora:* b. II, l. 20: *Puta cum aliquis recordatur,* etc.
146	16–20	*S. T.:* p. I, q. 78, a. 4, reply to obj. 5; p. I–II, q. 74, a. 3, reply to obj. 1.

CHAPTER 6: *THE PASSIONS AND ACTIONS OF MAN*

147	1–	
148	–8	*Q. D. de Veritate:* q. 22, a. 1; q. 25, a. 1.
148	9–	
149	–5	*S. T.:* p. I–II, q. 26, a. 1.
149	17–21	*S. T.:* p. I, q. 81, a. 1.
149	29–	
150	–5	*S. T.:* p. I–II, q. 28, a. 1, reply to obj. 3.
150	23–29	*Q. D. de Veritate:* q. 25, a. 2.

PAGE	LINE	
150	29–	
151	–5	*S. T.:* p. 1, q. 81, a. 2.
151	22	*S. T.:* p. I–II, q. 24, a. 2.
152	5–12	*S. T.:* p. I, q. 80, a. 2; p. I–II, q. 22, a. 1.
152	25–30	*C. G.:* b. I, c. 90.
153	8–10	*Ethica Nichomachea:* 1174b.
153	15–23	*In Ethica Nichomachea:* b. X, l. 6: *Est enim delectatio,* etc.
154	9–14	Hartshorne, C. *The Philosophy and Psychology of Sensation,* c. 1. University of Chicago Press, 1934.
154	25–31	*S. T.:* p. I–II, q. 32, a. 1, reply to obj. 3.
155	1–17	*S. T.:* p. I–II, q. 22, aa. 2 and 3.
155	26–	
156	–24	*S. T.:* p. I–II, q. 23, a. 1.
156	25–	
157	–26	*S. T.:* p. I–II, q. 23, a. 4.
157	27–31	*S. T.:* p. I–II, q. 23, a. 3.
158	1–	
159	–26	*S. T.:* p. I–II, q. 27, a. 4; q. 28, a. 6.
161	19–24	*Q. D. de Veritate:* q. 25, a. 2: *Nam quod animal appetat,* etc.
		Ethica Nichomachea: 1149a 25—1149b 4.
162	8–19	*In Epistolam ad Romanos:* c. 7, l. 3.
		S. T.: p. I–II, q. 31, a. 5.
162	19–23	*S. T.:* p. I, q. 81, a. 3, reply to obj. 2.
162	29–31	*S. T.:* p. I–II, q. 77, a. 6.
163	20–	
164	–11	*De Potentiis Animae* (opusculum): c. 5: *Motiva animalis est,* etc.
		C. G.: b. II, c. 82: *Delectationes autem brutorum,* etc.; also: *Non enim movet anima brutalis,* etc.
165	23–	
166	–5	*S. T.:* p. I, q. 81, a. 2.
166	6–8	*S. T.:* p. I, q. 81, a. 3, reply to obj. 2.
166	16–17	*S. T.:* p. I, q. 81, a. 3: *appetitus sensitivus in aliis quidem animalibus,* etc.
166	18–21	*S. T.:* p. I–II, q. 9, a. 2, reply to obj. 2.

PAGE	LINE	
166	22–26	*In de Anima:* b. III, l. 4: *appetitus non patitur neque movetur,* etc.
168	4–26	*S. T.:* p. I, q. 81, a. 3.

CHAPTER 7: *THE INTELLECTUAL KNOWL-
EDGE OF MAN*

PAGE	LINE	
169	25–	
170	–1	*Q. D. de Veritate:* q. 2, a. 2.
170	4–7	*S. T.:* p. I, q. 80, a. 1.
170	7–13	*C. G.:* b. II, c. 98.
171	4–12	*De Natura Materiae et Dimensionibus Interminatis* (opusculum): c. 1: *intellectus ad plura se extendit,* etc.
171	23–28	*In Libros Sententiarum:* b. IV, d. 49, q. 3, a. 5, quaestiuncula 4: *sensus enim,* etc., and reply to obj. 2.
172	6–9	
	21–27	*Quodlibetum Septimum:* a. 2.
		Q. D. de Veritate: q. 8, a. 14.
		S. T.: p. I, q. 85, a. 4.
173	6–12	*C. G.:* b. I, cc. 44–45; b. II, cc. 46 and 98.
		In Libros Sententiarum: b. II, d. 16, q. 1, a. 2.
		S. T.: p. I, q. 26, a. 2.
174	22–25	*S. T.:* p. I, q. 89, a. 1.
175	1–	
176	–6	*S. T.:* p. I, q. 12, a. 4; q. 55, a. 2; q. 84, a. 7.
179	16–	
181	–13	*S. T.:* p. I, q. 75, aa. 2 and 5; q. 76, a. 1; q. 84, aa. 1–6; q. 85, aa. 1–2.
		C. G.: b. II, cc. 59–78.
		In de Anima: b. III, ll. 3–8.
181	26–27	Locke, J. *opus cit.,* b. I, c. 1, paragraph 8.
181	30–	
182	–14	*Q. D. de Veritate:* q. 10, a. 8, reply to obj. 2: *Sicut enim,* etc.
182	15–16	*C. G.:* b. II, c. 96.
185	24–27	*In de Anima:* b. III, l. 10: *quarta autem conditio est,* etc.
186	6–8	*Q. D. de Anima:* a. 5: *intellectus autem agens est qui facit,* etc.
		C. G.: b. II, c. 78.

PAGE	LINE	
186	26–	
187	–1	*S. T.:* p. I, q. 86, a. 1, reply to obj. 3.
187	7–13	*Q. D. de Anima:* a. 20, end, reply to counterobj. 1: *anima conjuncta corpori,* etc.
187	14–31	*S. T.:* p. I, q. 84, a. 7.
188	5–19	*S. T.:* p. I, q. 84, a. 8.
188	23–29	*In Analytica Posteriora:* b. II, l. 13: *quia formae essentiales,* etc.
188	30–	
189	–16	*S. T.:* p. I. q. 79, a. 2.
192	5–8	*In de Anima:* b. III, l. 13: end.
192	9–29	*In de Anima:* b. I, l. 2: *intellectus quodammodo,* etc.
193	5	*S. T.:* p. I, q. 84, a. 6.
		Q. D. de Veritate: q. 10, a. 6, reply to obj. 7.
193	9–31	*S. T.:* p. I, q. 75, a. 3, reply to obj. 2; q. 84, a. 7, and reply to obj. 1 and 2 of a. 8.
		C. G.: b. II, c. 79.
195	10–13	*In Libros Sententiarum:* b. II, d. 3, q. 1, a. 6: *ex hoc enim quod anima,* etc.
195	27–	
196	–9	*C. G.:* b. II, c. 66.
197	8–11	*S. T.:* p. I, q. 58, a. 3.
197	16–21	*S. T.:* p. I, q. 85, aa. 3 and 5.
197	31–	
198	–10	*S. T.:* p. I, q. 79, a. 2.
198	11–25	*S. T.:* p. I, q. 14.
199	1–9	*S. T.:* p. I, q. 85, a. 1, reply to obj. 1.
199	10–27	*S. T.:* p. I, q. 79, a. 4.
200	3–26	*S. T.:* p. I, q. 79, a. 6, reply to obj. 2.
		In de Memoria et Reminiscentia: l. 2.
200	29–32	*S. T.:* p. I, q. 79, a. 7.
201	8–	
202	–12	*S. T.:* p. I, q. 86, a. 1.
		Q. D. de Veritate: q. 10, a. 5.
		In de Anima: b. III, l. 8: *Sed oportet quod alia potentia,* etc.
		In Physica: b. I, l. 1.
		In Libros Sententiarum: b. IV, d. 50, q. 1, a. 3.

PAGE	LINE	
202	13–26	*S. T.:* p. I, q. 84, a. 7.
204	22–30	*Q. D. de Veritate:* q. I, a. 3.
205	11–	
206	–2	*S. T.:* p. I, q. 85, a. 1.
206	3–	
207	–19	*S. T.:* p. I, q. 85, a. 3.
208	1–12	*S. T.:* p. I, q. 85, a. 5.
208	13–	
209	–17	*S. T.:* p. I, q. 85, a. 6.

CHAPTER 8: *THE VOLITIONAL LIFE OF MAN*

PAGE	LINE	
210	1–2	*C. G.:* b. II, c. 47.
210	22–24	Augustine, *Confessions:* b. I, c. 1.
211	6–13	*Q. D. de Veritate:* q. 10, a. 1, reply to obj. 2.
211	22–28	*S. T.:* p. I, q. 81, a. 1.
212	1–12	*S. T.:* p. I, q. 27, a. 3.
212	12–	
213	–10	*S. T.:* p. I, q. 27, a. 4.
		John of St. Thomas: *Cursus Philosophicus Thomisticus: Phil. Nat.*, p. I, q. 13, a. 2.
213	12–16	*S. T.:* p. I–II, q. 28, a. 1, reply to obj. 3.
213	17–	
214	–15	*S. T.:* p. I–II, q. 28, a. 1, and reply to obj. 2.
214	16–	
216	–3	*S. T.:* p. I, q. 82, aa. 1–2; p. I–II, q. 10, a. 2.
216	4–16	*S. T.:* p. I–II, q. 6, a. 4.
217	6–10	*S. T.:* p. I, q. 83, a. 4.
217	11–22	*Q. D. de Veritate:* q. 22, a. 6.
		Q. D. de Malo: q. 6.
222	2–3	*S. T.:* p. I–II, q. 10, a. 2.
223	7–9	*S. T.:* p. I, q. 83, a. 1.
223	20–23	*S. T.:* p. I, q. 83, a. 1.
224	22–	
226	–33	*Q. D. de Veritate:* q. 24, a. 1: *Homo per virtutem rationis,* etc.
		John of St. Thomas: *Cursus Philosophicus Thomisticus: Phil. Nat.*, p. IV, q. 12, a. 2.

PAGE	LINE	
227	19–22	*S. T.:* p. I–II, qq. 76–78.
227	22–28	*Q. D. de Veritate:* q. 22, a. 6: *ubi non est defectus*, etc.
228	5–8	*S. T.:* p. I, q. 62, a. 8, reply to obj. 3.
228	8–9	Augustine, *Opus Imperfectum contra Julianum:* b. 5, c. 58.
228	11–21	*S. T.:* p. I–II, q. 27, a. 2, reply to obj. 2.
228	24–26	*Q. D. de Veritate:* q. 22, a. 11: *Perfectius autem est*, etc.
229	1–2	*In de Anima:* b. II, l. 7: *appetitivum non constituit*, etc.
229	19–21	*S. T.:* p. I–II, q. 27, a. 2, reply to obj. 2.
229	25–30	*S. T.:* p. I–II, q. 28, a. 2.
230	1–17	John of St. Thomas: *Cursus Theologicus Thomisticus:* p. I, q. 19, *disput.* 5, a. 6. (*cf. S. T.:* p. I, q. 19, a. 6).
230	25–30	*S. T.:* p. I, q. 105, a. 4, reply to obj. 3.
230	30–	
231	–5	*S. T.:* p. I, q. 22, a. 4, reply to obj. 3.
231	13–24	*S. T.:* p. I, q. 83, a. 1, reply to obj. 3.
		Garrigou-Lagrange, R. *God, His Existence and Nature* (translated by Bede Rose): volume 2, pp. 75–81. St. Louis, Herder, 1936.
232	1–6	*S. T.:* p. I–II, q. 10, a. 3, reply to obj. 3.
232	7–27	*S. T.:* p. I–II, q. 10, a. 2.
233	3–19	*S. T.:* p. II–II, q. 25, a. 1.
233	25–30	*S. T.:* p. I, q. 23, a. 1.
233	31–36	*S. T.:* p. I, q. 62, a. 2.
234	3–7	*Q. D. de Veritate:* q. 22, a. 7: *homini inditus est*, etc.
234	8–16	*S. T.:* p. I–II, qq. 11–16.
234	17–21	*S. T.:* p. I–II, q. 15, a. 3, reply to obj. 3.
234	22–	
235	–5	*In de Anima:* b. III, l. 14: *quaeritur quare in appetitu sensitivo*, etc.
		S. T.: p. I, q. 82, a. 5.
235	6–13	*S. T.:* p. I–II, q. 9, a. 1, reply to obj. 3.
235	14–	
236	–6	*S. T.:* p. I, q. 83, a. 3.
236	25–	
237	–28	*S. T.:* p. I, q. 82, a. 3.

PAGE	LINE	
		CHAPTER 9: *THE POWERS OF MAN*
238	14–23	*De Anima:* 415a.
238	25–	
239	–6	*S. T.:* p. I, q. 77, a. 3.
241	18–26	*Q. D. de Veritate:* q. 10, a. 1, reply to obj. 2.
		S. T.: p. I, q. 78, a. 1.
241	27–	
242	–2	*S. T.:* p. I, q. 77, a. 3.
242	3–8	*S. T.:* p. I, q. 78, a. 2.
242	9–12	*Q. D. de Veritate:* q. 22, a. 10.
242	19–23	*S. T.:* p. I, q. 78, a. 1.
243	1–11	*S. T.:* p. I, q. 59, a. 2.
243	23–	
247	–19	*Q. D. de Anima:* a. 13.
244	15–18	*S. T.:* p. I, q. 59, a. 2, reply to obj. 2.
246	20–22	*Q. D. de Anima:* a. 13: *Vis autem motiva,* etc.
249	31–32	*C. G.:* b. II, c. 91.
250	15–18	*S. T.:* p. I, q. 14, a. 1.
250	20–	
256	–10	Brennan, R. E. *General Psychology,* pp. 432–38. New York, Macmillan, 1937.
256	9–10	*S. T.:* p. I, q. 77, a. 6.
257	2–3	*In Libros Sententiarum:* b. I, d. 8, q. 5, a. 2, reply to obj. 6.
257	4–7	*In Libros Sententiarum:* b. II, d. 32, q. 2, a. 3.
257	8–16	*S. T.:* p. I, q. 85, a. 7.
258	19–	
259	–36	*Q. D. de Anima:* a. 13.
		CHAPTER 10: *THE HABITS OF MAN*
262	25–27	*Metaphysica:* 1022b.
262	29–	
263	–2	*S. T.:* p. I–II, q. 49, a. 1.
263	11–	
264	–24	*S. T.:* p. I–II, q. 51, aa. 1–3.
264	6–7	*Cf. Ethica Nichomachea:* 1097b; 1103a–1103b.

PAGE	LINE	
264	25–	
265	–27	*Q. D. de Virtutibus in Communi:* a. 1: *Ex his etiam potest patere,* etc. *S. T.:* p. I–II, q. 49, a. 4.
265	28–	
266	–22	*S. T.:* p. I–II, q. 50, aa. 4–5.
266	23–	
267	–21	*S. T.:* p. I–II, q. 50, a. 3.
268	11–20	*S. T.:* p. I–II, q. 49, a. 2.
268	21–	
270	–9	*S. T.:* p. I–II, qq. 52–53.
268	27–	
269	–4	*S. T.:* p. I–II, q. 52, a. 3.
269	8–16	*S. T.:* p. I–II, q. 53, a. 1.
269	27–	
270	–2	*S. T.:* p. I–II, q. 53, a. 3.
270	10–	
272	–7	*S. T.:* p. I–II, qq. 55–56.
271	8–9	*Metaphysica:* 1022b.
271	22–23	*Ethica Nichomachea:* 1106a.
272	8–	
273	–10	*S. T.:* p. I–II, q. 57.
273	11–	
274	–2	*S. T.:* p. I–II, qq. 58–61.
274	3–	
276	–5	Brennan, R. E. *General Psychology:* pp. 396–400. New York, Macmillan, 1937.
276	15–	
277	–5	*S. T.:* p. I–II, q. 50, a. 3, reply to obj. 2.
277	6–32	*S. T.:* p. I–II, q. 54, a. 1.
278	5	Cicero: *Tusculanae Disputationes:* b. II, c. 18, section 43: *Appellata est enim ex viro virtus; viri autem propria maxime est fortitudo.*
278	25–33	*Ethica Nichomachea:* 1103a—1103b.
279	1–28	*S. T.:* p. I–II, q. 58, a. 5.

CHAPTER 11: *MAN: THE PERSON*

281	10–27	Müller, Max. *Biographies of Words and the Home of the Aryas:* c. 3 Persona. London, Longmans, Green, 1888.

PAGE	LINE	
281	28–	
282	–5	*S. T.:* p. I, q. 29, a. 3, reply to obj. 2.
282	6–7	Boethius: *De Persona et Duabus Naturis:* c. III.
282	9–	
288	–24	*S. T.:* p. I, q. 29; p. III, q. 2, aa. 1–3; p. III, q. 16, a. 12.

Q. D. de Potentia Dei: q. 9, aa. 1–3.
Q. D. de Unione Verbi Incarnati: a. 1.
C. G.: b. IV, c. 35.
Quodlibetum Nonum: a. 2.
John of St. Thomas: *Cursus Philosophicus Thomisticus: Log.,* p. II, q. 15; *Phil. Nat.,* p. I, q. 15.

PAGE	LINE	
282	9–	
283	–5	*S. T.:* p. I, q. 29, a. 2.

Q. D. de Potentia Dei: q. 9, a. 1.

PAGE	LINE	
283	6–8	*S. T.:* p. I, q. 29, aa. 1 and 4.
283	14–16	*Q. D. de Potentia Dei:* q. 9, a. 2, reply to obj. 6.
285	1–2	*S. T.:* p. III, q. 2, aa. 1–2.

Q. D. de Potentia Dei: q. 9, a. 2.

PAGE	LINE	
285	16–17	*S. T.:* p. I, q. 29, a. 2, reply to obj. 3.
285	27–31	*S. T.:* p. III, q. 2, a. 2.
286	11–13	*De Ente et Essentia* (opusculum): c. 1: *Nomen autem naturae,* etc.

S. T.: p. III, q. 2, a. 1.
Cf. Aristotle's *Physica:* 192b—193b.
St. Thomas says that "the word *nature* was first used to signify the coming into being of things by birth; and thence it was transferred to indicate the principle of this kind of generation: and then further still to signify the intrinsic principle of movement in a movable thing. And since [in corporeal substances] this principle is either matter or form, nature also stands for the matter or form of a natural thing having within itself the principle of its movement. Moreover, since matter and form constitute the essence of a natural thing, the meaning of the word *nature* is made to extend to the essence of anything

PAGE	LINE	
		existing in nature." (*C. G.:* b. IV, c. 35.) Because nature can be used synonymously with form, therefore, Boethius defines it as "the specific difference giving its form to each thing." (*De Persona et Duabus Naturis:* c. I.) If it be asked why we do not use the word *essence* instead of the word *nature* in the definition of person, the answer is that the specific difference completes a definition and confines the thing thus defined to its proper species. Accordingly, "the term *nature* is more suitable in the definition of person which is special to certain substances, than the term *essence* which is common [to all substances]." (*Q. D. de Potentia Dei:* q. 9, a. 2, reply to obj. 11. *Cf.* also *S. T.:* p. I, q. 29, a. 1, reply to obj. 4.)
287	6–	
288	–24	*S. T.:* p. III, q. 2, a. 2, reply to obj. 3; q. 16, a. 12, reply to obj. 2.
288	3–9	*S. T.:* p. I, q. 29, a. 1, reply to obj. 2.
288	29–	
289	–3	*Cf.* Gerdil, H. S. *Institut. Log., Metaphy., et Eth.: Ontol.,* q. I, c. 4.
289	9–12	Cajetan: *In Summam Theologicam Thomae de Aquino Commentarium:* p. III, q. 2, a. 2. Garrigou-Lagrange, R. De Personalitate juxta Cajetanum. *Angelicum,* 1934, pp. 407–24.
289	13–14	*Q. D. de Potentia Dei:* q. 9, a. 3. Also, q. 9, a. 2, reply to objections 1 and 2.
296	1–5	*S. T.:* p. I, q. 119, a. 1, reply to obj. 2.
299	5–10	*S. T.:* p. III, q. 2, a. 3.
299	18–	
300	–8	*S. T.:* p. I, q. 29, a. 2, reply to obj. 3.
300	9–18	*S. T.:* p. III, q. 2, a. 1.
300	19–	
301	–10	*S. T.:* p. III, q. 2, a. 2.
301	11–32	*Q. D. de Potentia Dei:* q. 9, a. 4.
302	21–29	Cajetan: *Super Tractatum de Ente et Essentia Commentarium:* c. 4.

PAGE	LINE	
		CHAPTER 12: *THE SOUL OF MAN*
307	15–	
309	–25	*S. T.:* p. I, q. 75, a. 2; q. 84, a. 7.
		Q. D. de Anima: aa. 1 and 14.
		C. G.: b. II, c. 65.
309	26–	
311	–3	*Q. D. de Veritate:* q. 1, a. 1.
		Q. D. de Potentia Dei: q. 3, a. 8: *accidentia magis proprie,* etc.
		In Physica: b. I, l. 1.
		S. T.: p. I, q. 5, a. 2; q. 79, a. 7.
311	4–	
312	–17	*C. G.:* b. II, c. 49.
312	18–	
313	–6	*S. T.:* p. I, q. 76, a. 8.
		C. G.: b. II, c. 72.
		Q. D. de Spiritualibus Creaturis: a. 4.
		Q. D. de Anima: a. 10.
313	15–16	*De Generatione Animalium:* 736b.
313	17–	
314	–28	*S. T.:* p. I, q. 90, aa. 2–3; q. 118, aa. 1–2.
		Q. D. de Potentia Dei: q. 3, aa. 4, 8, 9.
		Quodlibetum Nonum: a. 11.
		Compendium Theologiae (opusculum): cc. 92–93.
314	31–33	*S. T.:* p. I, q. 90, a. 1.
315	1–	
316	–7	*S. T.:* p. I, q. 90, a. 4; q. 118, a. 3; p. III, q. 6, aa. 3–4.
		C. G.: b. II, cc. 83–84.
315	21–22	*S. T.:* p. I, q. 90, a. 4.
316	4–6	*S. T.:* p. I, q. 89, a. 7.
316	8–	
317	–15	*C. G.:* b. II, c. 81.
		In de Anima: b. II, l. 1: *Similiter etiam nulla forma,* etc.
		Q. D. de Anima: a. 1, reply to obj. 2.
317	9–11	*C. G.:* b. II, c. 81: *Hujusmodi autem commensurationes,* etc.

PAGE	LINE	
317	16–	
320	–9	Hugon, E. *Cursus Philosophiae Thomisticae: Phil. Nat.*, p. II, tract 2, q. 4, a. 2. Paris, Lethielleux, 1927.
317	16–	
318	–8	*C. G.:* b. II, c. 89.
		Q. D. de Potentia Dei: q. 3, a. 9, reply to obj. 9.
		S. T.: p. I, q. 118, a. 2.
322	3–23	*S. T.:* p. I, q. 75, a. 6.
		In Libros Sententiarum: b. II, d. 19, q. 1, a. 1.
		C. G.: b. II, cc. 78, 79, 82.
		Q. D. de Anima: a. 14.
322	24–	
323	–8	*S. T.:* p. I, q. 8, a. 1; q. 50, a. 5, reply to obj. 3; q. 104, aa. 3–4.
		Q. D. de Potentia Dei: q. 5, aa. 3–4.
323	9–27	*S. T.:* p. I, q. 75, a. 6; p. I–II, q. 3, a. 8.
		C. G.: b. II, c. 55: *Impossibile est naturae desiderium*, etc.
		Q. D. de Anima: a. 14.
323	30–	
324	–25	*Compendium Theologiae* (opusculum): c. 104: *ultimo fine adepto*, etc.
325	21–	
326	–33	*S. T.:* p. I, q. 89.
		C. G.: b. II, cc. 81 and 96; b. III, c. 45.
326	9–14	*De Ente et Essentia* (opusculum): c. 6: *et ideo dicit Avicenna*, etc.
327	1–11	*C. G.:* b. II, c. 81: *quum anima humana . . . sit in confinio*, etc.
327	15–26	Brennan, R. E. *General Psychology:* pp. 306–12. New York, Macmillan, 1937.
327	26–	
328	–5	*Q. D. de Potentia Dei:* q. 3, a. 4, reply to obj. 7.
328	17–20	*S. T.:* p. I, q. 91, a. 2.
328	24–	
329	–3	*S. T.:* p. I, q. 65, a. 1, reply to obj. 1.
		Q. D. de Potentia Dei: q. 5, a. 10.
329	4–17	*S. T.:* p. III (supplement): q. 75.

PAGE	LINE	
330	1–	
331	–16	*S. T.:* p. I, q. 76, a. 8.
331	17–25	*S. T.:* p. I, q. 75, a. 3.
332	9–16	*S. T.:* p. I, q. 75, a. 6.
332	17–24	*S. T.:* p. III (supplement): qq. 82–85.

INDEX

Abstraction, 179–80, 199
  degrees, 35–38
    mathematical, 36
    metaphysical, 36–37
    physical, 36–37
  power, 247, 259
Accidental form, *v.* form
Ach, N., 59, 343
Achilles, 131
Act psychology, 178
Action and passion, 161
Active intellect, *v.* intellect
Adler, A., 220, 353
Adler, M. J., 60, 62, 141
Adlerian psychology, 220, 353
Aesthetic, *v.* sensitive
Agent intellect, *v.* intellect
Agility of glorified body, 332
Aisthesis, 11, 21, 366–67
Anabolism, 96
Anger, passion of, 157, 158
Animal inferior to man, 195–96
Animal prudence, *v.* estimative
Anschauungsbilder, 348
Anthropology, 356–59
Appetite, 21–22, 28, 147–68, 210–37
  habits, 31
  imperative offices, 40
  intellectual, 21, 28, 149, 370
    immaterial nature, 212
    object, 156, 210, 214–16
    single species, 234–35
  meaning, 148
  natural, 148, 214
  sensitive, 21–22, 148–49, 370
    concupiscible, 21–22, 150–51, 156–57, 158, 165–66, 369
    in man and brute, 161–62
    irascible, 21–22, 150–51, 157–58, 165–66, 369
    motives, 166
    object, 156
    psychosomatic nature, 159–60
    and conation, 165
    and knowledge, 147–48
    and locomotion, 163–64

Appetitive union, 149–50, 212–14
Apprehension, simple, 208
Arabian philosophers, 39
Aristophanes, 214
Aristotelian influence in modern psychology, 339
Art, habit of, 30, 272, 274, 371
Association, laws of, 19, 130, 131
Associational psychology, 177, 305
Atomism, 41, 154
Auditory sense, *v.* senses
Augustine, 159, 178, 199, 210, 228, 276, 307, 382, 383
Autonomic, *v.* nervous system
Averrhoism, 218
Aversion, passion of, 157, 158
Axones, 100

Bain, A., 177
Basedowoid types, 348
Bechterev, V., 346
Behavioristic psychology, 55, 177, 219, 222, 252, 274, 305, 306, 349–51
Benussi, V., 345
Beneficent love, 213
Bergson, H., 294, 307, 344
Berkeley, G., 181
Binet, A., 202, 344
Blood
  cells, 91–92
  corpuscles, 91–92
  plasma, 91–92
Body of man
  destiny, 328–29
  evolution
    ontogenetic, 327
    phylogenetic, 327
    and pre-dispositive action of nature, 328
  instrument of knowledge, 173–76
  origin, 327–28
  resurrection, 328–29
    dotes, 332
  sacramental character, 86–87, 109–10